Making Worlds: Art and Science Fiction

Edited by Amelia Barikin & Helen Hughes

Surpllus

Contents

Introduction: Making worlds in art and science fiction

Amelia Barikin

When Robert Smithson first saw Donald Judd's 'pink plexiglas box' in 1965, he thought it resembled 'a giant crystal from another planet'.[1] By the time I encountered Judd's work as a teenager in the 1990s, Smithson's observation had already been burned into my mind. Was he tripping? The comment seemed so far removed from everything that art historians would have had me believe about minimalism that I wondered if, perhaps, Smithson's revelation was acid-fuelled. But it was through Smithson's reading of Judd that I subsequently discovered J.G. Ballard, and his 1966 book *The Crystal World*—a world infected with zones of solidified time that slowly consume and finally crystallise all objects and living material. In the crystallised forest, time petrifies and splinters. Tree branches are sheathed in hard light, their efflorescent casing illuminating rivers solidified into lattices of sharp matted spires: 'The long arc of trees hanging over the water seemed to drip and glitter with myriads of prisms…'.[2] The 'scientific' explanation for this terrifying yet visually hypnotic process is finally given by the character of the Doctor, who, in classic Ballardian style, is also a specialist in leprosy:

> We know now that it is time…that is responsible for the transformation. The recent discovery of anti-matter in the universe inevitably involves the conception of anti-time as the fourth side of this negatively charged continuum. When anti-particle and particle collide, they not only destroy their own physical identities, but their opposing time values eliminate each other, subtracting from the universe another

> quantum from its total store of time...As more and more time 'leaks' away, the process of supersaturation continues, the original atoms and molecules producing spatial replicas of themselves, substance without mass, in an attempt to increase their foothold upon existence...The process is theoretically without end.[3]

It is not hard to see why Robert Smithson was so fascinated with *The Crystal World*, to the point that when he wrote about Judd's minimalist sculptures the objects took on the status of Ballard's crystallised artefacts.[4] Science fiction here becomes the lens through which the world—including the world of art—is able to be grasped anew.

The essays in *Making Worlds: Art and Science Fiction* have developed out of the many conversations we have had with artists, curators, art historians and writers who are self-confessed science fiction fans. The linking point between these conversations was the idea of science fiction as a platform for the building of alternate art histories. This collection is as such concerned less with how science fiction is referenced by artists, than with how works of art have begun to actually embody the operating systems of their content; how science fiction might be performed, materialised or enacted within a contemporary context. The territory covered is broad and diverse: time travel, geophilosophy, loops, apocalyptic landscapes, telepathy, dark matter, alien aesthetics, philology, science fiction as non-fiction, anthropology, dystopias, contemporary installation practices, and zones of fabulation. Writings on R.A. Lafferty and Aboriginal art find their counterpart in essays on de-territorialisation, empathy, and copy-worlds. Anthony White considers why ceramic objects play such an important role in Philip K. Dick's works, while Matthew Shannon and Helen Johnson both confront the philosophical implications of alien ontology, to very different ends. Methodological tactics of science fiction—extrapolation, montage and world-building—are further engaged by OSW and Soda_Jerk, who, through processes of construction and presentation, have both contributed texts with a science-fictional format.

The authors' approaches are at times personal (Arlo Mountford wanders around an English moor and thinks of Tarvovksy; Dylan Martorell recognises in Samuel Delany's *Dhalgren* the dissolving landscape of '60s counterculture in which he grew up; Charles Green locates in Frank Herbert's *Dune* a mode of contemporary disembodiment akin to a quasi-Buddhist demolition of the sublime), while others seek to unravel and recontextualise histories of ideas from a science-fictional perspective (Justin Clemens on the emergence of the new sciences; Chris McAuliffe on Robert Smithson's 'decrepit margins of time'; Ryan Johnston on Paolozzi and Roussel; Rex Butler on the paradoxes of time travel). Although the book is designed as something like an extended fan letter to the enduring presence of sci-fi as a mode of thought, it is also intended to function as a future archive: a collection of notes that capture something of the complex linkages, networks and shared connections between art and science fiction that are fast becoming a major trope in contemporary artistic practice.

Why science fiction, and why now? In 2003, artist and writer David Robbins published an essay called 'Warm Science Fiction' in which he considered the interpolation of reality and fiction as a key principle of contemporary life. 'The illusion-generator', Robbins wrote, 'is now too weak to launch imagined narratives free of the gravitational pull of reality and into the self-completing orbit known as "fiction"':

> Prevented from reaching this condition of full-on, illusionistic make-believe, 'story', now grounded and weakened, is infiltrated by a host of earth-bound

> narratives — reality's narratives. Fiction and non-fiction contaminate each other. The contamination destabilizes each category until, eventually, between them a new equilibrium is attained.[5]

Robbins was here ruminating on the widespread move toward what he called 'fictionalising the present' in contemporary societies: the production of a new equilibrium between hard reality and soft fiction that makes it difficult to distinguish the one from the other. This condition is historically specific — emerging as it does out of an era in which the rich and acute tension of ficto-reality touches all aspects of contemporary existence. As architects R&Sie have observed, 'science fiction has shifted neither forward nor backward but into the here and now. The books of Stephenson, Gibson, Sterling and others, while marketed as speculative fiction, were in fact live broadcasts, and the funhouse mirror that that the genre tended to create expanded throughout a universe of plausibilities and melted into the news, with all of its social dimensions.'[6]

Philip K. Dick already knew this, writing in his journal in 1978 that 'we're in a *condition*, not a world', and admitting that what he liked to do most was to create universes that were designed to fall apart.[7] For artists, confronting the 'condition' of the present often begins not with a question of delineation but of navigation: how to work with rather than work out the powerful tension between a limitless fantastical wilderness and the real business of being-in-the-world. The drive to generate and create science-fictional encounters, sensations and experiences, rather than simply illustrate science fiction narratives, has pulled science fiction off the page or the screen and into the real world. In contemporary art, 'science-fictionality' is most often articulated in real space, in real time.[8] It unfolds amongst durations and spaces as a principle of engagement that questions the platforms that permit its existence. Working through overlaps between fiction and non-fiction, the real and the imagined, science fiction is here valued for its capacity to construct alternate realities out of the very stuff from which the present is made.

That art disorients in productive ways is critical, and speaks also to one of the founding definitions of science fiction by Darko Suvin: the theory of cognitive estrangement. In the early 1970s, Suvin suggested that one of the most revolutionary elements of sci-fi is its ability to render thought itself strange, revealing the fragility of perception in the making of meaning.[9] But this kind of aesthetic and cognitive dissonance is not always a rigorously intellectual or even theoretical process. It is more often recognisable as a sensation, a kind of sensual, vertiginous pleasure invoked by the opening of a chasm, the creation of a hole through which another reality might emerge. The new territories of art, then: can they be accessed through the delirium of estrangement, through the vortices of science fiction, in 'no-knowledge zones'?[10]

Dealing with things not yet to come, with images charged with a state of future potential or spaces infused with a radical temporality, puts us in touch with the ability to imagine, and with the imaginary's capacity to build new worlds. As the artist Tom Nicholson has signalled, this is 'something that is not only really important to art, but also to our behaviour politically. We need not accept the world as it is because we can imagine it—and reshape it—otherwise.'[11] Although it may seem that we are a long way from the cover art of magazines such as *Amazing Stories*, or the fictions of Jules Verne and H.G. Wells from the 1800s, in some respects we haven't travelled far at all. The core principles of science fiction—alternate temporalities, extrapolation, speculation, consciousness of mutability, imagined possibilities—are all still clearly operating within the field of contemporary art, albeit within different formats and contexts. What *Making Worlds: Art and Science Fiction* suggests is that the presence of science fiction in art is now more readily determinable through analyses of behavioural structures and methodologies rather than through the investigation of icons, signs and objects. This shift not only presents a major revision of science fiction art outside of an iconographic domain, but it also offers another way of understanding the work completed by a vast selection of artists: a means of identifying patterns as yet unrecognised in the science fictions of contemporary art.

Notes

1 Robert Smithson, 'The Crystal Land' (1966), reprinted in Jack Flam (ed.), *Robert Smithson: The Collected Writings* (Berkeley: University of California Press, 1996), 7. On Smithson's interest in science fiction, see Eugene Tsai, 'Robert Smithson: Plotting a Line from Passaic, New Jersey to Amarillo, Texas', in Eugene Tsai and Cornelia Butler (eds), *Robert Smithson* (University of California Press and The Museum of Contemporary Art, Los Angeles: Berkeley and Los Angeles, 2004), 20. See also Chris McAuliffe's essay in this book.

2 J.G. Ballard, *The Crystal World* (New York: Berkeley Medallion Books, 1967), 61–2.

3 Ballard, *The Crystal World*, 75.

4 For Ballard's influence on American and English art in the 1960s and '70s, see Valérie Mavridorakis (ed.), *Art et science-fiction: La Ballard Connection* (Genève: Mamco, 2011).

5 David Robbins, 'Warm Science Fiction', in Pierre Huyghe, *Le Château de Turing* (Dijon: Le Consortium Dijon and Les presses du réel, 2003), 174.

6 R&Sie, '(Science) Fiction & Mass Culture Crisis', *New Territories*: http://www.new-territories.com/

roche%20text.htm. Accessed 22 April 2013.

7 Philip K. Dick, in Pamela Jackson and Jonathan Lethem (eds), *The Exegesis of Philip K. Dick* (Boston, New York: Houghton Mifflin Harcourt, 2011), 429.

8 On the idea of 'science-fictionality', see Istvan Csicery-Ronay: 'This widespread normalization of what is essentially a style of estrangement and dislocation has stimulated the development of science-fictional habits of mind, so that we no longer treat sf as purely a genre-engine producing formulaic effects, but rather as a kind of awareness we might call science-fictionality, a mode of response that frames and tests experiences as if they were aspects of a work of science fiction'. Istvan Csicsery-Ronay Jr, *The Seven Beauties of Science Fiction* (Connecticut: Wesleyan University Press, 2008), 2.

9 Darko Suvin, 'On the Poetics of the Science Fiction Genre', *College English*, 34.3 (Dec. 1972), 372–82.

10 On no-knowledge zones, see Amelia Barikin, *Parallel Presents: The Art of Pierre Huyghe* (Cambridge, MA: MIT Press, 2012), 207, 218.

11 Tom Nicholson, in Ryan Johnston (ed.), *Raafat Ishak and Tom Nicholson: Proposition for a Banner March and a Black Cube Hot Air Balloon* (Shepparton: Shepparton Art Museum, 2012), 35.

Crash and the aesthetics of disappearance

Andrew Frost

In April 1970, the exhibition 'Crashed Cars' opened at the New Arts Lab in Camden Town, London. On display were three crashed cars: a Pontiac, an Austin Cambridge A60 and a Mini. At the opening, an actress was hired to wander topless through the gallery and interview members of the crowd for a live feed to CCTV monitors. Jim Ballard's debut as a gallery artist was provocative: visitors poured their wine on the cars and smashed the glasses on the gallery floor. According to some accounts of the evening, the actress was sexually assaulted. After the opening the installation continued to provoke acts of vandalism, from the breaking of windscreens and mirrors to paint being daubed on car bodies to seats being urinated upon.[1] Although the work was designed to elicit just such a reaction, the ferocity of the response was surprising—not least to the creator of the work, the artist otherwise known as the science fiction writer, J.G. Ballard.

Ballard's foray into gallery exhibition validated many of the ideas underlying the novel *Crash* (1973) that was, at the time of the exhibition, a work in progress. Ballard's exhibition came at the end of a period of multimedia experimentation, including his 1970 collage novel *The Atrocity Exhibition* (which contained a chapter entitled 'Crash!'), poster and print advertising works, collaboration on a play and participation in an experimental documentary on his work screened on the BBC in 1971. The tenor of the time was towards radical forms and gestures, from Carl Andre's sculpture *Equivalent VIII* (1966)—denounced in the UK press when the Tate Gallery bought it in 1972—to the controversial provocations of COUM Transmissions' exhibition/performance at the ICA in 1976. In this context, Ballard's exhibition was surprisingly un-radical. Where Andre's infamous pile of bricks was an example of inscrutable minimalism, and COUM's proto-punk exhibition of bloodied tampons, knives and syringes tested the limits of publically presentable art objects, Ballard's artworks were sourced from a wrecker's yard and were simply smashed up cars, claimed as found objects and presented for the audience's consideration. Yet these objects, long since consigned back to the scrapyard to be melted down, remain radical as an *idea* because Ballard's gesture eschewed the trappings of experimental modernity for the cool surface of the contemporary object.

Like many things that are experienced when you're young, *Crash* had a profound influence on me when I finally got a hold of a copy in 1979, my second last year of high school. I had read about the book and its reputation as an avant-garde text in SF magazines, and in a chapter on the New Wave in the *Encyclopedia of Science Fiction* edited by Robert Holdstock published in 1978. I bought my copy of *Crash* from Galaxy Bookshop in Sydney, and as I gazed at its lurid cover as I travelled home on the train to the suburbs, I took in its details: a naked woman in front of a crashed car, its bonnet raised up like a gaping mouth, the woman's possibly lifeless head lolled to one side, her lower torso obscured by a twisted piece of metal. The cover seemed appropriate to the novel's uncredited (and no doubt unofficial) subtitle: A BRUTAL, EROTIC NOVEL.

Crash's cult reputation preceded my firsthand experience of it, but its reality was something quite different to what I had expected. Certainly, all the advertised violence was there, so too the dark satire of celebrity, and the strange meetings of sex, violence and cars, yet what was remarkable about *Crash* was just how approachable Ballard's prose style turned out to be. It certainly wasn't self-consciously *avant-garde* in any obvious stylistic sense: it deployed none of the cut up experimentation of William

Burroughs, nor the adventurousness of the *nouvelle roman*, nor even the fragmented prose of Ballard's own experimental phase. Its content was provocative, certainly, but its delivery was deliberately effaced and novelistic in the English tradition. The opening sets out its themes and its stylistic method:

> Vaughan died yesterday in his last car-crash. During our friendship he had rehearsed his death in many crashes, but this was his only true accident. Driven on a collision course towards the limousine of the film actress, his car jumped the rails of the London Airport flyover and plunged through the roof of a bus filled with airline passengers. The crushed bodies of package tourists, like a hemorrhage of the sun, still lay across the vinyl seats when I pushed my way through the police engineers an hour later. Holding the arm of her chauffer, the film actress Elizabeth Taylor, with whom Vaughan had dreamed of dying for so many months, stood alone under the revolving ambulance lights. As I knelt over Vaughan's body she placed a gloved hand to her throat.[2]

The precision of Ballard's prose is evident here. The novel proceeds in flashback from this scene, slowly building back to a dramatic recursion, but as an opening it sets the stage of its action—the roads and flyovers of London, the peripheries of Heathrow Airport—and the actors of the piece, the now-dead bystanders divided into two categories, both depersonalised groups: airline passengers, package tourists. A startling analogy describes a horrific scene without detail, but one rich with suggestion: *the bodies like a hemorrhage of the sun*. A dead body of the fictional antagonist Vaughan juxtaposed with the presence of a real world person, Elizabeth Taylor, and the 'gloved hand to her throat'.

Ballard's imagistic writing has the clarity of a photograph and the dramatic counterbalance between extremes is underscored by the matter-of-factness of its delivery. Even in the oft-quoted sequences of the book where Ballard's prose turns to 'pornographic realism', the text gains its most profound emotional effects in the slow accumulation of disturbing images:

> The volumes of Helen's thighs pressing against my hips, her left fist buried in my shoulder, her mouth grasping at my own, the shape and moisture of her anus as I stroked it with my ring finger, were each overlaid by the inventories of a benevolent technology—the molded binnacle of the instrument dials, the jutting carapace of the steering column shroud, the extravagant pistol grip of the handbrake. I felt the warm vinyl of the seat beside me, and then stroked the damp aisle of Helen's perineum. Her hand pressed against my right testicle. The plastic laminates around me, the colour of washed anthracite, were the same tones as her pubic hairs parted at the vestibule of her vulva. The passenger compartment enclosed us like a machine generating from our sexual act an homunculus of blood, semen and engine coolant.[3]

Jean Baudrillard observed that in *Crash*, 'everything is hyper-functional: traffic and accidents, technology and death, sex and simulation are all like one single, huge synchronous machine'.[4] For Baudrillard, Ballard's book was the 'first great novel of the universe of simulation' where the moral gaze, 'the critical judegmentalism that is still part of the old world's functionality', is absent, an absence framed by the functionality of the text itself:

> *Crash* devours its own rationality, since it does not treat the dysfunctional. It is a radicalized functional-

> ism, a functionalism that reaches its paradoxal limits and then burns them away. Thus, it becomes an undefinable object, and hence fascinating.[5]

For Baudrillard, *Crash* was an artifact of a 'non-symbolic universe' where images attained their power through the reversal 'of its mass-mediated substance (neon, concrete, cars, mechanical eroticism) [that] seems truly saturated with an intense initiatory power'.[6]

It's well noted that Ballard has given his name to a particular kind of image, the 'Ballardian' image or site. Jeanette Baxter argues that the term 'functions as a kind of trigger for conjuring up a series of distinctive images and landscapes which capture the contemporary condition in all of its violence and ambiguity; murdered celebrities, crashed cars, surveillance technologies, media politicians, gated communities'. To this list, Baxter adds 'vast shopping malls, drowned cities, nuclear weapons ranges and testing sites, landscaped business parks'.[7]

These are the sites of Baudrillard's notion of an 'initiatory power' that provoke a profound awareness of our sense of everyday reality, a process that connects Ballard's science fiction to the corpus of the genre. One of Ballard's major achievements as a SF writer was to widen the scope of his imagery from the obligatory Golden Age props of spaceships and aliens to the landscape of the contemporary world. Ballard was neither first nor alone in that project, but with the aid of his precise and focused prose, and a predilection for a particular array of images, his name has become indelibly associated with them.

Science fiction operates as a language of realism. In both its literary and filmic manifestations, narratives are framed by an effaced mimesis where effects, visual or textual, are rendered in the context of the believable, the everyday. This is one of the genre's most significant features, and examples of experimentation with representation, from anti-realist languages and *avant-garde* approaches to poetic, fantastical or compacted narratives are exceptions to a field of discourse marked by a strict adherence to realism: experimental SF novels such as John Brunner's *Stand on Zanzibar* (1973), Samuel R. Delany's *Dhalgren* (1975) or John Clute's more recent *Appleseed* (2001) are rare examples that challenge this orthodoxy. It is hard to think of any recent examples of SF cinema that might equate to the stylistic adventurousness of Jean-Luc Godard's *Alphaville* (1965) or *Weekend* (1967).

Another opening, another time: Richard and Stephanie Nova Milne who exhibit art as the art-making duo Ms&Mr unveil their installation video work *Occult To Do List 1988/2012* at Alaska Projects in Sydney, September 2012. The gallery is unusual—it is a single, small room on the sixth floor of a concrete multi-story car park in Kings Cross, Sydney, an exhibition space accessible via a long set of echoing stairs, or by car, located at the bottom of the hillside structure. At the opening, the crowd is exceedingly polite. They drink beer and wine, smoke and chat behind bright yellow plastic bollards erected by the gallery to protect visitors from any potential vehicular mishap. In the gallery space itself, mounted on a wall that leans away from the viewer at a 45-degree angle, is a three-screen video work displayed on monitors. On an adjacent wall is a watercolour that places the word 'CRASH' over what appears to be a crudely painted landscape, the text rendered in exact replica of the lettering on the first UK edition of Ballard's novel. The watercolour is spot-lit not by gallery lights but by the beam of a parked car that shines into the room. Nearby, adjacent to the gallery, is the same text again, this time rendered in two-metre-high polystyrene letters: 'CRASH'.

The images on the three screens need some decoding. On the right-hand vertical screen is the side-on image of a car slowly rising and falling, its body lifted up, its tail to the ground, its body slowly disappearing (and then reappearing) into the floor of the picture. It is a quote of David Pelham's 1974 Penguin edition cover for Ballard's *Drought* (1962), itself a pop art–inspired quote of Ant Farm's *Cadillac Ranch* (1974). The middle screen has two components: the background is a direct quotation of Chris Foss's cover for the 1975 Panther edition of *Crash*—the very same paperback version I had bought back in the late 1970s—while in the foreground the figure of a young boy is holding out his hand in mock pain, the hand covered in tomato sauce, the boy acting out the charade of being an accident victim. On the left screen, another image of the boy is seen; this time the context is more ambiguous, seen from the side, vertical screen format. He is perhaps asleep, perhaps pretending to be dead. The rendering of the images in all three screens accentuates pinks and reds, the individual elements have been collaged together and they shift, drifting apart, components slowly realigning: a deliberate gesture on the part of the artists to demonstrate the provisional nature of the composition, individual elements appropriated from various temporal locations and recontextualised into the here and now. Ms&Mr use elements of personal history in the form of old home movies and videos that they cut up and reuse—the image of the boy is in fact a sequence of Richard that has been placed into an entirely new temporal location. Later, after the show is finished, Ms&Mr retitle the work *Videodromes For The Alone: Amputee of the Neurotic Future 1988/2012*.

'Video art' is an imprecise term that refers to an array of technologies, from the long-defunct studio-bound tech of six decades past, through the development and release of portable gear and offline editing to the contemporary setting of HD mobile phone cameras and edit suites in every computer. As the technology of 'video art' has developed and dispersed, it has been marked by its disappearance from our collective consciousness. To notice a projector or a flat screen set up in a gallery space is completely unremarkable, but what is all the more startling is the fact that we cannot 'see' this technology. Like the 'frame' of realist prose, the representation of most video art exists in a cognitive space that appears to be quite separate to its delivery mechanism: we simply cannot sense the space between our eyes and the screen as we focus on images conjured in the soft light of a projection or the in the flow of HD plasma.

A number of artists working with screen technologies have experimented with the aesthetics of science fiction in what I would define as an aesthetic zone between the SF genre proper (and its manifestations in cinema and literature) and the edges of contemporary art practice. In this category we might include works by Anne Lislegaard, an artist who has examined in detail the potential of adapting themes from SF novels into installation works, including a work based on Ballard's *Crystal World*, or Aernout Mik, whose screen works such as *Middlemen* (2000) or *Pulverous* (2003) touched on elements of dystopic SF themes. Ms&Mr's engagement with Ballard's text eschews the conceptual 'stability' of faux-cinematic montage for a more discursive and 'unstable' visual collage, and an exhibition staging that further enhances and highlights the audience's mode of viewing the work. In a very real sense, Ballard's novel anticipated our contemporary moment, not because of the disruption of order, or the intrusion of symbolic desire into a waking state, but because these strategies of estrangement have been so comfortably absorbed by media. Where *Crash* remains provocative is in its unflinching will to expose the apparatus of its making, a will not wholly resolved in its form, an uncertainty that powers its effect.

Notes

1 Simon Ford, 'A Psychopathic Hymn: J.G. Ballard's "Crashed Cars" Exhibition of 1970', *Seconds*: http://www.slashseconds.org/issues/001/001/articles/13_sford/index.php. Accessed 22 November 2012.
2 J.G. Ballard, *Crash* (London: Panther, 1975), 3.
3 Ballard, *Crash*, 68.
4 Jean Baudrillard, 'Two Essays', *Science Fiction Studies*, Vol. 18, No. 55, Part 3 (November 1991): http://www.depauw.edu/sfs/backissues/55/baudrillard55art.htm. Accessed 22 November 2012.
5 Baudrillard, 1991.
6 Baudrillard, 1991.
7 Jeannette Baxter, 'J.G. Ballard and the Contemporary', in Jeanne Baxter (ed.), *J.G. Ballard: Contemporary Critical Perspectives* (London: Continuum, 2008), 2.

Not such a crap artist

Helen Hughes

In what follows, I conduct a science-fictional thought-experiment: I discuss Philip K. Dick's literary invention of an empathy box in *Do Androids Dream of Electric Sheep?* (1968) as a contemporary artwork, analysing it vis-à-vis Claire Bishop and Boris Groys's theories of installation art. At the centre of inquiry for both Bishop and Groys is the formulation of a community around contemporary installation art. For them, what constitutes the success or failure of contemporary installation relates to the level of self-awareness of the viewing community produced by the installation artwork. There is a parallel to be drawn here between such communities of installation art and the community produced by Dick's empathy boxes in *Do Androids Dream*. While an empathy box is not an artwork—it is, rather, a quasi-religious tool that is used to psychically unite the human community in the novel—it functions, I argue, analogously to certain contemporary artworks as described by Bishop and Groys. The narrative motif of the reveal, which is in some ways paradigmatic of Dick's science fiction, much of which is premised upon telescoping realities (*Valis*, 1981, or *The Three Stigmata of Palmer Eldritch*, 1965, are perhaps the best examples), is shown to be a feature shared with contemporary installation art. The reveal, I argue, is the circuit-breaker in the closed loops of centred and unified modes of self-identification within both the science-fictional and contemporary installation art communities. Put otherwise, it is the reveal that prompts self-reflexive viewing in both the communities described in Dick's science fiction and those produced by contemporary installation art. This analogy is offered as an example of classical science fiction anticipating a key theme in contemporary art.

The closed loop: Claire Bishop

In her famous response to Nicolas Bourriaud's concept of 'relational aesthetics' (the essay 'Antagonism and Relational Aesthetics', first published in *October* in 2004, and republished in 2005 as the final chapter of her book *Installation Art: A Critical History*), Claire Bishop argued that the 'microtopian' communities brought into being by projects such as Rirkrit Tiravanija's pad thai openings and Liam Gillick's discursive 'backdrops' effectuate a type of closed circuit of self-identification. Bishop suggests that these microtopian communities are myopic, trapped in a closed loop of self-identification wherein like-minded people—such as art dealers and critics—get together and talk about what they share in common.[1] Of Tiravanija's 1996 Cologne project *Untitled (Tomorrow is Another Day)*, a wooden reconstruction of his apartment in a gallery that visitors could occupy and use as they pleased, Bishop writes: 'This may be a microtopia, but—like utopia—it is still predicated on the exclusion of those who hinder or prevent its realization'. To iterate her point, she adds in parentheses: 'what might have happened if Tiravanija's space had been invaded by those seeking genuine "asylum"?'[2]

Because the relational artwork or art object in question is comprised by the interactions between its viewers, and these viewers, according to Bishop, are largely like-minded people and are definitely not asylum seekers, no outside perspective needs be confronted. That is to say, all identification within this type of relational artwork is a type of self-identification, and no meta- or outside perspective is integrated into the work. That this self-identification eschews any real internal difference is a problem for Bishop because this relational structure is not, then, politically emancipatory, as Bourriaud suggests. And nor does it reflect the fragmented and decentred nature of contemporary subjectivity—after feminism, colonialism, and structuralism. '[T]he relations set up by relational aesthetics are not intrinsically democratic, as Bourriaud suggests', writes Bishop, 'since they rest too comfortably within an ideal of subjectivity as whole and of community as immanent togetherness... [relational aesthetics] produces a community whose members identify with each other, because they have something in common'.[3]

According to Bishop, Bourriaud's microtopian community is a myopic community because it cannot truly see itself. Bourriaud's community is blind to the frictions and inequalities that make up actual politically emancipatory, democratic communities. Bishop quotes Rosalyn Deutsche—'Conflict, division, and instability, then, do not ruin the democratic public sphere; they are conditions of its existence'—to describe the way a democratic community necessarily includes rupture and dissent.[4] A microtopian community, in contrast, excludes or suppresses rupture and dissent and is therefore a type of monoculture: it is bound by a closed circuit of self-identification, rather than a more confronting 'non-identification' with the political other. The work of Santiago Sierra and Thomas Hirschhorn, which often stages encounters between typical viewers of contemporary art (educated, upper-middle class) and people who are usually excluded from the contemporary art institution (such as refugees, migrant communities, prostitutes, street vendors), is more successful to Bishop's mind because it foregrounds a form of non-identification that underlies contemporary subjectivity—after feminism, colonialism, structuralism.[5] Of Sierra's 2001 work for the Venice Biennale, *Persons Paid to Have Their Hair Dyed Blond*, which comprised a cast of recent Senegalese, Chinese and Bangladeshi immigrants to Italy, Bishop writes: 'Sierra's action disrupted the art audience's sense of identity, which is founded precisely on unspoken racial and class exclusions'.[6]

In her 2005 monograph on installation art, Bishop argues that installation as an artistic medium is a priori well disposed to deal with the inherently fragmented and decentred nature of contemporary subjectivity. This is because installation art, emerging alongside theories of poststructuralism which proliferated in the 1970s, is defined by the fact that there is no central or correct vantage point from which to view the multidimensional installation artwork—as opposed to a traditional painting or sculpture. '[P]oststructuralist theory argues that each person is intrinsically dislocated and divided, at odds with him or herself. In short, it states that the correct way in which to view our condition as human subjects is as fragmented, multiple and *decentered*.'[7] As such, the related perspectives offered by installation art, which has a greater capacity to mirror decentered, fragmented contemporary subjectivity, and 'relational antagonism', which affords a clearer reflection of a functioning democratic community, can be seen to produce self-aware viewing subjects.

The closed loop: empathy boxes and Mercerism

The inwardly focused, closed-loop community that comes into being in Bishop's analysis of [bad] relational artworks seems to me to be paralleled in a subplot surrounding the religion of Mercerism and the associated device of an empathy box in Philip K. Dick's 1968 novel, *Do Androids Dream of Electric Sheep?* In the novel, the state religion to which all human beings belong is called 'Mercerism'. Mercerism pivots around the suffering of a man named Wilbur Mercer who, like Sisyphus, is destined to walk endlessly up a mountain while he is abused by assailants who throw stones at him. Followers of Mercerism use empathy boxes to tap into a collective consciousness with Mercer at the centre; this centralised suffering of Mercer is broadcast to the community at large via the 'small black screen' on their empathy boxes. When tuned in, which is done by holding the box's handles, users of empathy boxes are inflicted with the same pains as Mercer, hence the name 'empathy' (as opposed to 'sympathy') box. Mercerists have empathy boxes in their homes, and they can tap into Mercer's suffering when in need of spiritual gratification:

> as he clutched the handles, John Isidore gradually experienced a waning of the living room in which he stood; the dilapidated furniture and walls ebbed out and he ceased to experience them at all. He found himself, instead, as always before, entering into the landscape of drab hill, drab sky. And at the same time he no longer witnessed the climb of the elderly man. His own feet now scraped, sought purchase, among the familiar loose stones; he felt the same old painful, irregular roughness beneath his feet and once again smelled the acrid haze of the sky—not Earth's sky but that of some place alien, distant, and yet, by means of the empathy box, instantly available... physical merging—accompanied by mental and spiritual identification—with Wilbur Mercer had reoccurred. As it did for everyone who at this moment clutched the handles, either here on Earth or on one of the colony planets. He experienced them, the others, incorporated the babble of their thoughts, heard in his own brain the noise of their many individual existences. They—and he—cared about one thing; this fusion of their mentalities...[8]

Through this process of 'fusion', the multiple subjectivities of empathy box users are 'condensed into the singularity of Mercer'.[9] A closed loop with no outside is created, thus giving rise to the term 'post-individual' that is frequently invoked to describe the human collective in *Do Androids*

Dream.[10] Mercerism, then, is a religion grounded in empathy. Empathy ('the intellectual identification with or vicarious experiencing of the feelings, thoughts, or attitudes of another',[11] as opposed to sympathy, feeling pity, sorry or compassion for another's misfortune) is the emotional capacity that literally binds humans together via the empathy box. Human empathy in the novel is concentrated on the figure of Mercer who, like Christ, is the Vine that connects and nurtures all believers.[12]

Importantly, in the world of *Do Androids Dream*, the capacity to empathise is also what distinguishes humans from androids, who by definition cannot empathise with others. Indeed, the understanding of humanity itself in *Do Androids Dream* is premised entirely on its 'psychic distance' from androids who are not naturally empathetic.[13] Mercerism is the theology that unites and defines all humans by excluding all androids from that definition (of humans as inherently empathic subjects, and androids as hard-wired to be without empathy). The Voigt-Kampff test administered by bounty hunters seeking out replicants (also known as androids) masquerading as humans measures the timing of empathic responses in its subjects: for humans, an empathic response is automatic, whereas in replicants it is fractionally too-slow (because it is a logical not an automatic response). We are all familiar with the famous *noir* showdown between a bounty hunter and the Nexus-6 replicant Leon in *Blade Runner* (1982), Ridley Scott's film adaption of the Dick novel, in which Leon the replicant immediately kills the bounty hunter upon realising that he has failed the Voigt-Kampff test (and will thus be revealed as a replicant and promptly executed, or 'retired').

The reveal: Al Jarry

The closed loop of self-identification in *Do Androids Dream*, however, is not left intact by the book's plot.

By the end of the novel, Mercerism is partly undone as Mercer himself is revealed to be a fake. A popular TV personality called Buster Friendly, whose image is broadcast twenty-three hours per day via his television show *Buster Friendly and His Friendly Friends*, reveals Wilbur Mercer to be an alcoholic, B-grade actor whose real name is Al Jarry,[14] and the desert mountain landscape in which he toils is shown to be a cheap, Hollywood sound set (the sky a painted backdrop, and the rocks hurled at him made of light-weight plastic). Friendly, himself a closet android, gleefully announces: '...as we theorized, the "rocks" did consist of rubber-like plastic. The "blood" was catsup, and...the only suffering Mr. Jarry underwent was having to go an entire day without a shot of whisky.'[15] In this way, the reveal, Dick's plot device that unmasks a greater or truer reality in which the earlier, self-contained events of the novel were seen to be taking place all along, ruptures the coherent self-identification of Mercerists.

The reveal: Boris Groys

This ousting of Mercer as a fake, the reveal that exposes the self-identification of the 'post-individual' community in *Do Androids Dream* as a closed loop, functions analogously to what Boris Groys describes as the shift in perspective effected by contemporary installation art. That is, the shift in perspective that enables the closed collective to see itself as such (a closed community) from an outside perspective.

Groys describes this shift best in his 2009 essay 'Politics of Installation', where he juxtaposes the viewer of mass culture and the viewer of contemporary installation art.[16] He explains that although a type of community comes together in the experience of mass culture (through a film screening, or a rock concert), that community cannot self-reflexively see itself because it is 'forward-oriented': toward the film screen, or the musicians performing. 'Mass culture', Groys argues, '...cannot fully reflect...because the communities it creates are not sufficiently aware of themselves as such'. Therefore, he concludes, 'they do not constitute any *politea*'.[17] Viewers of installation art, by contrast, *can* view themselves and reflect on the structure of the community of which they are a part because:

> The relative spatial separation provided by the installation space does not mean a turn away from the world [as with forward-oriented mass culture], but rather a de-localization and de-territorialization of mass-cultural transitory communities—in a way that assists them in reflecting upon their own condition, offering them an opportunity to exhibit themselves to themselves.[18]

In other words, the viewer of installation art is trained to look not at a discrete art object—a painting, a sculpture—but rather at the broader art context; they are trained to adopt a meta-perspective that includes other viewers wandering around the space who are also adopting a meta-perspective. The viewer of installation art, then, is able to see mass-culture from an outside perspective that includes a vision of their place, and the place of their community, within it. As such, according to Groys, the community that forms around an installation artwork is self-reflexive. Though, and typically of Groys's writing, he does not give an actual example of this effect in contemporary installation art. (Indeed his conception of 'installation art' remains entirely a linguistic proposition throughout the essay: basically an expanded definition of the readymade—nominalism.) However, one explicit manifestation of this kind of self-reflexive viewer can be seen in Bruce Nauman's installation *Live-Taped Video Corridor* of 1970.[19] Here, Nauman uses CCTV technology to film viewers of the work as they walk down a series of narrow, makeshift corridors towards a television screen onto which this CCTV footage is being broadcast live. As the viewer inches closer towards the TV screen, the image (of the back of this viewer walking towards the TV set) gets smaller and smaller, since the fixed-angle camera is mounted at the opposite end of the corridor.

Certain correlations between a forward-oriented, mass-cultural community as opposed to the self-reflexive community of installation art are readily apparent in *Do Androids Dream*: empathy boxes are thinly-veiled references to TV sets (aka 'idiot boxes'), reaching their peak commodification in 1960s America when and where Dick was writing. Moreover, Dick's invention of empathy boxes, as nearly every commentator on *Do Androids Dream* has pointed out, roughly correlates with the emergence of Marshall McLuhan's theory of a 'global village', in which television viewers are physically isolated but psychically connected to one another via 'the box' in their lounge room. In *Do Androids Dream*, the protagonist Rick Deckard's wife Iran, for instance, is characterised as superficial, unenlightened, and forward-oriented (hooked on her empathy box and her Penfield mood organ).[20] She is depicted in an unflattering light, constantly spitting venom at her husband ('get your crude cop hands off me!'), and completely beholden to her suite of mass-produced domestic items—like the empathy box and mood organ. (At one point, Deckard sets Iran's emotional dial to 594 on the mood organ: 'pleased acknowledgement of husband's superior wisdom in all matters'.)[21]

Once the reveal of Mercerism as a sham takes place, Mercerists are forced to confront, or see, the nature of their self-identification as locked in a groove. Like the viewer of installation art according to Groys, these subjects are given the opportunity to become reflexive, aware and 'enlightened'—they are now able to see mass culture and their place within it at a remove; the collective sees itself as performing a closed loop of self-identification from an outside perspective. This part of the plot is tracked more clearly through the character J.R. Isidore, a 'special' or 'chickenhead', whose world literally begins to collapse after Buster Friendly's revelation:

> Mercer is gone; he saw the dust and the ruin of the apartment as it lay spreading out everywhere—he heard the kipple coming, the final disorder of all forms, the absence which would win out. It grew around him as he stood holding the empty ceramic cup; the cupboards of the kitchen creaked and split and he felt the floor beneath his feet give.[22]

Buster Friendly, his voice still booming from the TV set, continues to antagonise Isidore by articulating the real impact of the Mercer–Jarry exposé:

> But ponder this…Ask yourselves what is it that Mercerism does. Well, if we're to believe its many practitioners, the experience fuses…men and women throughout the Sol System into a single entity. But an entity which is manageable by the so-called telepathic voice of 'Mercer'. Mark that. An ambitious politically minded would-be Hitler…[23]

Therefore, the self-identification of Mercerists not only serves to demarcate humans from androids, but also to render human users of empathy boxes wholly compliant as political subjects (i.e., un-reflexive, unaware, unenlightened). Put another way, pre-reveal empathy box users are like Groys's mass-cultural viewers (forward-oriented towards the 'little black screen'), and post-reveal empathy box users are like Groys's installation art viewers (gifted with a meta-perspective on their relationship to mass-cultural objects). In Bishop's framework, the reveal also functions analogously to installation art because it forces empathy box users to abandon the idea of subjectivity as unified (literally, through 'the singularity of Mercer') and of community as a form of 'immanent togetherness'.

Friendly *v.* Mercer

What would it mean, finally, to think of the empathy box and the related religion of Mercerism as an installation artwork, and of Wilbur Mercer and Buster Friendly as artists (perhaps video artists)?[24] In the scenario I have sketched above, it would seem that Mercer—in Bishop's eyes—is the lesser artist, the Gillick or Tiravanija, whose conception of 'community' operates as a microtopia by excluding any real difference or threat to unified identity; and Friendly is the greater artist, the Sierra or Hirschhorn, who foregrounds radical difference and non-identification as the underlying principles of subjectivity itself.

However, in a final turn of the screw in *Do Androids Dream*, Dick does not let the unmasking of Wilbur Mercer as the alcoholic, bit-part actor Al Jarry destroy human communion with the God. Indeed, in the pages that follow the revelation, J.R. Isidore and Rick Deckard continue to merge with Mercer and seek his advice. In response to the suggestion that Mercer is a fake, Deckard famously declares that Mercer couldn't possibly be fake—'Unless reality is a fake'.[25] Many humans continue to believe in Mercer simply because they want or need to: perhaps, Dick finally seems to suggest, it is belief, or the need to believe in something, that is the operative process that unites and defines humanity.

Here, I am reminded of an artist, indeed a contemporary installation artist, also a fan of Philip K. Dick, and a long-time thinker on the topic of empathy boxes: Mike Nelson. Speaking of his total installation *The Coral Reef* from 2000, Nelson said the work was about 'the impossibility of believing in anything but wanting to believe in something'.[26] *The Coral Reef* comprised a series of fifteen interconnecting rooms, joined by a winding corridor loosely modelled on the shape of a swastika—with each new wing of the installation folding back in on itself. As viewers of the installation wandered between rooms, they were faced with a series of manifestations of zealous belief in various different ideologies: ranging from mainstream and alternative religions (evangelical, Islamic and satanic), to motorcycle gangs, to socialism, to drug use. Typical of his approach to sculpture, Nelson represented these different ideologies through a series of small, shrine-like constellations of objects: a pair of black horns and a newspaper clipping about Aleister Crowley in the satanic room; an upturned milk crate with some aluminium foil and a cigarette lighter in the heroin room; a cluster of books on communism in the 'Mexican Revolutionaries' room. Importantly, however, the journey through all these rooms and their attendant ideologies began with art: the first of all these rooms was the small reception area of Nelson's primary gallery, Matt's Gallery, in London.[27]

Nelson derived the spatial structure of *The Coral Reef* from the book *A Perfect Vacuum*, written by the Polish science fiction writer Stanislaw Lem in 1971. *A Perfect Vacuum* is an anthology of reviews of made-up books, and its first chapter is a review of itself—completing the circular logic of the book much in the manner of Ouroboros the Serpent, who is forever chasing his own tail. In this way, Nelson's gallery reception area functions as an apposite 'introduction to itself' since, as Claire Bishop has suggested in her reading of the work, 'art is a belief system, the same as heroin or Islam or the biker gang'.[28]

As in the science fiction of Philip K. Dick, the reveal plays a central role in the installation art of Mike Nelson, whose ultra-realistic total installations can be described as a succession of telescoping realities in which the installation and the world at large bleed seamlessly into one another in a mutually enlightening manner. In *The Coral Reef*, the first of these successive reveals occurs when the art gallery reception area gives way to the first of Nelson's constructed rooms, an Islamic mini-cab office, and the last reveal occurs when a second, simulacral Islamic mini-cab office at the other end of the installation gives way to the gallery's storeroom — replete with the offcuts of wood and MDF board, as well as the half-empty paint tins that were used to construct the rest of the installation. The reveals in *The Coral Reef*, then, are highly self-reflexive artistic strategies that repeatedly point back to the installation's status as installation art: a constructed or fabricated reality, one made of MDF and recently hand-painted by the artist. And all this despite the highly convincing artifice (the realism) of the rooms and corridors. In this way, the community of viewers produced by Nelson's installation are doubly self-reflexive: they see themselves not only looking, but believing.

Notes

1 Speaking of American critic Jerry Saltz's review of a Tiravanija work, Bishop suggests that 'the review only tells us that Tiravanija's intervention is considered good because it permits networking among a group of art dealers and like-minded art lovers, and because it evokes the atmosphere of a late-night bar.' Claire Bishop, 'Antagonism and Relational Aesthetics', *October*, No. 110 (Fall 2004), 67.

2 Bishop, 'Antagonism and Relational Aesthetics', 68.

3 Bishop, 'Antagonism and Relational Aesthetics', 67.

4 Quoted in Bishop, 'Antagonism and Relational Aesthetics', 63: Roslayn Deutsche, *Evictions: Art and Spatial Politics* (Cambridge, MA: MIT Press, 1996), 295–6.

5 'Poststructuralist theory argues that each person is

intrinsically dislocated and divided, at odds with him or herself. In short, it states that the correct way in which to view our condition as human subjects is as fragmented, multiple and decentred.' Claire Bishop, *Installation Art: A Critical History* (London: Tate Publishing, 2005), 13.

6 Bishop, 'Antagonism and Relational Aesthetics', 73.

7 Bishop, *Installation Art*, 13.

8 Philip K. Dick, *Do Androids Dream of Electric Sheep?* [1968] (UK: Millennium Publications, 1999), 20.

9 Christopher A. Sims, 'The Dangers of Individualism and the Human Relationship to Technology', *Science Fiction Studies*, Vol. 36, No. 1 (March, 2009), 80.

10 See, for instance, Kevin R. McNamara, '*Blade Runner*'s post-individual Worldspace', *Contemporary Literature*, Vol. 38, No. 3 (Autumn, 1997), 422–66, and Sims, 'The Dangers of Individualism and the Human Relationship to Technology'.

11 'Empathy', *Dictionary.com*: http://dictionary.reference.com/browse/empathy?s=t. Accessed 29 June 2013.

12 John 15:5. [Jesus said] 'I am the vine; you are the branches. If you remain in me and I in you, you will bear much fruit; apart from me you can do nothing.'

13 Nexus-6 replicant Irmgard explains: '... it's that empathy... isn't it a way of proving that humans can do something we can't do? Because without the Mercer experience we just have your [human] *word* that you feel this empathy business, this shared, group thing...'. Dick, *Do Androids Dream of Electric Sheep?*, 179–80.

14 A reference to the pataphysicist, Alfred Jarry.

15 Dick, *Do Androids Dream of Electric Sheep?*, 179.

16 Boris Groys, 'Politics of Installation', *e-flux journal*, No. 2 (January 2009): http://www.e-flux.com/journal/politics-of-installation/. Accessed 6 June 2013.

17 Groys, 'Politics of Installation', 05/08.
18 Groys, 'Politics of Installation', 05/08.
19 Thank you to Amelia Barikin for this example.
20 A Penfield mood organ is a device in *Do Androids Dream of Electric Sheep?* that allows users to dial-up desired emotions or feelings, such as: 'business-like professional attitude'; 'self-accusatory depression'; 'the desire to watch TV, no matter what's on it' (dial 888); 'creative and fresh attitude toward job'; or, my favourite, 'more venom'. See Dick, *Do Androids Dream of Electric Sheep?*, 4–6.
21 Dick, *Do Androids Dream of Electric Sheep?*, 6.
22 Dick, *Do Androids Dream of Electric Sheep?*, 181.
23 Dick, *Do Androids Dream of Electric Sheep?*, 179.
24 Incidentally, in another essay called 'Comrades of Time' (2009), Groys suggests that Camus's Sisyphus is a 'proto-contemporary-artist whose aimless, senseless task of repeatedly rolling a boulder up a hill can be seen as a prototype for contemporary time-based art'. A better candidate would be Mercer, who, unlike Camus's Sisyphus, literally performs his relentless ascent *for a camera* (for an audience). Boris Groys, 'Comrades of Time', *e-flux journal*, No. 11 (December 2009): http://www.e-flux.com/journal/comrades-of-time/. Accessed 29 June 2013.
25 Dick, *Do Androids Dream of Electric Sheep?*, 201.
26 Bishop, *Installation Art*, 48.
27 When Nelson rebuilt this work for exhibition at the Tate Britain after it was purchased for the Tate collection in 2009, he rebuilt a facsimile of this room instead of using the readymade room when it was first exhibited in 2000 at Matt's Gallery in London.
28 Claire Bishop, 'Master of Reality', *Untitled* (Spring 2000), 6.

Eduardo Paolozzi: Surrealism, sci-fi and pop

Ryan Johnston

In 1966, the critic David Irwin published an article in *Studio International* titled 'Pop Art and Surrealism' in which, via a series of short case studies based on stylistic comparison, he raised the broad question of how the two movements might be related.[1] In the almost half century since the publication of Irwin's essay, however, it is the relationship between pop art and dada that has attracted the majority of art historical attention, while the precise legacy of surrealism remains relatively ill-attended. With this paper I seek to begin addressing this lacuna by focusing upon one of the artists Irwin identified as manifesting both pop and surrealist tendencies: Eduardo Paolozzi. Rather than stylistic analysis, my method is principally one of intellectual biography. By tracing in some detail the idiosyncratic reception of surrealism by Paolozzi, I will suggest that while it was certainly no longer considered a revolutionary or emancipatory project, its proclivity for fantastical, science-fictional world-making both provided a pathway to, and indeed some correspondence with, pop.

Paolozzi is today more frequently associated with pop than surrealism, and most accounts of pop—from Mario Amaya's influential 1965 book *Pop Art... And After* through to Hal Foster and Mark Francis's 2005 Phaidon monograph—begin with reference to his 1950s collages, comprised predominantly of mass cultural sources, and known collectively as *Bunk!*.[2] However, while the artist always remained ambivalent about his status as a 'Father of Pop', he did consistently affiliate with surrealism. For example, in a lengthy 1971 interview with his good friend, the science fiction author J.G. Ballard, Paolozzi insisted that his practice needed to be understood as 'an extension of radical surrealism'.[3] In order to begin coming to terms with what he and Ballard may have meant by this nomenclature, this article takes as a case study a small series of Paolozzi's sculptures and examines in some depth the precise nature of their surrealist heritage.

—

The works in question are the anthropomorphic bronze sculptures, produced between 1956 and 1959, for which Paolozzi first earned an international reputation. Apparently comprised of mass-produced objects and endowed with archetypal or otherwise mythological titles that convey a gravitas seemingly at odds with their own shaky architecture (*Jason*, 1956, *Icarus*, 1957, and *Cyclops*, 1957), these works visualise an apparently broad, profound and grotesque transformation in the relations between the human body and environment. In works like *Robot* (1956), the first of these sculptures, the body is in a state of dissolution and dilution: the figure is pockmarked and bitten, the arms and right hip have dissolved almost entirely, and gaping holes have opened the upper torso and head to the surrounding space. At the same time, the body has begun absorbing external characteristics: the legs resemble metal coils or springs, while on the right side of the head, a cog or some type of lens forms a lone eye emerging from the otherwise lax facial musculature. As the series progressed, correlation between biological function and artificial appendage was abstracted more or less totally, and any vestiges of psychology evaporated accordingly. By the time the series reached its conclusion with the *St Sebastian* sculptures (1957–9), the subject was reduced to a monumental yet shambolic husk seemingly at risk of collapse under the weight of its own over-articulated yet inexplicable form.

While there is considerably more to be said about the iconography of these works, the present essay instead focuses on the unusual process by which the sculptures were made, as it is in this respect that their fundamental surrealist and science-fictional influences can be detected most clearly. Although commonly mistaken for the type of welded or otherwise constructed metal sculpture so prevalent at the time, these works were in fact produced via a convoluted sculptural procedure that has gone undiscussed in the literature to date, despite Paolozzi's own efforts to foreground process in the reception of these works from the very beginning. For example, in a 1958 public lecture he explained that these sculptures were made by first selecting a range of found objects from everyday life (including food tins, electrical componentry, domestic gadgets and children's toys), taking their impressions in clay or plaster slabs, and then filling these impressions with molten wax.[4] Once dry, the wax was removed as a single and highly detailed sheet that could be heated, bent and shaped around clay cores to form figures that were finally cast in bronze via the *cire perdue* technique. The most striking aesthetic implication of this procedure is that while from a distance or in reproduction the sculptures appear hard and mechanical, upon closer inspection their surfaces appear as soft and organic (due to the use of wax models). The organic appearance belies both the metallic medium and the mass-produced materials from which the sculptures appear to be constituted. And this is an effect that, somewhat paradoxically, became more pronounced the more artificial objects were incorporated into the process. The encounter with these sculptures, most of which are slightly larger than life-size, is thus one of disturbingly simultaneous familiarity and otherness, or of self- and dis-identification.

Despite Paolozzi's efforts to distinguish his work by emphasising this procedure, these sculptures were nonetheless quickly subsumed within the neo-expressionist/existentialist discourse of the period, an eventuation due in no small part to their inclusion in MoMA's 'New Images of Man' exhibition in 1959. As this alleged shift from mass-cultural collage to expressionist sculpture constitutes an inversion of the privileged teleological trajectory of 1950s art, these works have tended to be dismissed as a reactionary turning away from the more progressive pop agendas of colleagues like Richard Hamilton, and resultantly they have received relatively little sustained art historical attention. Those accounts we do have are characterised both by an expressionist thematic as well as an historical displacement that figures them as images of past trauma (i.e., World War II and Korea), future catastrophe (i.e., nuclear or otherwise technologically inflicted) and/or a kind of schlock sci-fi primitivism (i.e., the Creature from the Black Lagoon meets the African tribal fetish).[5] By focusing on the paradoxically organic and metallic surface effects of these sculptures, and the implications of the technique by which this was achieved, I will argue that rather than expressionistically figuring a traumatic past or a catastrophic future, these works redeployed a sci-fi inflected surrealism to face up to the newly dawned age of pop.

—

At this point it needs to be clarified that the use of the term 'pop' in this context connotes not simply 'pop art', but is, in the spirit of Paolozzi's friend Lawrence Alloway, intended to encompass the broader historical shift of which the artistic practice was but one manifestation. Indeed, this shift from the austerity of the immediate post-war period to a new pop present in Britain c. 1956 was propelled by a variety of historical forces. These included the influx of Hollywood movies and American magazines (heightened under the conditions of the Anglo-American loan agreement); the belated but rapid institution of a largely American commodity and consumer culture, a culture that was in turn driven in no small part by a government-led automation program that dramatically reconfigured the practice of labour and leisure; and the displacement of British geo-political influence (for example the Suez Canal crisis) amid increasing Cold War insecurities. And the most useful place to start explicating how a science-fictional surrealism was summoned to deal with this historical moment is another paradigmatic event of 1956, the exhibition 'This is Tomorrow' at the Whitechapel Gallery.

—

'This is Tomorrow' opened at the Whitechapel Gallery in August 1956, at more or less exactly the same time Paolozzi began making these new sculptures. It was, of course, a seminal moment in the history of pop art, however it was also a moment when several key figures of the Independent Group, Paolozzi included, had begun to rethink their artistic practices in response to recent history. As Paolozzi's collaborators, the architects Alison and Peter Smithson, said of *Patio and Pavilion*, their sombre contribution to the exhibition, 'we were taking position in the acquisitive society as it began its run'.[6] For the purposes of this article, however, the exhibition itself is of less relevance than the events of the opening night party.

As is well known, 'This is Tomorrow' was launched by an actor dressed as Robby the Robot, the star of MGM's science fiction film *Forbidden Planet*, who, according to the organisers, was the first robot to open an art exhibition. Unfortunately this auspicious moment was marred when the costume's poor ventilation caused the domed visor to fog up as the actor, struggling for air and unable to read his lines, was heckled by the unappreciative crowd. What has gone unremarked, however, is how similar accounts of that night were to those of another famous exhibition that opened in London exactly twenty years earlier with a near identical sartorial misadventure:

the 'First International Surrealist Exhibition'. On that occasion, Salvador Dali took to the stage dressed not as a robot but an aquanaut, only for his address to be curtailed in similar fashion when he began to asphyxiate and had to be cut from his costume as, once again, the crowd heckled. Notably, while there were numerous witnesses to the Dali episode, we are reliant on the organisers of 'This is Tomorrow' for reports of its opening.[7] The question that thus emerges is: why was what is arguably the first exhibition of pop framed by surrealism?

The dysfunctional prosthetic body was, of course, a fairly common surrealist trope. As Hal Foster has argued, it provided a vehicle with which to dialectically engage the Fordist reorganisation of French society that transpired contemporaneously with the movement's emergence.[8] Robby played a similarly critical function at 'This is Tomorrow', as Lawrence Alloway explained in an article strategically placed in *Art News and Review* to coincide with the exhibition. In his text, titled 'The Robot and the Arts', Alloway explained that Robby's presence at the exhibition was 'a gimmick, of course, but a gimmick with resonance, with implications'.[9] The implications were outlined as follows:

> Robby's presence at 'This is Tomorrow' pin-pointed the problem: who makes the machine age art, the fine artists or the popular artists?...At a time when many artists are looking for iconographies with which to express 'the times' with a high degree of accessibility the popular arts have it. At the disposal of pulp magazine artists, comic book staff, film studios, their publicity departments, toy manufacturers, is a tool of amazing...strength.[10]

'The times' to which Alloway referred were of course different to those of the surrealists, but, as I have already outlined, no less paradigmatic. And if for the surrealists the mechanical prosthesis was an icon of the era of mass production, then the robot, by 1956, had assumed a similar status. It was the symbol, Alloway argued, that could best accommodate the complex historical matrix of the new pop age, and, as he well knew, an image with increasing currency in the popular media of the period, where it denoted not the new industrial and cultural technologies of pop, but the very people whose everyday life was increasingly mediated by them.[11]

—

Seen against this backdrop, it seems hardly coincidental that the first of Paolozzi's new sculptures was titled *Robot*, and these works should thus be considered a direct response to, or even collusion with, Alloway's call. However, Paolozzi's personal deployment of surrealism was both more specific and idiosyncratic than a straightforward updating of Dali's iconography. When asked in 1958 by the critic Edouard Roditi to elaborate on an earlier claim to the surrealist influence on these works, Paolozzi named two artists who, although not actually surrealists, were valorised and claimed by the group nonetheless: the first was the Italian renaissance painter Piero di Cosimo and the second was the French avant-garde author Raymond Roussel. Despite the apparent improbability of this pairing there are a number of correlations between Piero and Roussel that shed some light on these sculptures.[12]

—

Paolozzi first encountered Piero in the mid-1940s when, as an art student, he worked as a night watchman at the Ashmolean Museum in Oxford which had recently acquired the painting *Forest Fire*, a work he took the opportunity to observe at length.[13] *Forest Fire* depicts a large forest bursting into flame as its inhabitants flee, and is characterised by extraordinary detail and realism yet also a sense of strangeness derived from both the inclusion of fantastical creatures and odd spatial construction. Piero's work was celebrated on several occasions by the surrealists, including in a collage by Max Ernst and a lengthy 1938 essay in *Minotaure* by Georges Pudelko, which Paolozzi read while resident in Paris a decade later.[14] In his essay, Pudelko argued that the fantastic realism of *Forest Fire* combined with the odd pictorial space to suggest a world governed by the 'pell mell of chance…[and] determined by a mysterious order…that harmonises things which have no reasonable relation between them'.[15] This surreal-esque quality of Piero's painting was also registered by subsequent art historians. Writing one year after Pudelko in an essay Paolozzi would also likely have read, Erwin Panofsky observed that if Piero's worlds seem fantastical and 'emanate a pervasive atmosphere of strangeness', it is 'not because the elements are unreal, but…because the very veracity…is convincingly evocative of a time remote from our potential experience'.[16] In 2006, Renaissance scholar Dennis Geronimus similarly interpreted the perspectival oddity of *Forest Fire* as Piero's refusal to 'impose reason on his orchestrated lapses from the accepted order of things'.[17] Now, while the significance of Piero for these sculptures could be elaborated much further, here it is worth simply noting that this strategy—wherein lapses in reason were harmonised via extreme veridic detail—was a strategy Piero shared with Raymond Roussel.

Paolozzi first encountered Roussel during the war, when he read the serialised English translation of the novel *Impressions of Africa* (1908) that was published in *View* over the summer of 1943–44. The experience prompted him to seek out copies of this and Roussel's other books, such as *Locus Solus*, when the war ended.

Like most of Roussel's novels, these books combine well established, even mundane, genre types (shipwrecked castaways or a country house visit) with detailed, hyper-realistic prose. Yet Roussel's mundane realism is rendered utterly strange by narratives that feature fantastical, often bio-mechanical, beings and contraptions: a family of singers who can project their voices over long distances by echoing them off each others' emaciated thoraxes; a machine that aerially propels itself around a field on which it composes a giant mosaic from human teeth and, most tellingly in this context, an artist who devises a way of translating his etchings into highly detailed sculptures by taking their negative impression in a special type of black wax. As Michel Leiris put it, in terms very similar to the discussion of Piero above, Roussel's books are like 'the re-creation of the universe, the construction of a special world that replaces the ordinary world'.[18]

So, like Piero, Roussel harmonised unreasonable relations via the use of extreme artistic detail and veridity. This was a technique comparable to the surrealist principle of juxtaposition but not identical, insofar as the result was not a jarring flash of the marvellous, but the uncanny apprehension of an utterly recognisable world in which the order of things had been mysteriously recalibrated, or in which reason had suddenly lapsed. It was, in other words, an effect very similar to the encounter with Paolozzi's sculptures which, as noted earlier, engendered a disarming experience of simultaneous familiarity and otherness, or self- and dis- identification through the highly detailed organic rendering of mass-produced goods. However, as the apparent inspiration taken from Roussel's wax sculptor suggests, Paolozzi was ultimately less interested in his iconography than his compositional technique.

Paolozzi also made this clear in the aforementioned interview with Roditi, explaining that with these sculptures 'I have attempted to adapt... to the plastic arts some of the principles of Roussel's Poetics'.[19] Paolozzi's reference to Roussel's poetics stemmed from his having read the author's final, posthumously published text prosaically titled *How I Wrote Certain of My Books* (1935). The essay did precisely as promised and revealed in a matter-of-fact way the complex and laboured linguistic system Roussel employed to compose his fantastical novels:

> I chose two almost identical words (reminiscent of metagrams). For example, billard and pillard. To these I added similar words capable of two different meanings, thus obtaining two almost identical phrases... The two phrases found, it was a case of developing narrative which could begin with the first and end with the latter.[20]

Over the course of Roussel's career, this procedure was increasingly complicated. By the time he wrote *Impressions of Africa*, one half of the homonymic equation was left out, or submerged beneath, the narrative which was nonetheless elaborated around, just as it ghosted, these now absent stimulus phrases. As Jacob S. Fisher has observed, the entire book 'unravels according to whole scenes that everywhere bear the mark of the initial phrase although it is nowhere visible'.[21] Or, as Michel Foucault described it (noting the literality of the word 'impressions' in the title), *Impressions of Africa* 'is no more than letters... written in the negative... then brought back to the black words of a legible and common language'.[22]

It is in this Rousellian play of negative and positive impressions not of Africa but of the very stuff of pop culture that the implications of Paolozzi's sculptural process become, I think, somewhat clearer. Just as Roussel would select phrases, double them, and then elaborate these ghostly doubles into worlds simultaneously veridic and strange that everywhere echoed the absent motivator, so too Paolozzi would select objects, double them, and then elaborate these into images of the body that were simultaneously familiar and other. As he underscored to Roditi, 'the found objects are not present in these sculptures, but survive only as ghosts of forms that still haunt the bronze'.[23]

How Paolozzi may have understood this ghosting effect is unclear and requires some speculation. Roussel exerted considerable influence over a large number of post-war artists, with greatly divergent results (we need only think, for example, of the French *noveau roman*, the OuLiPo group, or the Australian surrealist painter James Gleeson to get a sense of this diversity).[24] Paolozzi's interest in the ghosting effect of this technique was shared in particular, however, by Foucault, who at the same time that Paolozzi was making these sculptures, was writing his only long work of literary history on Roussel's technique.

For Foucault, the ghosting aspect of Roussel's writing revealed the logic underpinning his orchestrated lapses in reason. Whereas both Piero and Roussel's unreasonable visions had previously been considered at a remove from potential experience, for Foucault, Roussel's unreason communicated 'undoubtedly with the reasoning of our world'.[25] It did this insofar as this method of homonymic ghosting or splitting, into which unreasonable narrative was inserted, revealed the unreason of language itself. That is, by constituting his unreason as a linguistic interrelationship, Roussel was revealing that this unreason was in fact immanent to language itself. And, Foucault continued, if it is via its representation in language that we recognise our own world as reasonable, then Roussel's play on language holds up to us our own negative, or 'deathly', mirror image.[26] Or, as Pierre Macherey summarised Foucault's position, Roussel's writing ultimately 'displays the unreason of our reasoning' by 'flushing out the monstrous, irrational figures that haunt' it.[27]

If Roussel's writing thus 'flushed out' an irrationality immanent to language itself, the stakes of Paolozzi's sculptures were somewhat different. For Paolozzi, Piero and even more so Roussel's orchestrated lapses in reason provided an example by which to exorcise the irrational monsters that haunted his own particular historical moment. That is, rather than an expressionistic retreat from his mass cultural collages of the early 1950s, with these sculptures Paolozzi followed the lead of Roussel's own prodigious sculptor to capture the negative impression of works such as *Bunk!* in three dimensions. By constituting his sculptures from the ghosts of the everyday stuff of the new age of pop, Paolozzi held up a negative mirror to its own historical rationale: the automation of labour to commodify leisure; economic stability through planned obsolescence; and of peace via the guarantee of mutually assured destruction. In so doing, these sculptures confront the viewer with their own 'deathly image' as a burnt up, hollowed out, reified and confounded subject on the verge of near total dissolution.

—

And it is at this point that the broader, iconographic significance of these sculptures referred to at the very beginning of this essay lies. The image of a subject in a state of environmental interpenetration emerged in the work of many writers and artists reflecting on the pop age. For example, in 1957, Roland Barthes, writing in *Mythologies*, diagnosed a contemporary 'crisis of bodily consciousness', while in 1958 Hannah Arendt wrote of the manner in which technology increasingly relates to 'the biological process itself, so that the apparatuses we once handled freely begin to look as though they were "shells belonging to the human body as the shell belongs to the body of a turtle".'[28] In 1959, the Swiss novelist Max Frisch published the science fiction novel *Homo Faber*, in which the technophile protagonist, an American engineer, endured a malaise with symptoms virtually identical to those endured by these sculptures. But perhaps most pointedly, these sculptures anticipate the technologically extended, networked and dynamic pop sci-fi subjects soon to be envisioned by Marshall McLuhan, as if to warn that the flipside of the emerging global village he imagined them populating was always already a devastating short circuit. Thus, by way of conclusion, if these sculptures are, as I am contending, a quintessential image of the new pop subject, it was an image Paolozzi arrived at only by negotiating an idiosyncratic, science-fictional trajectory through surrealism.[29]

Notes

1 David Irwin, 'Pop Art and Surrealism', *Studio International*, 877 (1966), 187–91.
2 Mario Amaya, *Pop Art... And After* (New York: The Viking Press, 1965), and Hal Foster and Mark Francis (eds), *Pop* (London: Phaidon Press, 2005).
3 Frank Whitford, 'Speculative Illustrations: Eduardo Paolozzi in Conversation with J.G. Ballard and Frank Whitford', *Studio International*, 182 (1971), 136.
4 Eduardo Paolozzi, 'Notes from a Lecture at the Institute of Contemporary Arts' (1958), in Robin Spencer (ed.), *Eduardo Paolozzi: Writings and Interviews* (London: Oxford University Press, 2000), 80–6.
5 For readings of these sculpture as a reactionary and/or naive turning away from pop see, *inter alia*, Foster and Francis (eds), *Pop*, 58; and Rosalind Krauss, '1959' in Hal Foster, Rosalind Krauss, Yve-Alain Bois and Benjamin H.D. Buchloh, *Art Since 1900:*

Modernism, Antimodernism, Postmodernism (London: Thames and Hudson, 2004), 421–2.

6 Alison and Peter Smithson, 'The "As Found" and the "Found"' in David Robbins (ed.), *The Independent Group: Postwar Britain and the Aesthetics of Plenty* (Cambridge, MA: MIT Press, 1990), 201.

7 On Dali's speech, see Richard March, 'The Swallow's Egg: Notes on Contemporary Art', *Scrutiny*, No. 3 (1936), 252. The only contemporary published account of the 'This is Tomorrow' opening is: Reyner Banham, 'Not Quite Architecture, Not Quite Painting or Sculpture Either', *The Architects' Journal*, 124, No. 3207 (1956), 61–3. Lawrence Alloway also made a brief and retrospective allusion to this event in his seminal 1961 Third Programme broadcast, later published as: Lawrence Alloway, 'The Development of British Pop' in Lucy Lippard (ed.), *Pop Art*, (London: Thames and Hudson, 2001), 201, n23.

8 Hal Foster, *Compulsive Beauty* (Cambridge: MIT Press, 2003), 152–3.

9 Lawrence Alloway, 'The Robot and the Arts', *Art News and Review*, 8, No. 16 (1956), 1.

10 Alloway, 'The Robot and the Arts', 1, 6.

11 For example, when 11,000 workers in Coventry walked off the job in early 1956 in protest at the Standard Motor Company's partial automation of the plant, the media immediately dubbed them the 'robot men' and their protest the 'robot strike'. For an indicative example of the numerous reports of the strike to adopt this use of the term robot see *The Daily Express* (Monday 7 May, 1956), 1. Likewise, even the government's own official report into industrial automation adopted this usage when the authors ambivalently concluded that despite inaugurating an inevitable decline in skilled labour 'automation would not make robots of us all'; Dept. of Scientific and Industrial

Research, *A Report on the Technical Trends and Their Impact on Management and Labor* (London: Her Majesty's Stationary Office, 1956).

12 Edouard Roditi, 'Interview with Eduardo Paolozzi', *ARTS*, 33 (1959), 42–7.

13 Roditi, 'Interview with Eduardo Paolozzi', 1959.

14 Paolozzi discusses reading *Minotaure* while living in Paris, and makes reference to this specific article, in his National Life Story Collection interview with Frank Whitford. See Frank Whitford and Eduardo Paolozzi', 'Sir Eduardo Paolozzi', MS. British Library: National Life Story Collection, 1993, 96, 110.

15 Georges Pudelko, 'Piero di Cosimo, Peintre Bizarre', *Minotaure*, 11 (1938), 23–4. (Author's translation.) Pudelko's essay was drawn from his unfinished book on the artist.

16 Erwin Panofsky, *Studies in iconology: Humanistic Themes in the Art of the Renaissance* (New York: Oxford University Press, 1939), 67.

17 Dennis Geronimus, *Piero di Cosimo: Visions Beautiful and Strange* (New Haven: Yale University Press, 2006), 141.

18 Leiris quoted in Pierre Macherey, *The Object of Literature* (Cambridge: Cambridge University Press, 1995), 216, n14.

19 Roditi, 'Interview with Eduardo Paolozzi', 1959.

20 Raymond Roussel, 'How I Wrote Certain of My Texts', in Trevor Winkfield (ed.), *How I Wrote Certain of My Books and Other Writings by Raymond Roussel*, (Cambridge, MA: Exact Change, 1995), 4.

21 Jacob S. Fisher, *Foucault and His Authors* (PhD diss., University of California, Berkeley, 2001), 225.

22 MF, 34 (new version).

23 Roditi, 1959.

24 The best surveys of Roussel's various reception following the publication of *How I Wrote Certain of*

My Books are: Rebecca Graves, *Writing Machines: Villiers de Isle Adam and Raymond Roussel* (PhD diss., Princeton University, 2002), 221–39; and Stephanie Jennings Hanor, *Jean Tinguely: Useless Machines and Mechanical Performers, 1955–1970* (PhD diss., The University of Texas, Austin, 2003), 83–96.

25 Foucault, 166. It is important to note that 'unreason' was not clearly defined by Foucault and is the subject of some scholarly contestation. This lack of clarity has also been exacerbated by the manner in which *Madness and Unreason: History of Madness in the Classical Age* (1961) was abridged as *Madness and Civilisation: A History of Insanity in the Age of Reason* (1964), in which form it was then translated into English. This process essentially obscured the etymology of the term within Foucault's oeuvre (particularly within English language scholarship) until very recently. My own reading of 'unreason' here is indebted to that of Pierre Macherey in 'Foucault reads Roussel: Literature as Philosophy', *The Object of Literature*, (Cambridge: Cambridge University Press, 1995), 211–27, the best of the surprisingly sparse literature on *Death and the Labyrinth*. The other notable but brief account is in Gilles Deleuze, *Foucault* (London: Athlone, 1988). On the disappearance of 'unreason' during the abridgement of *Madness...*, see Ian Hacking's foreword to the unabridged version of this text, published in English as Michel Foucault, *History of Madness* (London & New York: Routledge, 2006), ix–xii. For an excellent discussion of the significance of the concept of unreason within Foucault's earlier and later writings see Nigel Dodd, 'Foucault's Void', *The British Journal of Sociology*, Vol. 58, No. 3, (2007), 477–93.

26 Foucault, 166–7. 'Deathly' is Macherey's phrase.

27 Pierre Macherey, *The Object of Literature* (Cambridge:

Cambridge University Press, 1995), 32.

28 Hannah Arendt, *The Human Condition* (Chicago: University of Chicago Press, 1998), 153. Arendt's turtle shell analogy is drawn from the writing of German physicist Herner Heisenberg.

29 McLuhan, *Understanding Media*, 3, and Marshall McLuhan, 'The Agenbite of Outwit' (1963), in McLuhan, *Media Research: Technology, Art, Communication*, ed. Michel A. Moos, (Amsterdam: G+B Arts International, 1997), 123–4. For a fascinating discussion of this aspect of McLuhan's writings in regards to pop art, see Brandon Joseph, '"My Mind Split Open": Andy Warhol's Exploding Plastic Inevitable', *Grey Room*, No. 8 (2002), 80–107.

Lafferty looper

Adrian Martin

I am thinking of the SF writer I loved most at the age of fifteen—by which time I had already accumulated an encyclopaedic familiarity with the genre, by way of weekly book-exchanges of novels and anthologies, the excellent shelves of the East Melbourne library, my Talmudic readings of the local (and rather intellectual) fanzine *SF Commentary*, and my attendance at conventions devoted to the SF religion (not quite yet the fan/commerce/*Star Wars* orgies they were to become).

In fact it was, in part, hearing the film critic John Flaus speak (at great length) at one of these spacey-con events—and learning that there was a culture of SF films by people named Godard, Tarkovsky and Marker, revered by people like George Turner and Stanislaw Lem, who also quoted people like Elias Canetti—that I made my teenage switch from SF to cinema. A fickle moment, but a sustaining passion...as it turned out.

I got rid of almost all my SF books (and I had accumulated quite a library) at that moment. Got rid of all the comics, too. Only a few of each I have kept. And the word order in that last sentence is a clue to the guy I'm talking about: R.A. Lafferty (1914–2002).

I have always been amazed, a bit dismayed, at the very narrow range of SF authors to whom modern art/culture theory pays homage. J.G. Ballard and Philip K. Dick, Dick and Ballard, from A to B and back again. Later there was the cyber-generation (William Gibson et al.), but that was a continuation of the same line; it was fiction for the McKenzie Wark era of fast theory. Earlier, much earlier, there had been a less cool generation, given to quoting Asimov or Heinlein or Arthur C. Clarke or Clifford D. Simak. That generation peaked with Kubrick's

2001. Over and out. Pre-*October* magazine, around 1968, Annette Michelson wrote the last great phenomenological art-theory manifesto for Kubrick's film.[1] *Artforum* (where her piece appeared) peaked then, too. So did Michael Snow with *Wavelength*, and a whole bunch of other cats (Hollis Frampton et al.) doing their sensual-conceptualist-structuralist thing. Godard and Marker and Varda and Fassbinder and all those others were waiting in the wings for a change-up of theory to the post-structural. It came, it saw, it conquered. At least Godard keeps paying homage to Simak's *City* (1952) in his brightly-coloured screen fantasies of dogs and llamas and donkeys and suchlike overrunning his gas-station world.

Lost in these lifting and falling fogs of fashion was R.A. Lafferty. I put this perception into a footnote in *Tension* magazine—Utopia edition, 1985—where no one would notice or read it or take it seriously. But I meant it. I called on the world of groovers to start quoting Lafferty as their Theory Master, their privileged source of handy allegories and metaphors. They didn't. They still don't. Walter Benjamin emerged from even greyer ashes to beat him at that. Damn him!

But is my own vision blurred now? I am Bruce Willis looking at myself, shot/reverse-shot, in the face and body of Joseph Gordon-Levitt, and something is not quite right here. I am looking up the Nets and Webs and I am learning that R.A. was a staunch conservative, and deeply, fanatically religious to boot. I must turn away from these horrible revelations. I didn't know or intuit any of that when I was fifteen, and I refuse to know it now. It's not in the texts, I'm telling you.

I have only the faintest clue what Steampunk is (Edward Colless knows, I'll ask him), but I am nonetheless absolutely certain that R.A. Lafferty invented it. In a story of 1961 (I think: even the attributions of provenance are eccentric and confusing) called 'Rainbird', collected in a 1973 Daw SF paperback titled *Strange Doings*. (That proves it: in '73 I was thirteen going on fourteen.) Which is the greatest book-work of World Literature Then or Now, as far as my fifteen-year-old, Gordon-Levitt self is concerned.

'Rainbird' spins a very typical Lafferty tale. It's a far-out time travel story where the central character, self-styled inventor Higgston Rainbird—who keeps encountering himself at different ages, on top of a mountain, and having a knowing yarn with himself—keeps re-doing the time-warp trick with his self-made time-machine, and rewriting the earth's (or just his own) destiny, over and over. Yes, a little like in *Looper*!

Except that Lafferty only ever wrote shaggy-dog stories with droll, deflating conclusions: so, the more that Higgston travels back and forward in time to instruct himself better as to what he should invent, the more he cocks up the whole show. He ends his days as the little-known inventor of variations on the plow, the nutmeg grater, and the log-splitter. 'He is known for such, and no more', that's the last line of the tale (it's a cheap book, so the next story starts right on the same page). Which is worse, even, than being buried in a footnote in *Tension* magazine.

Where was I? Ah yes, Steampunk. Lafferty himself worked, for much of his life, as an electrical engineer. In this story 'Rainbird', during one of Higgston's looper-ascensions, we read:

> The milestones that Higgston left are breathtaking. He built a short high dam on the flank of Devil's Head Mountain, and had hydroelectric power for his own shop in that same year (1779). He had an arc light burning in Horse-Head Lighthouse in 1781. He read by true incandescent light in 1783, and lighted his native village, Knobknocker, three years later. He

drove a charcoal fuelled automobile in 1787, switched to a distillate of whale oil in 1789, and used true rock oil in 1790. His gasoline powered combination reaper-thresher was in commercial production in 1793, the same year in which he wired Centerville for light and power. His first diesel locomotive made its trial run in 1996, in which year he also converted one of his earlier coal burning steamships to liquid fuel.[2]

You get the idea. And you get a sense of the wild, ridiculous, preposterous language of Lafferty: words upon words in trance-like, dazed repetition (power, light, oil, fuel), minimal variations (from whale oil to true rock oil). Endless lists, which are neither quite descriptive nor narrative. Syntax from another time, another world: many times and worlds, in fact.

Stories don't go forward in Lafferty. They loop, they twist. They are more like anecdotes or jokes than fully-fleshed-out narratives. Lafferty knew that he was no good for stories. He regarded his novels as just bloated-out versions of his short tales, or gimcrack machines to string a whole bunch of them together. I'd read all the novels he had out (like *Pastmaster*, his utopian fantasia) by the time I was fifteen, but I can't remember any detail of them now. It's the short pieces I remember, and mainly the ones in *Strange Doings*: 'Continued on Next Rock', 'Sodom and Gomorrah, Texas', 'The Transcendent Tigers', 'Camels and Dromedaries, Clem', 'Cliffs that Laughed'—even the titles are nutso-baroque.

I guess he wrote fantasy, or speculative fiction, or thought-experiments, or something else that has no tidy generic name. Magic Realism? Nah. Not space operas, which I hate and he hates, too. He seemed to mainly be motivated by a love of word-play—with silly person and place names (like Knobknocker) fully allowed. He started late (when he was forty); but he wrote a lot, and he wrote fast. He wrote histories and a multi-volume autobiography too. I have the impression that his writing was so odd that no sub-editor, even of the dreary old-school SF sort ('Rainbird' is early '60s, remember), dared fiddle with it—and in this, I deeply admire him. I pictured him (insofar as I needed a picture at all when I was 15: I've never seen a photo of him until now) as some rolling, Irish drunkard, and in some of these details, the Webs inform me, I was not entirely wrong: he was an all-American who lived most of his days in Tulsa, but he did indeed drink a lot.

Who cares? I'm remembering how John Cale described Dylan Thomas's Welsh-flavoured language (which he set to music) as 'rambunctious'; and I'm thinking about how I came to love (once I had converted to cinema) the screwball dialogue in Preston Sturges's films (with their Kockenlockers and Ginglebuschers), and the dense, knotted-up, back-and-forth impressionism of the film critics Manny Farber or Bill Routt or Raymond Durgnat. Swampy writings, obsessive, murky, impenetrably obscure and cryptic and private-keyed sometimes: but flying on a rhythm that carried and sustained you. Something like what I like to be writing here.

Michel Serres said of a particular Tintin comic (I can quote this one without looking it up, I left it back in an '80s issue of *Art & Text*): 'The fable is profound, and without ostentation'. Hergé cannot be mine, for he is Spielberg's now, poor thing. But I can say it of a story by R.A. Lafferty. Once again, I must risk the loop, and actually confront my sweet memory of this tale with what is on the pages of my yellowing and slightly smelly 1973 paperback.

—Here is what I remember, an incredible image that is better and more beautiful than any metaphor/allegory I ever drew from the shallow wells or short-memory banks of Theory: there are climbers who brave this incredibly difficult mountain that curves right at the top—plunging them to their death. Just before they fall, they notch out a bit of graffiti on the rock face. They die; the cliffs laugh at them. To write a little more, a little further along, is just to get one tiny fraction of a second more of life before certain death in the valley below. That's what writing, and life, are: a little scratch or scribble of shit on a rock, meaning nothing communication-wise (just 'blah-blah was here'), just that hopeless, quixotic gesture, and that's all, before the end. But the gesture you have to do, have to perform: why else be born in the first place? Cosmic befuddlement of this sort is the ground-tone of Lafferty's fiction.

I don't remember any specific characters, any developed plot as such (I never do in his stuff, which also says something about the types of cinema I will come to love): only that image of the clamber, the graffiti and the laughing cliff, repeated and built-up mercilessly. Who even tells the tale? Narrators are always strange confabulations in his stories, either omniscient gods or just nerds reading out of some diary they can't fathom, and which they throw away at the end.

—Here is what I discover, forty years later: that, in fact, I cannot even correctly recall the title of this story! I thought it was 'Cliffs that Laughed'; it's not. Then I checked 'Continued on Next Rock'; nope. (But I enjoyed reading them, immensely.) I still can't figure it out on this deadline—and the Internet, although teeming with Lafferty fans and tribute-pages these days, can't solve it for me in a hurry. Bad luck.

But, leafing frantically through the pages of *Strange Doings*, I realise that so many of Lafferty's cherished motifs and word-games, images and situations, even the associations struck by their titles, are virtually interchangeable, from item to item. So many of the pieces turn out to be structured a bit like a Raúl Ruiz film (of course)—like *The Three Crowns of the Sailor* especially.

Narrations within narrations; false starts; parodies of the fan worlds of comics and SF, and of theory too (there's even someone named 'Foulcault'); crackerbarrel wisdoms about the art and craft of storytelling itself. (All wisdom is of the crackerbarrel variety in Lafferty, but no less profound and unostentatious for that.)

Tales filled with fantastic-plastic exoticism, like Josef von Sternberg crossed with Jacques Tourneur: islands, native informants, pirates in the Indies, age-old mythology, ghosts and golems, spells and comas, mother–daughter teams specialising in fury, duplicity and voracious desire. Endless sea voyages. Landscapes that keep breaking apart and languages that keep mutating in translation. Jokes about countries and the people and customs and language-idioms in them: even Australia, where he travelled.

I remembered none of this in specific detail, but it all seems to have seeped into one hundred cinematographs that I later came to study and worship. Thank you, R.A. Lafferty.

We will be known for such, and no more.

Notes

1 Annette Michelson, 'Bodies in Space: Films as "Carnal Knowledge",' *Artforum*, Vol. 7, No. 6 (February 1969), 53–64.

2 R.A. Lafferty, 'Rainbird', in *Strange Doings* (New York: Daw, 1973).

Forward to the past: On the paradoxes of time travel

Rex Butler

At about the halfway point of James Cameron's *The Terminator* (1984), Sarah Connor is stopped by the police after a high-speed chase, along with Kyle Reese, the agent who has been sent from the future to save her. Reese is arrested and interviewed back at the station by the police psychiatrist, who declares him crazy. Meanwhile, the Terminator, who has been chasing them, returns and begins shooting up the station, killing everyone in sight. Sarah is put into a darkened room by one of the officers and told to remain under the desk. By some stroke of luck, the room she is in is among the last the Terminator gets to during his rampage, although he appears to walk past it several times. Just before he does finally arrive at it, Reese, who is being held in the room next door, enters and tells Sarah to come with him if she wants to live. Overcoming all of her instincts and disregarding everything she has just been told about him, Sarah decides to leave with Reese. A moment later, the Terminator breaks down the door of the room in which she had been hiding and sprays it with bullets.

Now together on the run from an unstoppable killer, Sarah and Reese decide to stop for the night. While Sarah patches Reese's wounds, he begins to tell her a far-fetched story about a future battle for the fate of the world between humans and machines, in which Sarah, at the time a humble waitress, will become the mother of the eventual saviour of humankind, John Connor. The homicidal maniac who is chasing them and who blew up the police station is a robot sent from the future through a time machine by computers to kill Sarah, while Reese was sent the same way by the humans to try to keep

Sarah alive. As this preposterous tale, told with absolute sincerity but without a shred of evidence, continues to unwind, along with all of the obvious questions—'Why me?'—and objections—'But if the time machine has been destroyed to prevent others getting through, you won't be able to get back'—Sarah suddenly has too much. 'Come on. We're talking about things I haven't done yet in the past tense', she says. 'It's driving me crazy!' she exclaims, standing up and backing away from Reese and putting her hands over her ears as though to hear no more.

But Sarah, despite all of the evidence—or, rather, despite the lack of evidence—continues to believe. Indeed, the next morning, attracted by Reese and realising that she has nobody else to turn to, nobody else with whom she can share this extraordinary new destiny that appears to be hers, she makes love with Reese in a hotel room. It is in fact this act that leads to the birth of John Connor. Reese, it turns out, is the father of the man he was sent to protect. However, while this quiet interlude is taking place, the Terminator finds out where Sarah and Reese are hiding, and the rest of the film is one long, expertly choreographed chase, with the Terminator at every moment gradually drawing closer. It is a chase that ends only when, in a factory ironically employing the very machinery that will eventually lead to computers taking over the world, as the now-disabled Terminator's finger reaches out towards a cornered Reese, Reese's own finger reaches out to hit a button that activates a press that crushes the Terminator, in a sequence that looks for all the world like a replay of Zeno's paradox.

At every moment of the film—and *The Terminator* is, of course, famously exciting—Sarah and Reese manage to evade the Terminator through a fortunate combination of luck and design. From that heart-stopping moment toward the beginning of the film when the Terminator scans a disco ready to shoot and Sarah ducks her head just in time, to the fact that the Terminator does not immediately go into that room in the police station in which Sarah is being held, to Reese's extraordinary driving skills around the streets of Los Angeles as they are being pursued, to Sarah's own unexpected ability to drive a high-speed vehicle while Reese throws improvised bombs, suggestive of her later destiny (and, of course, the initials of John Connor as the future saviour of humankind are not coincidental, with Reese playing the role of the angel Gabriel), the whole film is full of moments that, if they had turned out differently, would have meant not only the end of humanity but also that the whole story we are following would never have begun.

The entire film is filled with a tremendous narrative tension, the sense that any accident befalling the characters, any failure of their nerve or skill, and the world will come to an end. At any moment things could go wrong and the Terminator could kill Sarah and with that eliminate the future redeemer of humankind. At every twist and turn, only an extraordinary act of *will*—both the refusal of reflection Sarah calls for and a kind of suspension of disbelief in Reese's story—allows them to keep on going, to overcome all obstacles, to realise that destiny for which Sarah of all the women in the world has been chosen. And yet, if we think about it another way, Sarah does not really need to struggle at all. Her destiny has already come to pass. The future of humankind is already assured. For, of course, if Sarah does not live into the future as the mother of John Connor, then the computers would not have sent the Terminator back in time to prevent Connor's birth. That Terminator so implacably chasing them and getting closer and closer must ultimately fail if indeed it is to be sent back to undertake its mission in the first place.

This is the profound paradox of all science fiction time travel stories, of which *The Terminator* is perhaps the great modern revival. It is a paradox that is unthinkable but that every effective time travel story like *The Terminator* renders vivid and that constitutes what we might call its drama. We would say that it is true that events must have turned out exactly the way they did for what we are watching to be possible, and yet this is only because of the deliberate actions of the characters. That is, the events of the film are destined and could not have turned out in any other way, and yet this is only because this destiny has been willed by its characters. And this inseparability of will and destiny must be understood in two ways. Both—and this is the easier to grasp—that events are destined only because they are willed and—this is undoubtedly the harder—events are willed only because they are destined. It is not only will that produces destiny, but destiny that allows in the proper sense will, destiny that is the only proper object of the will.

But what could this mean? How are we to understand this circular if not self-contradictory series of statements? Science fiction, of course, had dealt with the question of time travel with something like H.G. Wells's *The Time Machine* (1895) before even the official designation of the genre. But, famously, even before Wells's masterpiece, Thomas A. Gutherie's *Tourmalin's Time Cheques* (1891) was grappling with the paradoxes of time travel, the logical problems that necessarily arise as a consequence of travelling back and forth in time. Two of these paradoxes in particular have become staples of science fiction, the explicit subject of stories that, in a manner befitting the 'speculative' nature of the genre, take the initial premise of time travel and attempt to devise more and more imaginative variations based on it. These paradoxes are increasingly subject nowadays to either scientific disproof or explanation as though they constitute a serious possibility for physics and have equally become the subject for analytic philosophy papers that try to think through the conundrums concerning human identity, parallel times and alternate universes they raise.[1] Many of the same problems appear in this essay with perhaps a special emphasis on the notion of time opened up by time travel stories, while hopefully coming up with 'solutions' not arrived at before (although priority, of course, is a difficult thing to assert with regard to time travel).

The first great variant of the time travel story is the 'closed loop'.[2] This is seen in those stories in which there is an apparently unbroken circle connecting past and present, or present and future. We find this when someone finds the plans for a time machine, builds it, sends themselves into the future, where they analyse the machine, write down the plans and send them back into the past so they can discover them. A classic example of this is 'The Gadget Had a Ghost' (1952) by Murray Leinster, in which the discovery of a message in the protagonist's handwriting in an ancient book sets off a long chain of events that leads to the writing of the message. We have something similar in P. Schuyler Miller's 'As Never Was' (1944), in which a strange artefact, a knife made from an unidentified metal, is discovered, investigated without success, displayed in a museum and eventually transported back in time to be discovered (and there is a beautiful metaphysical 'gloss' to the story, in which the knife sustains a small scratch during its attempted analysis). Finally, we have Mack Reynolds's astonishing 'Compounded Interest' (1956), a story described by fellow writer Barry Malzberg as 'one of the greatest and most terrifying in the history of sf', in which a man travels into the past to invest a few coins that, accumulating interest over the years, eventually yield the huge fortune he requires in order to build the time machine that will send him into the past to make his original investment.[3] (And at a certain point in the story it is suggested, in an insight worthy of Marx on the enigma of 'primitive accumulation', that the entire world economy is nothing less than the outcome of this investment.)

Each of these stories can undoubtedly be thought of as an instance of the future leading to the past or effect preceding cause, in a reversal of ordinary reality that could be fixed simply by relabelling past and future and cause and effect or running time backwards. But the problem is not so easy to correct. For the effect of these stories is not to highlight the continuity of things, how everything stays the same though reversed, but on the contrary to force us to consider how something *new* is created. Even though there is a connection between past and present and no identifiable moment where things begin, suddenly there is this extra object in the world: the message in 'The Gadget Had a Ghost', the knife in 'As Never Was', and money in 'Compounded Interest'. And even within these stories, there is often a twist, such as the scratch on the knife in 'As Never Was' that appears and disappears according to what point of the narrative we are at. Indeed, there is a great time travel story, Robert Heinlein's 'By His Bootstraps' (1941), that takes as its subject just this 'impossible' paradox of something arising out of nothing, or more precisely giving rise to itself, in the manner of the immortal Baron Münchhausen out of whose exploits the original expression arose.

The other type of paradox in time travel stories initially appears to be the opposite of the first. If in the first there is a loop seamlessly connecting past and present from which nothing can escape, in the second it is the *impossibility* of this loop that is the subject of the story. And this impossibility in turn takes two forms, both named after famous fictional examples. The 'grandfather paradox', which prevents the carrying out of any action by the time traveller in the past that would render the future act of time travel impossible, was first used in the *Le voyageur imprudent* (1943) by René Barjavel. It takes the classic form of a time traveller in the past killing their grandfather, as this would obviously mean that they themselves would not be born in the future.[4] And this leads to a whole series of stories in which this paradox is produced or brought about in more and more elaborate ways. To take just one contemporary example: in the episode 'Roswell that Ends well' (2001) from the television series *Futurama*, the protagonist locks his grandfather away in an isolated house in a desert in an attempt to protect him, only for the house to turn out to be at the centre of a nuclear testing site.

This logical impossibility is formalised in the critical literature in the so-called 'Novikov self-consistency principle', which forbids any action that might endanger the course of events that led to the original decision to travel back in time.[5] This doctrine not only functions as a putative narrative prohibition, which sets out either an explicit or implicit series of rules that cannot be broken, but again, as is typical of the genre, allows a series of hypotheticals playing on these prohibitions. In Mort Weisinger's 'Thompson's Time Travelling Theory' (1944), for example, we cannot be sure whether the attempted murder of the grandfather has taken place. In C.L. Moore's 'Tryst in Time' (1936), the protagonist repeatedly attempts to murder his grandfather, but each time something comes up (a gun jamming or a misidentification) that prevents this. And this, in turn, leads to a whole genre of 'time patrol' stories or novels, in which cosmic policemen enforce the upholding of the rules of time travel. Examples of this include Isaac Asimov's *The End of Eternity* (1955) and Poul Anderson's epic *Time Patrol* series (1955–91), in which we follow a team of intergalactic guardians who seek to identify and intervene in any breaches of historical sequence before they happen. Or, in another speculative twist on the grandfather paradox and its resulting prohibition, there is a whole series of stories in which a temporal rift that endangers the possibility of a successful return is 'healed' by the time our adventurers are scheduled to make their return trip. Examples of this include Eando Binder's *The Time-Cheaters* (1940), in which criminals who seek to take advantage of time travel meet their comeuppance, and Piers Anthony and Roberto Fuentes's *Dead Morn* (1994), in which nature itself rectifies any potential reordering of events.

The so-called butterfly effect is a variant or complement of the grandfather paradox (although, equally, it is the grandfather paradox that can be seen as a variant of the butterfly effect). It is named—not just in science fiction but more generally in chaos physics and popular culture—after that moment in Ray Bradbury's short story 'A Sound of Thunder' (1952) when a hunter who has travelled back in time to shoot dinosaurs accidentally kills a butterfly with the result that the present they return to is different from the one they left. Here, as opposed to the deliberate attempt to alter the past by killing one's grandfather, which can perhaps be prevented, we have inadvertent alterations that *necessarily* arise due to the presence of the time travellers themselves. (Although we might note that the other reason why the grandfather paradox arises with respect to the *grandfather* is that it is implied that it is always possible that we do not recognise him and thus could kill him accidentally.) There are several stories in which the smallest of causes—the archetypal beating of butterflies' wings in Bradbury's story—have the most dramatic of effects. We might think here, in an echo of Bradbury's story, of Henry Cowper's 'Mosquito's Choice' (1993), in which the decision of a humble mosquito as to which person to bite will lead or not lead to the death of Hitler. Or there are those alternate histories in which the presence of a seemingly 'neutral' observer or historian back in the past alters the outcome of the events they travelled back in time to see. There are any number of these, notable for the overturning or possible overturning of the outcome of well-known historical events, for example, Chad Oliver's 'A Star Above It' (1955), in which the Aztecs beat Cortez, Ward Moore's *Bring the Jubilee* (1953), in which the Confederates win the Battle of Gettysburg, and Philip K. Dick's *The Man in the High Castle* (1962), in which Germany and Japan win World War II.

But there is also a whole series of stories in which (and this is how this second, butterfly effect speaks to that first, grandfather paradox), despite the attempt not to alter events, everything nevertheless changes or, even more paradoxically, in which, despite the attempt to correct an earlier intervention in time, to put things back as they were, events are still ineluctably changed. An example of the first type of story is Barry Malzberg's *Chorale* (1978), in which a team of scientists travels back in time, aware of the dangers of their presence and seeking to avoid any intervention, but nevertheless find events ineluctably taking them away from the possibility of their return. An example of the second type of story is Fritz Leiber's *The Big Time* (1961), in which a group of soldiers, involved in a battle as to who will control time, attempt to correct a determination of history that will condemn them to oblivion, only for this correction itself to condemn them to oblivion. (And this second type of story is perhaps a variant on another subgenre of the time travel story, in which the protagonist seeks to avoid a prophecy of their future, but all of their efforts to do so only more surely bring it about.)

What conclusion can we draw from these different types of story? On the one hand, there is the 'closed loop', in which something comes out of nothing in the seamless connection between past and present. On the other, we have the 'grandfather paradox' and the 'butterfly effect', in which it is impossible to go from the past to the present, whether this detour is caused deliberately or accidentally and whether we attempt to correct it or not. At first sight, the two appear to be opposites, or even to have nothing to do with each other, and this is largely the way they have been understood in the critical literature.[6] Here, however, we want to suggest that they are in fact the *same* or at least cannot be separated. Each principle is always to be found in every time travel story in order to make up the two indivisible halves of its logic. Each act of time travel at once succeeds and fails, reaches its destination and does not, changes everything and changes nothing. Or, more precisely, it succeeds but only because it is possible it failed, reaches its destination but only because it is possible it did not, changes nothing but only because it is possible everything is changed.

How can we actually see this in the stories? Let us begin by looking at a particular subgenre that is seen across all types of time travel science fiction and that we would argue has the profoundest connection with it: the self-fulfilling prophecy story. Of course, virtually all time travel narratives involve some element of prophecy. The instructions for building a time machine that are sent into the past are themselves a kind of self-fulfilling prophecy that necessarily has to come true. We have, to begin with, the general ability to see into the future available to all time travellers, as seen in Ray Bradbury's 'The Toynbee Convector' (1984), in which a vision of utopia brought back from the future actually leads to the citizens of the present working to realise this vision. Or, on a more personal level, there are stories like Louis Marlow's *The Devil in Crystal* (1944), in which characters are given predictions of future success that they must attempt to fulfil, or, conversely, stories like G. Hunter's 'Journey' (1951), in which they are given warnings of future danger that they must seek to avoid. But there are also more interesting variants, in which we see a prophecy of failure that is fulfilled even in the attempt to avoid it, and its necessary converse, a prophecy of success that seems impossible to fulfil, even as we follow its instructions.

An example of the former is the novel *Many Mansions* (1973) by Robert Silverberg, in which after the prophecy of a future marriage breakup the main characters do everything possible to avoid it, even contemplating killing each other and each other's parents. Obviously enough, however, it is exactly through these attempts to avoid the prediction that it comes to pass. And, needless to say, there are many equivalents—at least with regard to the grandfather paradox—of that most famous instance of the self-fulfilling prophecy in Western culture: Oedipus's murder of his father Laius, despite his own attempts to avoid it. In both of these cases we might say that it is only by seeking to do something *different* from the prophecy that the prophecy comes about. But these narratives are matched by what appears to be their opposite, which is an *inability* to bring a desired prophecy about. This is obviously a variant on the butterfly effect, but in the novel *Changing the Past* (1989) by Thomas Berger a character is given several different opportunities (and several different personae) to change his life for the better, but each time he seems to be getting closer, something unexpected occurs and the prediction appears to be further away than ever.

What these time travel stories reveal is that even so-called self-fulfilling prophecies cannot be fulfilled directly. That is, even though the prophecy seems clear, something simply awaiting its realisation in the future, in fact it is only in the past, *after* it has been realised, that we can say what it was. We never actually realise a prophecy in the present: it is always too soon or too late. The prophecy, as it turns out, is not only always different, but different from itself. In a sense, we end up realising a prophecy only by *not* realising it. The prophecy comes to be realised as it always was, in the only way it could be to allow time travel into the future, only by being for at least part of the time different. It is not that it is ever actually different because it does come to be realised in the only way it could be, in the predicted form it had from the beginning, but this only through a certain passage of difference and misrecognition. And this is not ultimately opposed to those stories in which we fail to realise the prophecy because, as we know, this failure is possible only because of its ultimate success, and would not even take place unless the protagonist returned again to their destiny. This failure can be only a certain preliminary or present-tense view of what will come to be, which from a later perspective will be judged to be a success.

In order to try to elaborate this and to begin to think beyond the strict confines of time travel stories, let us take an example of what we might regard as a self-fulfilling prophecy in 'theory'—although we would argue that 'theory' always takes the form of such self-fulfilling prophecies (and thus always involves a form of time travel). It is a well-known 1984 essay by Jean Baudrillard entitled 'The Year 2000 Will Not Take Place'.[7] Of course, we cannot but think—as with his even more famous claim that the first Gulf War in 1991 did not take place—that Baudrillard's prediction has obviously been refuted and overtaken by events. However, we would argue against all of the evidence that what Baudrillard is saying here is essentially true and, like all self-fulfilling prophecies, is not refuted but in fact confirmed by everything that appears to go against it. That is, it proceeds not directly but only through the detour of difference, of being different from itself. The statement is not true at the moment it is said or read, but only before (when the year 2000 has not yet taken place) and after (when the year 2000 has already taken place). But what can this possibly mean?

How are we to justify this series of seemingly extravagant claims, this argument presented not in the realm of fiction where it might be licensed or at least explained by a certain 'suspension of disbelief', but in the realm of sociology or theory, which are notionally subject to the claims of empirical truth?

Baudrillard begins 'The Year 2000', in a way typical of his more general arguments concerning simulation, by referring to the end of history. History has ended, he suggests, because of three different reasons, between which, importantly, he does not choose. His first hypothesis is that history ends because there is *too much* history: 'Events no longer have consequences because they go too quickly—they are diffused too quickly, too far, they are caught up in circuits—they can never return as testimony for themselves or their meaning'.[8] His second hypothesis is that history ends because there is *not enough* history. Here, on the contrary: 'Progress, history, reason, desire are no longer able to find their "escape velocity". They can no longer pull away from this too-dense body that irresistibly slows their progress.'[9] And his third hypothesis, in a kind of combination of the other two, is that history ends *as* history, in the completion of the logic of history itself: 'History will not disappear for want of history. It will disappear for having exceeded that limit point, vanishing point. It will disappear in the perfection of its materiality.'[10] In the first hypothesis, we might say, history is over because history has already ended; the end arises before the beginning. In the second hypothesis, history is over because history can never get to its end; we have a beginning but not an end. And in the third hypothesis, history is over because history is its own end; history arises at the same time as the end of history.

These are undoubtedly complex and commonsensically challenging ideas, admittedly presented here in a very summary fashion, but to help us to try to explain them we might turn to the next part of Baudrillard's essay, in which, as some attempt to elaborate how we got to where we are today, Baudrillard offers a brief 'history' of the end of history, or at least outlines two different ways of understanding the end of history. The first is what Baudrillard calls 'ceremonial' time, and he associates it with what he calls (in typically French fashion) 'primitive' or at least pre-Christian societies. This is a circular time in which we do not advance towards some preordained goal and in which, as he says, 'everything is completed in the beginning and where the ceremony retraces the perfection of the original event—perfect in the sense that everything is complete'.[11] The second is what he calls 'linear' time, and he associates it with the rise of Christianity and modern industrial society. It is a time in which 'events are thought to follow one another like cause and effect' and where even 'eschatological processes, the Last Judgement or revolution, salvation or catastrophe, is at once the time of the end and of its unlimited suspension'.[12] And, again, even though 'historically'—precisely the category in question—linear time has superseded circular time, Baudrillard does not finally choose between these two different possibilities. Indeed, as he says—and we would even like to think of this in terms of the battle between the cyborg and Kyle Reese in *The Terminator*—human history is nothing but the immortal rivalry between the two forms. In general, it has been linear time that has been dominant, but periodically there have been outbursts of circular time, in which the end is either deferred or brought forward.[13]

But, again, what is at stake in these two seemingly opposed conceptions of time, and why does Baudrillard not choose between them? In fact, 'The Year 2000' is not so much about the *end* of history as about the *conditions of possibility* of history. In a brilliant allegorical fashion, Baudrillard uses the idea of the end of history actually to speak of time. The essential paradox of time was first set forth some twenty-five centuries ago by Zeno of Elea. In a famous thought-experiment — familiar to anyone who has ever watched a Roadrunner and Coyote cartoon — Zeno suggests that any movement from A to B is impossible because before getting to B we must cross a point C halfway between A and B, and before getting to C we must cross a point D halfway between A and C, and so on… And it can indeed appear as though we can never get to B until we realise that Zeno is allowed to construct his argument only because he has supposed that in some way we are already at B: 'before getting to B we must cross a point C'. In other words — and this is beginning to get close both to the enigma of those time travel stories and to the final scene in *The Terminator* — it is *only because we are already at B that we cannot get to B.* It is not so much that we cannot get from A to B as it is that looking back from B we cannot imagine how we got there. And the same paradox can be stated in terms of time. The classic spatial representation of time is something like the digital numbers on a clock radio, of the kind weatherman Phil Connors wakes up to every morning in the film *Groundhog Day* (1993). It is as though the successive moments of time are points strung along a line, just as at a certain moment in *Groundhog Day* 5:59 becomes 6:00. But it is here that a well-known philosophical objection is raised. Is it 5:59 that disappears to allow 6:00 to appear or is it 6:00 that appears to allow 5:59 to disappear? The problem with the first alternative is that in 5:59 disappearing before 6:00 appears a gap or hole in time opens up. The problem with the second alternative is that in 6:00 appearing before 5:59 disappears we have two moments on top of each other.

The solution, of course, is that 5:59 must disappear *as* 6:00 appears. Running alongside actual time in which one moment succeeds another there must always be a virtual time in which two moments are *at the same time*. It is not a virtual time that could ever be realised because we only ever have actual time, but it is this impossible simultaneity of two moments that makes possible actual time. Or to put this another way, each successive moment in the linear unwinding of time takes the place of that virtual moment between it and the next, but this moment in turn is possible only because of a moment after that. In this sense, linear time takes the form of a perpetual falling short of an end that has already occurred. It is because that second moment has arrived that there is always another moment between us and this second moment; we can only ever reach the end because there is another moment that comes after the end that allows the end to arrive. And if we return to Baudrillard's essay, this is exactly what he argues there too. If we read that first hypothesis concerning the end of history again, it is suggesting that the end has already occurred, that the end comes before the beginning. If we read that second hypothesis again, it is suggesting that the end is never attained, that we have a beginning without an end. And he does not choose between the two hypotheses because both are necessary for history, for the linear advance of time: every actual present moment in historical time stands in for a virtual absent moment, which is his third hypothesis. And again Baudrillard does not choose between these linear and circular modes of temporality because both are necessary for time. If there is only linear time in which one moment follows another and we can never get to the end, this is nevertheless possible only because of a circular time in which all moments are the same moment and the end precedes the beginning.

Is this not the fundamental condition of all time travel narratives? It is not just at the moment of the return to the past but *at every moment* that things can go wrong, that we cannot see how we will get from beginning to end, that it is possible that the original decision to travel back in time will not be taken; but this is only because everything has happened as it must, the end comes before the beginning, the original decision to travel has already been made. This is why in every time travel story—and not just in *The Terminator*—the characters do not simply lie back and await their eventual transportation. It is only by an extraordinary act of will that we can get from one moment to the next. As with John Connor and his father Kyle Reese in *The Terminator*, it is not just a matter of destiny because destiny must be willed. It is not just a matter of resurrection because resurrection requires the overcoming of doubt through faith. And is this not—a whole other topic—the fundamental lesson of Nietzsche's Eternal Return, which is often mentioned in the context of time travel stories? It is not that everything is destined and that nothing further needs to be done. This was the mistake of the Ancient Greeks and their unbroken ring of *Ouroboros*. Nor is it even a matter of willing this destiny, as though from somewhere outside of it. This was the mistake of Zarathustra and his single but not repeated affirmation. Rather, it is essential both that destiny is willed and that will is destined. This is the final insight of Nietzsche's Dionysius and his doubled or repeated affirmation. And it is exactly at this point that the Eternal Return becomes a doctrine that 'breaks the history of the world in two', becomes both the unavoidable and unrealisable basis for the world just as it is.[14]

And we perhaps see something of this doubling or self-fulfilling quality in time travel stories themselves, for in a sense they *are* those objects they feature being transported within them (ancient message, knife, money). The so-called grandfather paradox, as we have seen, attempts to prohibit the time traveller doing anything that might endanger their eventual return. But, of course, they must *always* do something that leads to their destiny taking another course, as the butterfly effect tells us. The time traveller's very presence is enough to alter events. Indeed, even the decision not to kill the grandfather because of the so-called Novikov prohibition is itself enough to prevent a possible return. Even our knowledge of the fact of time travel is itself enough to render it impossible. All of this is one side of time travel stories: the fact that they cannot be thought or narrated. But, of course, all of this is possible only because the act of time travel *has occurred*. Moreover, we would say that it is precisely through something like the butterfly effect that events lead to the original decision to travel being undertaken, just as it is our very inability to think time travel that is its proof. In an absolutely paradoxical way, then, the same events both prohibit and enable time travel. The original or eventual decision to return is allowed only by what makes it impossible, and this impossibility is possible only because of this return. Not just the specific objects (like the scratch in the knife in 'As Never Was') but everything in these stories miraculously appears and disappears at the same time, as though we were looking through what is to what lies beneath, but that what lies beneath is able to be seen only through what stands in for it.

We see all of this in Baudrillard's 'The Year 2000'. Baudrillard begins there with a citation from Elias Canetti, a novelist coming out of a post-Marxist world view, to the effect that 'our task and our duty is to discover that point [after which history is no longer real]'.[15] That is, Canetti imagines, in an admittedly 'angelic' way, an eventual restoration of history in which we can go back to the past and make right what was lost. For Baudrillard, however, this recuperation is impossible. Not only can we not say what was lost, insofar as the effect of this loss of history is that there is more history than ever; but the result of this loss is we cannot even realise the loss of history, insofar as there is no longer any real history with which to compare it. Indeed, we might even propose the paradox that for Baudrillard the sign that the end of history has taken place is our inability to realise it, just as the sign that it has not yet taken place is that we can still think about it. The same paradox is at work in time travel stories, for time travel as we have suggested is nothing but time itself, nothing but the insight into that impossible virtual time that makes possible actual time. There can be no evidence for this except for actual time itself, but after the hypothesis is stated it is true: the fact that there is only linear time is possible only because of this other circular time. In this sense, time travel exists only through its narration, even though this narration is also its impossibility. The contradiction marks Baudrillard's essay, too, in which he claims that the truth of what he says is that we cannot realise it, while of course he claims to realise *this* himself. And all of this points to the fugitive or esoteric status of those insights into this other form of time throughout the history of philosophy: Nietzsche's Eternal Return, Bergson's déjà vu, Spinoza's notion of the 'adequate idea', in which effects explain causes…

We can see all of this in that great time travel story with which we conclude here: Harold Ramis's *Groundhog Day* (1993). In the film, weatherman Phil Connors, played by Bill Murray, relives the same day over and over again in rural Punxsutawney, Pennsylvania, while those around him continue on unaware. After robbing banks when he knows the guard is not looking, preventing elderly people having accidents he knows will occur in advance and all the other things his mystical experience allows him, he eventually decides to seduce his attractive producer Rita, played by Andie MacDowell. But, in the film's version of the butterfly effect, even though he can have the same date with Rita night after night, hoping to follow that single, labyrinthine thread of action and conversation that will lead to her bed, he is finally unable to. At some point, a glitch inevitably occurs that takes events off in unexpected directions, not least Phil's own consciousness that he is saying the same thing over and over again. Of course, the only way this endless cycle is broken is when Phil abandons his goal of sleeping with Rita and is simply 'himself' without any ulterior motive. The irony is that in the final scene of the film, Phil actually wakes up the next morning with Rita in his bed next to him, the digital clock clicks over to a new day, and Rita and he have a whole future life together.

This ending might appear to suggest a comfortable return to normality, but it actually represents the most terrifying possibility of all. For what the film ultimately suggests is that ordinary everyday time is possible only through the conscious forgetting of the experience of time travel. The paradox is that, just as the pursuing of our destiny is enough to ensure it will not happen, so not knowing of it is exactly how it takes place. And this is the true effect of time travel as a self-fulfilling prophecy: that what is, even in its apparent absence or refutation, is possible only because of it. Again, we discover that our destiny comes to pass only through a detour and that this detour is our destiny. The time travel narrative at once defers what it speaks of or renders it impossible, and is this very time travel and is possible only because of it. And we see this, finally, in perhaps the great fictional equivalent to Baudrillard's 'The Year 2000'. It is the story 'The Man from When' (1966) by Dannie Plachta, in which a time traveller arrives from the future to reveal that the energy required to send him back in time has destroyed the world from which he came. To this, at the end of his brief tale, he adds that he has travelled back all of 18 minutes. Of course, here—like Scheherazade in *1001 Nights*—it is only the narrative itself that defers the events it speaks of; it is only so long as the time traveller speaks that the apocalypse of which he speaks will not happen. But in another way the story itself *is* this end, opening up the hypothesis of time travel, which once it has been proposed cannot be refuted.

Like 'The Year 2000', then, as long as we can speak that of which we speak will not take place, while this speaking itself is the end it speaks of. This is the true at-the-same-timeness of time travel, which is the very at-the-same-timeness of time itself.

Notes

1 Paul J. Nahin, *Time Machines: Time Travel in Physics, Metaphysics and Science Fiction* (New York: American Institute of Physics, 1993).
2 Peter Nicolls (ed.), *The Science Fiction Encyclopedia* (New York: Doubleday, 1979), 605.
3 Barry Malzberg, 'Introduction', in Mack Reynolds, *The Best of Mack Reynolds* (New York: Pocket Books, 1976), 4.
4 Nahin, *Time Machines.*
5 Allen Everett and Thomas Rosman, *Time Travel and Warp Drives: A Scientific Guide to Shortcuts through Time and Space* (Chicago: University of Chicago Press, 2011), 134.
6 George Slusser and Robert Heath, 'Arrows and Riddles: Scientific Models of Time Travel', in Gary Westfahl, George Slusser and David Leiby (eds), *Worlds Enough and Time: Explorations of Time in Science Fiction and Fantasy* (Westport, Connecticut: Prager, 2002).
7 Jean Baudrillard, 'The Year 2000 Will Not Take Place', in Elizabeth Grosz, Terry Threadgold, David Kelly and Alan Cholodenko (eds), *Future*Fall: Excursions into Post-Modernity* (Sydney: Power Publishing, 1986), 19.
8 Baudrillard, 'The Year 2000', 19.
9 Baudrillard, 'The Year 2000', 20.
10 Baudrillard, 'The Year 2000', 21.

11 Baudrillard, 'The Year 2000', 23.
12 Baudrillard, 'The Year 2000', 23.
13 Baudrillard, 'The Year 2000', 24.
14 Pierre Klossowski, *Nietzsche and the Vicious Circle* (London: Athlone, 1997), 66–73.
15 Baudrillard, 'The Year 2000', 18.

Homage to the Zone

Arlo Mountford

> Intelligence is a complex instinct which hasn't yet fully matured. The idea is that instinctive activity is always natural and useful. A million years will pass, the instinct will mature, and we will cease making mistakes which are probably an integral part of intelligence. And then if anything in the universe changes we will happily become extinct—again…[1]
> —*Roadside Picnic*, Arkady and Boris Strugatsky, 1972

The Zone is a sight of alien visitation in Arkady and Boris Strugatsky's 1972 Soviet science fiction novel *Roadside Picnic*. This is the same Zone made famous in Andrei Tarkovsky's 1979 film *Stalker*. Although Tarkovsky never explains the origin of the Zone in such direct terms, the Professor character in the film does mention the possibility of a falling meteorite. More importantly for Tarkovsky perhaps, the Zone is simply another space, its origins unexplained. In both the book and the film, the Zone is a geographic space that was once like any other site but has now become altered, no longer complying with the laws of earthly physics. Inside the Zone, space and everyday objects take on new properties, becoming mystical, sometimes mythical.

According to the composer Eduard Artemyev, who also worked on Tarkovsky's other science fiction film *Solaris* as well as *The Mirror*, at the time of making *Stalker* Tarkovsky was interested in Zen Buddhism and asked him to write music which suggested a meeting of East and West.[2] Perhaps the more interesting contribution by Artemyev to the film is the electronic manipulation and inclusion of everyday sounds in his soundtrack. The most overt example of this is found in the scene in which the three central characters—the Stalker, the Writer and the Professor—first travel on the railway trolley from the everyday world into the Zone, the click-clack rhythm of the sleepers slowly morphing into an otherworldly atmosphere.

As I write this there is a storm overhead, thunder and lightning, heavy rain on the tin roof above. Like the click-clack of railway sleepers, perhaps a cliché but undeniably beautiful and somehow Zone-like.

Brian O'Doherty, in his series of essays *Inside the White Cube: The Ideology of the Gallery Space* first published in *Artforum* in 1976, describes the white cube as a space in which art can exist in an 'eternity of display, and though there is lots of "period" (late-modern), there is no time. This eternity gives the gallery a limbo-like status; one has died already to be there.'[3]

The power of the gallery space to act as a *limbo-like* Zone where time and subsequently the laws of physics do not exist but period does, where our knowledge of history and the world outside the Zone allows us to approach objects inside the Zone with alternative perspectives, is, of course, science fiction. Artists since Duchamp have disrupted and proven this conceit. But why shouldn't a suspension of disbelief also prevail? The same suspension is expected from writing, filmmaking and performance and if we allow it to, as many artists and the art industry have, the gallery space can also exist as a Tardis-like machine here on earth. That is, the gallery space is much larger than its physical dimensions, and is capable of transporting and transforming objects by the power of context.

The path is immediately quite muddy and it is necessary to jump the occasional stream caused by the extremely wet summer that the country has had this year. It's now October and autumn, but thanks to the water it feels as though the winter snow is thawing on distant peaks, the rivers running fast with white water. Of course, there are no such peaks and as it turns out the ground is just completely sodden, the peat allows the water to sit and the moor is covered in four inches of mud.

After a few hundred metres, the river moves close to some woods and a path a bit higher up. Better defined, this path threads through a tunnel of shrubs and smaller trees leading higher up the hill. Slowly the vegetation recedes, providing a view of the river and valley in the context of its surrounding hillocks and mounds.

The Zone is a dangerous site. By way of navigation, the Stalker uses a supply of nuts and bolts tied with string, throwing them ahead of him a few feet at a time to ensure the path is clear. Any variation in the nuts' flight path indicates something amiss. In the gallery Zone, perhaps the equivalent of these pathfinders are the room labels or room sheets, those snippets of information that steer you in the right direction? Much like the Stalker's companions, when I enter the gallery I feel insecure, an insecurity that manifests itself as bravado—*I'm an artist, I understand this space*. Maybe this bravado is more like the Writer's drunken courage? Usually I am forced to refer to the information, to step back and listen to the Stalker who, in this case, is most probably the curator, to read their nuts and bolts, to follow their navigational tools…

At one point in the film, the room that the travelers desire is only a few hundred metres away, however the Stalker explains that they must not head straight for it but instead circle around. The Writer, tired of following the Stalker and his strange manner, heads directly for their goal but is stopped twenty metres from the room. When he returns to the group he asks the others why they called him back. The Professor and the Stalker both insist they did not. This is an odd moment in the film. We are not given any visual clues that something unusual has occurred — there are no special effects or even the suggestion of some sentient force, such as the metaphysical swirling liquid shots used in *Solaris*. Instead, our suspension of disbelief is notched up another level. Something invisible has happened on screen. (Geoff Dyer, in his fantastic book *Zona*, points out that there is a disembodied voice that calls out 'stop' at this moment, which he finds annoying and unnecessary. In the confusion of the shot I hadn't even noticed it. On re-watching I also noticed a wind picks up quite dramatically as the Writer approaches the room but it all feels worldly, as though the Zone really just exists in their heads and we are along for the ride.)[4]

O'Doherty again: 'The ideal gallery subtracts from the artwork all cues that interfere with the fact that it is "art". The work is isolated from everything that would detract from its own evaluation of itself.'[5] This ability for the gallery zone to imbue objects with a power and mystique is most clearly exemplified by Duchamp's *Fountain* (1917). There is more than one version of this work in museums around the world, but *the first* is part of the Pompidou collection in Paris where it sits as an oracle of twentieth-century art history. The irony of this framing gesture can be lost on no one — the gallery space has the power to place this object in the appropriate context, exemplifying a period but not time.

In Bruce Nauman's 1966–7 photograph *Self Portrait as a Fountain*, which references Duchamp's work, time is again stopped and only the action is preserved. The recording of the action took place in the studio, an environment considered in Nauman's own philosophy as a separate zone of its own. By using the studio as the space in which to compose the photograph, Nauman chooses when the action itself is no longer temporal: when the flow of water from his mouth is suddenly made static. Creating the work in the studio also allows him to determine when it enters the atemporal zone of the gallery, after which point the work can also become 'isolated from everything that would detract from its own evaluation of itself'.[6]

After a few hundred metres the path descends back to the river and moves southeast around a small hillock. At this point two ramblers and a dog pass us whilst we leave the path towards the base of the hillock. We are convinced the hillock must be the location of the Iron Age fort marked 'Cow Castle' on the map. This is our first moment of disorientation although we don't realise it at the time. Accustomed to measuring distance in kilometres, we assume we have travelled more miles than we actually have.

Back on the path we round the hillock and return to the river which widens and is followed on our left by an ancient stone wall covered in moss, the trees growing through the stones acting as much like mortar to the wall's structure as a destructive force against it. After the wall and through more thick black mud we reach some stones which can act as a small bench where we sit and eat a premature lunch of cheese, tomato and cucumber sandwiches.

The Zone can only be navigated by a Stalker. The Stalker learns to do this empirically, developing knowledge and an instinct for the place over time. Other Stalkers have gone before them, some act as mentors as in the case of Porcupine, the Stalker's now-dead teacher. There is a case for mentorship in the art world but ultimately the sons/daughters must kill their fathers/mothers. There is no time in the Gallery Zone, so the artist is forced to see things in terms of *period*: one period succeeding the next. In the Zone, the Stalker follows and learns from the indicators left by previous stalkers. Eventually they will reach the room that grants all those who enter it their innermost wish.

In Tarkovsky's film, Alexander Kaidanovsky plays the Stalker as a nervous fool who appears permanently on edge, navigating emotionally. He sees his role as that of a Samaritan facilitating the passage of good people or pilgrims to a meeting with God. Inevitably, such meetings do not grant the pilgrim that which they desire. Is there an equivalent of the room in the Gallery Zone? The moment the Gallery Zone includes your contribution within its context, your artwork becomes part of the Zone. Perhaps this is the role of the critic: part 'room' and part visitor to the Zone.

In this way the gallery differs from the Zone. The gallery exists because of the contributions made to it and the suspension of disbelief. The Zone exists regardless of contribution; the room exists whether the Writer or the Professor enter it or not. Or does it? In the film there is doubt in both the Writer and the Professor's minds. During one of Geoff Dyer's early viewings of the film, it occurred to both him and his mate that perhaps the Zone portion of the film was just a huge acid trip (the trip being in colour, while the black and white sections of the film represented grim reality!).[7] There are very few physical indications that the Zone actually exists—the repeated flight of the bird, the dog (but this could just be a dog!). Predominantly it is the characters' belief that keeps the Zone intact.

O'Doherty refers to just two visitors to the Gallery Zone: the Spectator and the Eye. The Spectator is the clumsier of the two: 'arriving with modernism, with the disappearance of perspective', he or she is part of the Zone.[8] The Spectator exists the moment the framed picture plane (also a Zone) loses its power and the white cube becomes the context for the work. At this point we are no longer looking into the canvas but are aware of how the canvas affects the viewer.

The Spectator is all of us and none of us, a faceless

stand-in for the gallery experience. Unlike the Stalker, the Spectator is clumsy not instinctive and is constantly being manipulated by their context: '*the viewer feels... the audience is forced... the viewer must squint their eyes...*'. According to O'Doherty, the Spectator is the more 'real-world' of the two, kept in real space by the introduction of collage. For the Spectator, the realness and loss of traditional perspective and scale caused by the chair caning being physically stuck to the surface of Picasso's 1911 *Still Life with Chair Caning* forces the Spectator back out into the world, but not necessarily out of the Zone.

The Eye is much more highbrow than the Spectator. The Eye is guided across the picture plane, it investigates context. It is the educated audience aware of the manipulations that the artwork is attempting to perform. The Eye is excited by the splatters of Jackson Pollock and the colour fields of Barnett Newman and Frank Stella. Unlike the Spectator, the Eye leaves no shadow on the gallery walls. Disembodied, it floats in front of the two dimensional plane. It is not until minimalism that the Eye is forced back into the body, back into the clumsy, roaming Spectator in order to move around the minimal object. Like a Dalek negotiating steps for the first time, the Eye needed the body to appreciate the three-dimensionality of the minimal object in the context of the white cube or Gallery Zone.

After lunch we move away from the river again, passing around another small hillock which turns out to be Cow Castle, the Iron Age fort we thought we had discovered earlier, although we didn't know this at the time. Cow Castle is followed by a smaller hillock commonly referred to as 'Calf'. We pass between mother and child and come to a brook making its way towards the Barle River. Crossing a footbridge we follow this brook but veer southeast before the river and into a conifer plantation. There are mountain bike tracks through the mud.

The conifer plantation is death. A zone of muffled quiet where thin green needles on towering branches above suck the sunlight before it ever reaches the mud below. It is easy to turn evangelical here and protest the man-made, but in reality all of Britain is managed, these woods and moors have been kept for hundreds of years. The plantation is dark but not wild, inspired less by the grotesqueries of ancient Germany's wild woods than the horrors of shallow graves and English crime dramas.

Segueing from the plantation to the moor we slowly climb through a farmer's paddock, pass through a gate and over a bridle path. We then ascend more directly towards the top of the moor where it is still thick with mud, despite the altitude. To our left, wild ponies are grazing amongst the heath. They occasionally look up to monitor our progress. They don't care. They're concerned about putting on weight before the next winter, about being in the sheltered clearing amongst the heath for the cold evening. The Zone doesn't affect them. They are part of the Zone we've constructed but it's not real, at least not to them.

Trudging across the top of the moor, this time west in the direction we came from but higher up with views of the rolling hills and valleys. Again we pass through a gate and over a bridle path but this time we are confronted with a road, a driveway, it appears to fork but really we have just intersected with it at a corner. Confused, we consult the map: have we really only travelled this far? Or perhaps we are closer than we think? As we snatch at the map a car approaches up the hill, a Subaru Forester, mud caked up its sides, seats covered in rugs, junk in the back. A farmer's car. It gets closer and I expect it to stop, to offer directions, but as the farmer's wife passes I notice she is laughing.

Notes

1. Reprinted as Boris and Arkady Strugatsky, *Roadside Picnic*, trans. Olena Bormashenko (Chicago: Chicago Review Press, 2012).
2. Eduard Artemyev, in *Stalker: Disc 2, The Films of Andrei Tarkovsky* (Director's Collection, Distinction Series, Shock, 1991).
3. Brian O'Doherty, *Inside the White Cube, The Ideology of the Gallery Space* (California: First University of California Press, 1999), 15.
4. Geoff Dyer, *Zona: A book about a film about a journey to a room* (Melbourne: Text Publishing, 2012).
5. O'Doherty, *Inside the White Cube*, 14.
6. O'Doherty, *Inside the White Cube*, 14.
7. Dyer, *Zona*, 2012.
8. O'Doherty, *Inside the White Cube*, 35.

'On the decrepit margins of time': Robert Smithson's science fiction tactics

Chris McAuliffe

From across the room, Robert Smithson's *Four-sided vortex* (1965) reads as an understated exercise in minimalism. A waist-high, square extrusion in sheet metal, this stump of a column has neither the production-line seriality nor the *gestalt*-driven gigantism of more familiar minimalist installations. It reads, a little forlornly, as a plinth awaiting the arrival of a crowning sculpture.

Up close, it's a different matter. From above, the *Four-sided vortex* opens onto something that minimalist orthodoxy strenuously denied: an interior. The structure is lined with mirrors, angled to meet at its base and forming an inverted pyramid generating endless internal reflections. The *Four-sided vortex* is perceptually baffling and psychically unbalancing. The object seems bigger on the inside than it is on the outside and deeper than the gallery floor would allow. The kaleidoscopic shards of the interior contradict the planar exterior and trigger mild vertigo in the viewer.

The *Four-sided vortex* is not so much a specific object as a hall of mirrors. It is a manifestation of Smithson's mannerist take on minimalist syntax: idiosyncratic, hyperbolic, even parodic. Concealing an expansive, paradoxical, anti-*gestalt* experience within a baldly articulated cladding, it corrupts minimalism's machine-shop sobriety with mannerism's stylised excess.

A few years later, watching Stanley Kubrick's *2001: A Space Odyssey* on 17 April 1968, Smithson encountered the popular science fiction cousin of his mirrored vortex.[1] At the climax of Kubrick's epic, in another unholy union of mute geometry and hallucinogenic cacophony, the Monolith, which had stood sentinel over hominid development for the course of the movie, turned out to be neither singular nor stone. Opening onto some other dimension, not dissimilar to the psychedelic light show of a hippie venue like San Francisco's Fillmore West, the Monolith took the audience on a retina-searing, bum-numbingly boring trip culminating, after an excruciating interlude in an inter-galactic retirement home, in the birth of a cosmic star child.

Smithson himself had already paired the recondite forms of minimalism with the pulp/pomp of science fiction. In a May 1966 article in *Harper's Bazaar*, he remarked, 'The first time I saw Don Judd's "pink Plexiglas box," it suggested a giant crystal from another planet'.[2] Earlier still, in his first published artist's statement, Smithson suggested that his own Plexiglas and corrugated acrylic relief construction, *Quick millions* (1965), might be 'an anti-parody of obsolete science fiction architecture'.[3] In Smithson's hands, science fiction emerges from an uncertain cultural and temporal zone to sully the clean lines and avant-garde aspirations of contemporary art. Through the eyes of a science fiction fan, minimalism becomes a fragment of an abandoned B-movie set, the oxymoronic residue of a redundant futurism.

—

To ask what Smithson was doing with science fiction is to rediscover his tactical bent and reconnect with his historical moment. Between Smithson's time and our own is a subsidiary moment, one which honoured him as a poststructuralist *avant la lettre* while separating him from his context in the downtown scene of 1960s New York. With the first publication of Smithson's collected writings in 1979, coinciding with the emergence of postmodern theory in American art criticism, attention shifted from his roots in underground literature, countercultural thought and science fiction and towards affinities with

French theory. Writing in *October*, Craig Owens gave Smithson an updated pedigree:

> [W]hat is described by Smithson in this text is that dizzying experience of decentering which occurred 'at the moment when language invaded the universal problematic, the moment when, in the absence of a centre or an origin, everything became discourse' (Derrida). If this collection of Smithson's writings testifies to anything in our present culture, it is to the eruption of language into the field of the visual arts, and the subsequent decentering of that field—a decentering in which these texts themselves play a crucial part.[4]

From there, Smithson was characterised as a fundamentally discursive artist, whose writing, in particular, exemplified the allegorical mode in postmodernism.

But Smithson's engagement with science fiction was essentially tactical, tied to critical debates specific to his circumstances in the New York scene. Smithson's moment, and his intellectual milieu, was one in which science fiction ceased to be merely a pulp affront to high culture and became a weapon in a struggle against the dominant formalist aesthetic of the late 1960s. Inverting what English critic (and science fiction fan) Lawrence Alloway called the 'taste pyramids',[5] Smithson's take on science fiction embraced the cultural relativism of the 1960s. Confounding and parodying the models of history and time that propelled formalist criticism, it staked out an anti-formalist terrain. Celebrating repressed, anti-Cartesian and paradoxical knowledge, it embraced the sensibility of the counterculture and parodied the button-down Establishment. Inventively melding the popular and the avant-garde voice, it helped Smithson develop a provocative, non-institutional literary style.

Science fiction writers played a significant role in Smithson's conceptual, rhetorical and literary development. Postructuralist writers, on the other hand, were cited infrequently and often out of context.[6] Smithson's consistent evocation of writers such as J.G. Ballard, Brian Aldiss and Jorge Louis Borges signalled the tone of his writing—dry, melancholic, paradoxical—as well as his key similes—industrial decrepitude, environmental decay, the entanglement of time, and the implosion of reason into conundrum.

Among the many books and journals in Smithson's library, around fifty could be termed science fiction.[7] Some of the classics are there—Conan Doyle's *The Lost World*, Verne's *From Earth to the Moon*, Wells's *The Time Machine*—alongside emerging English voices such as Ballard and Aldiss, and the masters and hacks of such magazines as *Amazing*, *Analog* and *Galaxy*. In addition, there are authors such as Edgar Allan Poe and Borges whose fusion of fact, fantasy, paradox and the macabre paralleled the universe of science fiction. Of course, what remained of the library can't register everything that Smithson read.

The only of Aldiss's novels remaining in Smithson's library, *Cryptozoic!* (1967), is a veritable compendium of the artist's motifs.[8] Art, time and entropy are drawn together in the tale of Edward Bush, a late twenty-first-century artist able to 'mind travel' deep into the prehistoric past, using a drug named CSD. Here he makes artworks—spatial-kinetic groupages, or SKGs—in which he hopes to 'grapple with the new and fundamental problems of time perception' triggered by mind travel.[9] Now able to encompass past and present, the expanded consciousness of twenty-first-century humanity makes for a life that 'followed the scheme of a vortex... symbol of the way every phenomenon in the universe swirled round into the human eye, like water out of a basin'.[10]

The vortex represented not only Bush's 'warped emotions' but also an established artistic response to the temporal confusions of modernity: 'The painter who stirred [Bush] most was old Joseph Mallord William Turner; his life, set in another period where technology was altering ideas of time, had also moved in vortices, just as his later canvases had been dominated by that pattern'.[11]

Bush roams Devonian, Cryptozoic and Jurassic landscapes, encountering a growing number of mind travel tourists. Haunted by spectral visitors from future centuries, he becomes enmeshed in a trans-temporal conflict between agents of various twenty-first-century dictatorships and proponents of conflicting mind travel schools. Finally he is confronted with the revelation that the Western mind has consistently misconstrued time. The difficulty of Bush's journeys back to his twenty-first-century present—'up the entropy slope' as Aldiss puts it—arises because time flows in reverse, the future lies 'behind' us in the past rather than the other way around.[12] (And so, it is explained, Christ's resurrection is not a matter of his death and rebirth but rather his birth then death, moving from 'now' to 'then'. Of course, this reversed telling doesn't quite add up; Christ would still resurrect on one side of the crucifixion, whichever way the narrative was going. But never mind, what matters here is that classic science fiction device, the climactic mind fuck.)

Aldiss's novel traverses what we can recognise as a Smithsonian landscape. In the deep past—found 'down' the entropy slope, so to speak—are the confused layers of prehistoric time. 'Paleontological fragments, geology and time are piled haphazardly in jumbled strata. They lay heaped about meaninglessly… Everywhere about, they made a confusion of angles, while underneath them lay snares of shadow… It was as if they lay here on the decrepit margins of time embodying all the amazing forms the world was to carry.'[13]

But faith, reason and history are shattered in the realisation that what was once the past is now the future. These 'copromorphic fragments', which hinted at all imaginable animal and human forms, were found at the end of time, not at its beginning.[14] Time's arrow is reversed and speeds towards a pile of fossilised shit. The artist is left wandering in 'the blind desert of space–time'.[15]

What was it that made the reversal and confusion of conventional understandings of time so attractive to Smithson? Why was he so eager to conflate the prehistoric and the present, to find 'hide-outs for time',[16] to declare entropy an all-purpose metaphor for everything from Watergate to the Oil crisis?[17] There is more to this than the mind-bending premise of Aldiss's *Cryptozoic!*. For Smithson and a growing number of New York artists and critics, the refusal of linear time was a way of derailing the teleological impetus of then-dominant formalist criticism.

By 1967 the major textual elements of the formalist version of modernism—Clement Greenberg's 'Modernist Painting' (1961) and *Art and Culture* (1962); Michael Fried's *Three American Painters* (1965) and 'Art and Objecthood' (1967)—were in place. The criticism of Greenberg and Fried had established a paradigm of such authority that it was generally regarded as the dominant model for the explanation of contemporary practice. The intellectual substance of the Greenbergian paradigm and the imperious self-assurance of its texts were sufficient to make 'Greenbergianism', 'formalism', and 'modernism' interchangeable terms. The 'Greenberg gang' had succeeded in establishing an official history of modernism.[18] The state of art in New York in the mid-sixties was summed up as 'a kind of triumphant Greenbergian thing'.[19]

Smithson's thinking, and that of his peers, was shaped by an anti-formalist impulse. Minimal, conceptual and earthworks practices were a platform from which to declare: 'We have come to the end of the line...Formalist art is dead because its formalist aspect is, like chess, a game of no consequence, an image of nothing in which the same ground is gone over and over in the same way, to the vast indifference of nearly everybody but its dealers; and abstraction has declined to an empty and affluent spirituality at the level of consumer goods.'[20]

Here the failings of formalism are defined within the compass of the art world, but they were also related to a broader cultural and historical polemic. Cast as an official art, formalism could be painted as the aesthetic equivalent of the economic, cultural, and epistemological Establishment which the counterculture of the sixties disdained. What had once been an avant-garde art movement came to represent both an embrace of convention and a refusal of the broader social aims of the sixties project. Formalism seemed not only to reject certain artistic practices, but also to discard entire domains of experience and thought—just as the Establishment did.

An eclectic reader and a *bricoleur* of theory, Smithson took a heterological approach to contesting formalism. The temporal conundrums of science fiction—and the explicit reversal of time in *Cryptozoic!*—were one of several assaults on formalism's linear temporality, now seen as a relentless route march from Manet, through Picasso and Pollock to the doors of William Rubin's Museum of Modern Art.

Archaeologist George Kubler's 1962 book *The Shape of Time*, for example, had a brief surge of popularity among New York artists in the late sixties. Most of the text deals with the problem of style in archaeology, and the passages of interest to Smithson were those that argued against a biological or organic understanding of time as a determinant continuum or a natural flow of genetically linked events. Kubler argued that 'historical time...is intermittent and variable'. His claim that history was based not on organic development but on a collection of 'ruined fragments' offered contemporary artists another weapon to deploy against the 'Greenbergian thing'.[21]

Smithson was quick to exploit the opportunity. By asserting that 'the biological metaphor is at the bottom of all "formalist" criticism', he was able to use Kubler to question the integrity of the historicist bases of formalism.[22] '[T]he *one line* of the avant-garde is forking, breaking and becoming *many lines*', Smithson declared, for time was 'circular and unending'. Accepting and broadcasting Kubler's claim that actuality 'is the void between events',[23] Smithson could position the art object in a kind of stasis: a frozen, entropic present-ness. 'This reduction of time', he claimed, 'all but annihilates the value of the notion of "action" in art'.[24]

Multiple, circular and unending time is the stuff of science fiction. But it was equally the stuff of new theoretical paradigms of the 1960s, whether derived from Kubler's archaeological methodology, Borges's labyrinthine paradoxes or the New Novel of Alain Robbe-Grillet. Put simply, time could be turned against competing art critical paradigms such presence (Fried), action (Harold Rosenberg) or teleology (Greenberg).

Much of Smithson's reading — encompassing philosophy, archaeology, literary criticism, geology and art history as well as science fiction — was directed towards piecing together a theory of art distinct from formalism and allied with a countercultural sensibility. Of particular importance to Smithson was English art educator Anton Ehrenzweig's *The Hidden Order of Art* (1967). Ehrenzweig premised his discussion of the psychology of art and creativity on a division of the mind into the conscious (or differentiated) and the unconscious (or undifferentiated). In a culture in which the reality principle held sway, he argued, the ideal image was a gestalt, a reduction of the chaotic perceptions jostling together in the unconscious into a readily assimilable, stable form. In this rationalist schema, the unconscious was seen as having no order and no utility, it was repressed in favour of differentiated, hierarchical perception. This was a dominant order which Smithson could see articulated in minimalism, the museum and American technocracy as a whole.

It was the task of the artist, claimed Ehrenzweig, to refuse the dominance of the conscious. The unconscious, he suggested, had an order of its own which would open onto a realm of unrepressed freedom. Art, therefore, must not attempt to go beyond the initial, unconscious phase of perception where all is fragmentation, polymorphous desire and free play. The artist must learn to resist the fear of the apparent disorder of the unconscious that drove him to tidy up his work. What the artist should present to the viewer was not a rationalised, differentiated gestalt but the 'chaos' of the unconscious, 'a precision instrument for creative scanning that is far superior to discursive reason and logic'.[25] There must be no presentation of bounded form, no formalising of the perceptual field; 'the fatal bisection into figure and ground' must be avoided.[26] If the hidden order of the preconscious prevails, 'The surface gestalt lies in ruins, splintered and unfocusable, the undifferentiated matrix of all art lies exposed, and forces the spectator to remain in the oceanic state of the empty stare when all differentiation is suspended'.[27] The suspension of differentiation implied the refusal of rules, boundaries, distinctions of quality, restrictions on desire and individual expression; in short, the agenda of the sixties.

'A Tour of the Monuments of Passaic, New Jersey', Smithson's warped travelogue of a 1967 field trip, sets a string of binary oppositions into play: monumental versus banal, nature versus culture, motion versus stasis. When Smithson came upon a half-built road he claimed to have difficulty distinguishing between the completed and incomplete sections, both were 'confounded into a unitary chaos'.[28] The suspension of a distinction between completion and incompletion, the whole and the fragment, the differentiated and undifferentiated propelled Smithson's art and was mapped explicitly in the site/non-site rhythm of his texts, sculptures and film.

Aldiss, too, was part of the trip to Passaic. But his novel *Earthworks*, which Smithson bought to read on the trip, was not a determining factor in the piece, despite the promise of its title. Smithson typically drew together an ensemble of references. This was a literary device familiar in science fiction, the generation of an alternate world through an admixture of science, factoid, myth and fantasy. In its style, Smithson's picture of Passaic owes something to the flat intonation of Ballard's descriptions of ruined beach resorts, the hokey pedagogy of a tourist brochure and Poe's feigned pomposity. Conceptually, its challenge to the imperious pronouncements of formalism lies in Ehrenzweig's suspension of the differentiated/undifferentiated dyad in a state of 'dedifferentiation', a formulation that hints at the return of what formalism so vigorously repressed in art: surrealism. Here, Aldiss re-enters the picture. What haunted the players in *Cryptozoic!* was the dawning recognition that consciousness was shaped by a trans-temporal 'undermind'.

What holds this eclectic mix together is both its sense of purpose—its determination to open up a space within which post-formalist practice could be legitimated—and the enthusiasm of a fan. Smithson's texts are carefully crafted ripostes to formalism. But they are also what Lawrence Grossberg calls 'mattering maps'. These chart the points of intensity in a fan's consciousness, linking texts, artefacts, sites and behaviours, 'the places at which we can construct our own identity as something to be invested in, as something that matters'.[29] Science fiction texts offered Smithson a kind of counter-rhetoric to formalist critics, but the science fiction fan mentality offered a way of marshalling intensities into an internally consistent and motivating practice.

To embrace science fiction as something more than an enthusiasm, to give it purpose within art-critical discourse, Smithson adopted the leveling tactic of Lawrence Alloway who declared, 'Instead of the hierarchy we need a continuum'.[30] Watching monster movies such as *Tarantula* at the London Palladium with Eduardo Paolozzi, Alloway recalled, 'our feeling was never that we were slumming, or getting away from it all, or not being serious. It was our assumption that what we felt… was as serious and interesting and worthwhile as our other aesthetic feelings.'[31] Reversals of taste, camp, and the as-yet-unchristened 'trash aesthetic' are there in Smithson's collages: *Untitled (The time travelers)* (1964) coupled beefcake nudes with a still from the eponymous movie; *It's King Kong* (c. 1961–63) paired the giant simian with picture postcard images of New York monuments. Horror movies and 'landmarks of Sci-fic' were listed by Smithson in his article 'Entropy and the new monuments'.[32] However, his tactical use of science fiction quickly extended beyond the simple reversal of cultural hierarchies. Smithson's appointment book shows him bouncing back and forth between science fiction movies and hard science: *Alphaville* and a solar eclipse, *5,000 years to Earth* and the Apollo 11 moon shot.[33]

It wouldn't make sense to cast Smithson as a precursor to today's 'fan boy'—his embrace of science fiction was not an identity-defining participation in a highly specialised subculture—but it is clear that the fan mentality played a part in his practice, especially in the case of Borges. In texts like *Ficciones* (1962) and *Labyrinths* (1964), both of which Smithson owned, Borges constructed fictive philosophies, sciences, histories, and planets. He capped this relativist multiplication of knowledges with an exaggerated idealism which argued that systems of knowledge generated the world, rather than vice-versa. This anti-hierarchical philosophical bricolage held a strong appeal for artists like Smithson, who was especially struck by 'the way he would use leftover remnants of philosophy… That kind of taking a discarded system and using it, you know, as a kind of armature. I guess this has always been my kind of world view'.[34] While Borges's appeal lay in his oxymoronic combination of the tangible and the mystical, in his minute description of impossible phenomena, Smithson also declares the emotional investment and personal identification typical of a fan. 'In the words of Borges', he wrote in a letter of 1966, 'I have set out "to design that ungraspable architecture",' adding, as if it really needed to be said, 'he is one of my favourites'.[35]

This is a different relationship to that which Smithson had with Ballard, the author most commonly cited as evidence of Smithson's science fiction affiliation. The difference rests on a distinction between textual rhetoric and overarching conceptual ambition. Smithson's allusions to Ballard are manifold. His essay, 'The Crystal Land' (1966) borrows more than the title of Ballard's *The Crystal World* (1966); the narrative recounts the invasion of the African jungle by an organism that turns everything to crystal and slows down time (and features characters named Aragon, Peret, Tatlin, Balthus and Derain). Ballard's *The Terminal Beach* (1964) is chock full of Smithsonian devices: labyrinths, deserts, wreckage, radiation, decay, mirrors, hallucinations, and scientific experimentation. But Ballard figures primarily in terms of *mise en scène* and mood: industrial decrepitude and decaying seaside resorts are sets upon which entropic dramas shot through with lassitude, fatalism and resignation are played out.

Style mattered to Smithson and drove his engagement with writers and theorists. 'The Crystal Land' and

'Incidents of mirror travel in the Yucatan'[36] have their Ballardian motifs but are equally indebted to Alain Robbe-Grillet's descriptive techniques and deadpan style. In these articles the circumstances of travel, the minutiae of debris on the dashboard of Smithson's car and the distinguishing features of the landscape were catalogued with the mute exhaustiveness typical of Robbe-Grillet's novels: 'My eyes glanced over the dashboard, it became a complex of chrome fixed into an embankment of steel. A glass disk covered the clock. The speedometer was broken. Cigarette butts were packed into the ashtray. Faint reflections slid over the windshield.'[37]

Smithson's unemphatic, non-psychologistic descriptions echo the 'hyper-prosaism'[38] he identified in the work of Robert Morris, Dan Flavin, Sol LeWitt and Donald Judd, all of whom eliminated 'time as decay or biological evolution'.[39] The latter is another invocation of Kubler but the labyrinthine circularity and unrelenting objectivity of Smithson's style borrowed heavily from Robbe-Grillet. And the prominence of the French writer in avant-garde circles in New York may well have shaped Smithson's preferences in science fiction. As American artists of the 1960s became increasingly involved in writing, as texts became a more important part of their oeuvre, they began to attend to literary style more closely. It is telling that Smithson chose a very precise location in science fiction's many-roomed mansion. Not the gentleman adventurers of Verne and Wells, not the space-age cowboys of American pulp, not the paranoid simulacra-scape of Philip K. Dick, or the space opera of Asimov and Clarke. Instead Smithson was drawn to English authors like Aldiss and Ballard, who melded the world-weary elegance of Graham Greene and Somerset Maugham, and the matter-of-fact tradition of H.G. Wells, with a little kitchen-sink realism and post-Suez Crisis, end-of-empire angst. It was a position that made for a happy union of avant-garde credentials (the French New Novel) and pop-cultural *frisson*.

In understanding the historical character of both science fiction in Smithson's practice and its subsequent annexation to the 'discursive' version of Smithson, we can learn from the protagonist of Aldiss's *Earthworks*: 'I begin to get the feel of this writing. It's just a matter of recalling everything and omitting some things, only you have to get the proportions right.'[40]

Getting the proportions right means asking what Smithson was doing with a particular kind of science fiction within a particular cultural milieu. Answering that question—recognising how science fiction style and motifs had a role in the construction of a post-formalist discourse in the US—suggests why Smithson was so quickly canonised as a proto-postmodernist: he showed how an astute iconoclasm, driven by a union of high theory and popular culture, could open up territory for an upstart avant-garde. Which is not to say his posthumous postmodern epigones got Smithson wrong but rather that their fascination with the discursive element blinded them to the process by which he built that allegorical potential into a sustained body of writing.

To put it another way, Smithson might be better seen as one of a succession of artists (or art movements) who used the material of science fiction and the mentality of the fan to establish divergent streams within modernism. London's Independent Group preceded Smithson (if we set aside Aldiss's reversal of the time stream for the moment), as did Beat writers such as William Burroughs and *Nouvelle vague* auteurs like Jean-Luc Godard. Within popular music, a venerable genealogy runs from Sun Ra's Interplanetray Arkestra to Parliament/Funkadelic, through England's Pink Floyd and Hawkwind, and on into the obscure constellations of German 'space rock'. In Australia we have yet to properly explore how the character of vanguard art over the course of the 1980s was significantly shaped by the popularity of Ridley Scott's *Blade Runner* (1982) and the consequent rediscovery of Philip K. Dick's dystopian visions of the near-future.

Notes

1 Entry in Smithson's appointment book, Robert Smithson papers, Archives of American Art, Smithsonian Institute, roll 3832, frame 493.

2 Reprinted as Robert Smithson, 'The Crystal Land' (1966), in Jack Flam (ed.), *Robert Smithson: The Collected Writings* (Berkeley: University of California Press, 1996), 7.

3 Robert Smithson, 'Quick millions' (1965), in Flam (ed.), *Robert Smithson: The Collected Writings*, 3.

4 Craig Owens, 'Earthwords', *October*, No. 10 (1979), 122. The parenthetic naming of Derrida as author of the quotation is Owens's. The quotation is from Jacques Derrida, 'Structure, Sign and Play in the Discourse of the Human Sciences', in his *Writing and Difference*, trans. Alan Bass (Chicago: University of Chicago Press, 1978), 280.

5 Lawrence Alloway, 'Artists as consumers', *Image*, No. 3 (1961), reprinted in Richard Kalina (ed.), *Imagining the present: context, content, and the role of the critic*, (London: Routledge, 2006), 72.

6 In the United States, in the late 1960s and early '70s, Roland Barthes was encountered primarily as a commentator on the work of novelist Alain Robbe-Grillet. Michel Foucault was read within the context of the anti-psychiatry movement.

7 A copy of Valentin Tatransky's catalogue of Robert Smithson's library was included in Eugene Tsai (ed.), *Robert Smithson* (California: Museum of Contemporary Art, Los Angeles, 2004), 249–63.

8 Smithson carried Brian Aldiss's *Earthworks* (1965) on

his field trip tour of Passaic, New Jersey and cited it in his *Artforum* report on the project, 'The Monuments of Passaic', *Artforum*, Vol. 6, No. 4 (December 1967), 48–51.

9 *Cryptozoic!* was the American re-titling of the original English publication of Aldiss's novel as *An Age*, (London: Faber and Faber, 1967). All citations are from the English paperback edition by Sphere, London, 1969. The title of this essay is taken from the title of Book 2, Chapter 5, p. 141.

10 Aldiss, *An Age*, 15.

11 Aldiss, *An Age*, 15.

12 Aldiss, *An Age*, 25.

13 Aldiss, *An Age*, 148.

14 Aldiss, *An Age*, 148.

15 Aldiss, *An Age*, 32.

16 Robert Smithson, 'Entropy and the New Monuments' (1966), in Flam (ed.), *Robert Smithson: The Collected Writings*, 11.

17 Smithson makes a sweeping application of entropy to contemporary social and political crises in 'Entropy made visible: interview with Alison Sky' (1973), in Flam (ed.), *Robert Smithson: The Collected Writings*, 301–2.

18 Joseph Kosuth, '1975', *The Fox*, No. 2 (1975), 88.

19 Nad Rifkin, 'Interview with Lynda Benglis', in Lynn Gumpert et al., *Early Work: Lynda Benglis, Joan Brown, Luis Jimenez, Gary Stephan, Lawrence Weiner* (New York: The New Museum of Contemporary Art, 1982), 7.

20 David Antin, 'It reaches a desert in which nothing can be perceived but feeling', in *Earth, Air, Fire, Water: Elements of Art*, exh. cat. (Boston: Museum of Fine Arts, 1971), 17.

21 George Kubler, *The Shape of Time* (New Haven: Yale University Press, 1962), 13–4.

22 Smithson, 'Quasi-infinities and the Waning of Space' (1966), in Flam (ed.), *Robert Smithson: The Collected Writings*, 35.

23 Kubler, *The Shape of Time*, 17. Quoted by Smithson in 'Quasi-infinities and the Waning of Space' (1966), in Flam (ed.), *Robert Smithson: The Collected Writings*, 34.

24 Robert Smithson, 'Entropy and the New Monuments' (1966), in Flam (ed.), *Robert Smithson: The Collected Writings*, 11.

25 Anton Ehrenzweig, *The Hidden Order of Art* (Berkeley: University of California Press, 1967), 5.

26 Ehrenzweig, *The Hidden Order of Art*, 24.

27 Ehrenzweig, *The Hidden Order of Art*, 121.

28 Smithson, 'A Tour of the Monuments of Passaic, New Jersey' (1967) in Flam (ed.), *Robert Smithson: The Collected Writings*, 71.

29 Lawrence Grossberg, 'Is there a fan in the house?: the affective sensibility of fandom', in Lisa A. Lewis, *The adoring audience: fan culture and popular media* (London: Routledge, 1992), 56–7.

30 Lawrence Alloway, 'Artists as consumers', *Image*, No. 3 (1961), in Richard Kalina (ed.), *Imagining the present: context, content, and the role of the critic*, (London: Routledge, 2006), 72.

31 Lawrence Alloway, 'Pop art since 1949' (1962), in his *Imagining the present*, 83.

32 Smithson, 'Entropy and the New Monuments' (1966), in Flam (ed.), *Robert Smithson: The Collected Writings*, 16–7.

33 The entries, from the Robert Smithson papers, are respectively 12–14 April 1966 (roll 3832, frame 514), 22 January 1967 (roll 3832, frame 502), 2 June 1968 (roll 3832, frame 493), 20 July 1969 (roll 3832, frame 528).

34 Paul Cummings, 'Interview with Robert Smithson', in

Flam (ed.), *Robert Smithson: The Collected Writings*, 294.

35 Robert Smithson papers, Archives of American Art, roll 2832, frames 749–50.

36 Robert Smithson, 'The Crystal Land' (1966), in Flam (ed.), *Robert Smithson: The Collected Writings*, 7–9 and 'Incidents of Mirror Travel in the Yucatan' (1969), in Flam (ed.), *Robert Smithson: The Collected Writings*, 119–33.

37 Smithson, 'The Crystal Land', in Flam (ed.), *Robert Smithson: The Collected Writings*, 8.

38 Smithson, 'Entropy and the New Monuments' (1966), in Flam (ed.), *Robert Smithson: The Collected Writings*, 16.

39 Smithson, 'The Crystal Land', 11.

40 Brian Aldiss, *Earthworks* (1965) (New York: Signet, 1967), 13.

Pots in Dick:
Ceramic objects in Philip K. Dick's fiction

Anthony White

Ceramic objects play a surprisingly important role in Philip K. Dick's fiction. Surprising, perhaps, because Dick is one of the late twentieth century's pre-eminent writers of science fiction, a genre often associated with futuristic scenarios involving hyper-advanced technology, whereas ceramic objects such as jugs and pots are the product of some of the earliest technology known to humankind, the first evidence of which dates back to 20,000 BC.[1] Mundane objects such as pots and jugs also don't fit well within the common perception of Dick's work, renowned for its bizarre, paranoid and often haunting narratives featuring mental illness, telepathy, drug use, the manipulation of memory, androids, and time travel, set in a near or distant future both familiar and yet alien to our experience of the everyday. Moreover, in the film versions of his narratives, some of the more eccentric and anachronistic aspects of his fiction are not given their full due, such as the religion of Mercerism in *Do Androids Dream of Electric Sheep*, which did not make it into the final version of *Blade Runner*, thereby making his fiction seem more homogenous than it is on the page. The role of ceramicists and their work in Dick's writing has received some attention in the scholarly literature to date, for example in Aaron Barlow's 2005 study *How Much Does Chaos Scare You?: Politics, Religion, And Philosophy in the Fiction of Philip K. Dick*.[2] Unlike Barlow, here I concentrate less on the question of how ceramic makers express the ethical character of Dick's thought, and more on how the objects themselves function within the fictional worlds the author creates.

The clay objects that feature in many of Dick's stories

are just one among many different cultural forms that play a significant part in his narratives. From music, to writing, to fine art and artefacts, Dick gave a prominent role to the arts in his fiction, and reserved a special place for two kinds of objects. The first are those that require close manual attention in their production. Dick often found a way to celebrate the virtues of the handmade in his stories. As he once confessed, 'I've always had a great regard for men who worked with their hands. Craftsmen as it were.'[3] The other objects that Dick was keen to explore in his fiction were those artefacts that have a sense of history about them. For example, the jewellery and antiques central to the narrative of *The Man in the High Castle* (1962) are redolent of either the handmade or the historical. They are objects full of the kind of presence, authenticity, and materiality that the German critical theorist Walter Benjamin described as essential to the quality of 'aura'.[4] The function that such objects often serve in Dick's writings, at one level, is a counterpoint to the unreality, immateriality and ahistoricity that is depicted in his novels, a world in which all kinds of objects and experiences can be mass-produced at the flick of a switch, people can be transported instantly from one part of the world to another, to another time, or can even alter the flow of time itself so that reality itself becomes questionable.

The Man in the High Castle proposes an alternate history in which the Allies were defeated in WWII and the Nazis, who have colonised the Eastern half of the United States, have invented the means to fly across the Atlantic in forty-five minutes by rocket ship and to transport humans to Mars and beyond. Among the Japanese occupiers of the Western portion of the country are collectors who have a mania for pre-War Americana, objects such as the Colt .44 firearm, a signed picture of the Hollywood actress Jean Harlow, a civil war era recruiting poster. Such objects are bought and sold in the story as authentic artefacts with a deep sense of historicity, but, as we discover, many of them are mass-produced fakes posing as the real thing. We also encounter in the narrative a piece of hand-crafted, contemporary jewellery, which, according to a Japanese collector, in its irregular shape embodies the principle of *wu*, a Chinese term referring to a beauty discovered in imperfection. As the collector argues,

> The forces within this piece are stabilized. At rest. So to speak, this object has made its peace with the universe. It has separated from it and hence has managed to come to homeostasis... *wu* is customarily found in the least imposing places, as in the Christian aphorism, 'stones rejected by the builder'. One experiences awareness of *wu* in such trash as an old stick, or a rusty beer can by the side of the road... Here, an artificer has put *wu* into the object.[5]

In the world of the novel, historical objects of Americana are open to being faked because they are so desirable in a ruling Japanese culture which celebrates, at an aesthetic level, an earlier period of American political independence. As a piece of contemporary art, which possesses no historicity but rather embodies the quality of *wu*, the jewellery provides a still point in the novel against the rampant inauthenticity of the market for historical objects.

This potentially oppositional quality of the object emerges elsewhere in Dick's fiction in relation to ceramics. In *The Simulacra* (1964), two jug performers are the main protagonists of the story. The jug, a largish container usually made of stoneware with a narrow mouth and designed for holding liquids, was an instrument used in bands that played American folk music in the 1920s. The jug was played by being blown into at regular intervals to produce a rhythmic, bass sound. As Francis Davis argues, jug bands 'were a tribute to the ingenuity shown by impoverished rural blacks in expressing themselves musically on whatever they found at hand'.[6] In this sense, Dick's incorporation of the jug as a musical instrument in this story forms part of his broader interest in the 'least imposing' artefacts, objects that most people would pay no attention to, in accordance with the view expressed by one of Dick's characters in a related story that 'art can be found in the most mundane daily walks of life'.[7]

When the performers in *The Simulacra* are invited into the inner sanctum of the government as hired entertainers, however, the impact is somewhat unexpected: in the process a figurehead of the government is bitten by an alien creature that the performers have brought along with them. The figurehead argues after the incident:

> This whole jug business... it was just a cover-up for an action hostile to us, wasn't it? A crime against the state. We'll have to rethink the entire philosophy of inviting performers here... perhaps it's been a mistake. It gives too much access to anyone who has hostile intentions toward us.[8]

Even though the jug players in Dick's story had not been seeking the downfall of the government, and had only inadvertently become involved in an insurrection of sorts, the ceramic objects they play are implicated in a threat to the status quo. By inviting the quirky and eccentric performers in to provide entertainment that would be broadcast to the masses, the government had hoped to control the population with entertaining distractions but had instead been physically threatened. The incident, which plays a role in the narrative somewhat like that of the play within Shakespeare's *Hamlet*, suggests the potentially threatening dimension of art and its capacity to speak back to power.

Elsewhere, in *The Three Stigmata of Palmer Eldritch* (1964), one of the principal characters, Richard Hnatt, has a revelation while undergoing a radical medical procedure that produces effects similar to that of a rapid advance in human evolution. He ruminates on his attitude to his wife's ceramic works, and realises that one of the key factors leading someone to attain higher levels of consciousness is 'empathy':

> Grasping another, not from outside but from the inner. For example, had he ever really looked at Emily's pots as anything more than merchandise for which a market existed? No. What I ought to have seen in them, he realized, is the artistic intention, the spirit she's revealing intrinsically.[9]

Here the ceramic object is the occasion for the character to contemplate a profound connection not only to his wife but also to the artistic process and the meaning of art. Conversely, the pots also function as a way of registering when something is going wrong, such as when Emily undergoes the same evolution therapy as her husband but it backfires and she regresses on the evolutionary scale rather than moving forwards. The resulting regression leads to redundancy in her ceramic designs, as she begins to repeat work she has created before without realising it. The pots in this story, which are strangely anachronistic in a world where far more advanced technologies are freely available, stand for a sense of authenticity and presence that contrasts with a bewilderingly futuristic world in which interplanetary travel is routine and advertisements are disseminated by cleverly trained insects. At the same time, the redundancy in Emily's pot designs speaks to a regressive quality connected to the tragic consequences of submitting oneself to radical therapies that seek to artificially speed up human progress, itself an analogy for some of the more deleterious aspects of the supramodernity encountered in Dick's fiction.

In *Flow My Tears The Policeman Said* (1974), the famous television host and entertainer Jason Taverner finds himself stripped of his fame in an alternate reality. In the midst of his distress he meets a potter whose work is described by the narrator in the last lines of the book as something 'openly and genuinely cherished. And loved.'[10] This sentiment bears significant contrast to the shallow, attention-seeking personalities of several of the main characters including the protagonist. Indeed, when Taverner meets the potter, he professes his admiration and immediately offers to feature her work on his television show. Preposterously, he envisages having himself jump out of one her pots or convincing the audience, through the use of a false expert, that the work is superior to ancient Chinese ceramic ware, a suggestion against which the potter, Mary Anne, humbly protests. In response to his repeated insistence that she allow her work on his show, she complains:

> 'I know I'm a good potter; I know that the stores, the good ones, like what I do. Does everything have to be on a great scale with a cast of thousands? Can't I lead my little life the way I want to?' She glared at him, her voice almost inaudible. 'I don't see what all your exposure and fame have done for you—back at the coffee shop you said to me, "Is my record really on that jukebox?" You were afraid it wasn't; you were a lot more insecure than I'll ever be.'[11]

Mary Anne's life, with its humility, simplicity and respect for intrinsically good work is light years away from the artificial and unreal existence lived by the celebrities who are the book's central characters. Again the ceramic object stands in opposition to the lightness, insubstantiality and mendacity of the world around it.

However, there are complexities in Dick's accounts of these objects, in particular ceramic works, that upset easy dichotomies. Although Mary Anne avoids allowing her work to become part of a broader commercial spectacle, she nevertheless measures the worth of her work not intrinsically—as Richard Hnatt's revelation suggested one should—but in the fact that certain merchants are willing to buy it. Moreover, for every Mary Anne who eschews broader fame and engagement with electronic forms of entertainment, there are countless others who are actively engaged in bringing such objects to a marketplace of practices which are part of a diabolical spectacle culture using entertainment as population control. For example, in *The Three Stigmata of Palmer Eldritch*, Richard Hnatt is engaged in the business of attempting to have his wife Emily's ceramics accepted for use in drug-assisted mass hallucinations devised to distract the population from their dire living conditions—either on the overheated Earth or on Mars where the environment can barely sustain life. So for all the authenticity of the ceramic objects, the ultimate goal of some artisanal production in Dick's universe is to become part of an anaesthetic form of mind control.

Moreover, while historicity is perceived to be a value in Dick's accounts of crafted objects, it is often in their capacity to innovate, leave the past behind and create something completely unprecedented that the author sees value in jewellery or ceramics. Think, for example, of the way in which the jewellery in *The Man in the High Castle* has value precisely because of its contemporaneity, because of its escape from the market pressures associated with the rampant desire for antiques; or how Emily's regression in *The Three Stigmata of Palmer Eldritch* is registered by her inability to produce new designs. In both cases it is clear that historicity can never be a value in and of itself, and Dick does not seek to celebrate the historical quality of objects as a simple opposition to the futuristic world that he describes. Indeed, one of the signature qualities of his fiction is his scrambling of the oppositions between new and old, historicity and contemporaneity. One only has to look at the actual music played by the jug players in *The Simulacra*. Their bizarre adaptation of down-and-out folk music instruments used by African Americans in the 1920s to the purpose of performing compositions at the very pinnacle of classical musical culture by Schubert and Mozart is a baffling form of anachronism. It not only defies the imagination in terms of the technical skills required to pull it off, but is a wholly unexpected miscegenation of high and low, of different national cultures, and, of course, of historical periods. Even though both jug music and Mozart seem obsolescent within the futuristic culture of the novel, the sense of anachronism is just as great as that between the two traditions that the jug players collide in their performances. Here neither age nor newness is a value in and of itself.

Which brings us to *Galactic Pot-Healer* (1969), the only novel of Dick's in which a craftsperson working with pots is actually the central character. Interestingly, too, it's the only story in which the ceramic worker is male rather than female. Joe Fernwright, who lives in a future world, is trained as a pot repairer like his father before him, thus continuing a venerable tradition. However, the demand for his work has virtually dried up and he lives on a veteran's pension. Just as he contemplates giving up his profession he is contacted by a capricious alien being called The Glimmung and offered a huge sum of money to repair pots on a distant planet. This pot healing work is part of an enormous project to raise a colossal, ancient cathedral from a process of entropic decay in an oceanic swamp that, if not arrested, will have catastrophic consequences at a cosmic level. In the rather freewheeling and often comical narrative, ceramic objects are frequently invoked and a lot of technical or expert knowledge about different ceramic traditions from around the globe and their materials, glazing and firing techniques is paraded before the reader. At the end of the story, in which the cathedral is finally raised and Joe's work is completed, he decides to begin to create new pottery rather than focus on repairing old pieces. At this point in the story, we glimpse that recurrent theme in Dick's thought: the relationship between the historical and the contemporary, the old and the new. At his first attempt to create a pot from scratch, which is announced at the end of the novel with much rhetorical fanfare as a new beginning to the despondent character's life, Joe takes the first creation out of the kiln. The book ends on these words: 'The pot was awful'.[12] Dick was as sceptical about the concept of historicity as he was about the idea of abandoning the past and embarking on something entirely new.

However, for the main part the ceramic objects in his writing are conduits for channelling authentic experience, cultural complexity and spiritual profundity. The sense of deeper meaning emanating from such objects has its apotheosis in Dick's later fiction, such as *Valis* (1981), in which the protagonist, Horselover Fat, explains his religious conversion through a young drug dealer named Stephanie with whom he is in love:

> The means by which Stephanie brought Horselover Fat to God was by means of a little clay pot… It looked like an ordinary pot: squat and light brown, with a small amount of blue glaze as trim. Stephanie was not an expert potter… The pot was unusual in one way, however. In it slumbered God.[13]

Elsewhere in the story the same pot, which Dick names 'Oh Ho', and a clay water pitcher are described as having designs on them that promise to reveal the secrets of the universe by anachronistically merging ancient Christian thought with advanced alien technologies. In his later fiction Dick's thought becomes increasingly fanciful and yet, at least in relation to ceramic objects, similar concerns remain present, such as the relationship between the humility of the crafted object and the depth of the significance that lies within it and the wild anachronisms upon which these objects are founded.

To make a leap which may seem counter-intuitive but is perfectly in tune with the vertiginous, irreconcilable time registers and unusual merging of low fiction and high philosophy in Dick's writing, I would like to conclude by citing some German critical theorists on the topic of ceramic objects. In Ernst Bloch's poetic text 'An Old Pot' of 1918, the author speculates on the nature of a humble ceramic receptacle. Contemplating its insides, he argues that 'It is difficult to fathom how things look in the dark, spacious belly of these jugs'. In spite of this difficulty, Bloch argues that 'I can certainly become shaped like a jug, and can look on myself as a brown, strangely formed, Nordic amphora-like something... in such a way that I become richer for my part by doing so, more present, more educated to what I am through this work'.[14] In his commentary on this enigmatic text, Theodor Adorno notes how it celebrates the qualities of crudity, archaism and imperfection in a ceramic pot, and that it demonstrates something important about knowledge:

> What Bloch is after is this: if one only really knew what the pot in its thing-language is saying and concealing at the same time, then one would know what ought to be known and what the discipline of civilizing thought... has forbidden consciousness to

> ask. This secret would be the opposite of something that has always been and will always be, the opposite of invariance: something that would finally be different.[15]

The pot, with its mysterious interior, literally inaccessible but imaginatively rich with associations, promises for Bloch and Adorno another form of understanding and an alternative type of experience to that delivered by a philosophical tradition, culminating in Kant, primarily concerned with contemplating both objects and people as if from the outside and thereby reducing them to an abstraction. Where Dick's thought bears comparison with that of German critical theory is in the value placed on the humble, unassuming object and its ability to stand apart from the dominant currents of thinking and practice in the worlds he depicts. With the dizzying capacity for fungibility they exhibit at the level of both time and space, Dick's worlds are only an exaggeration of present-day commodity culture's capacity for the abstraction of material qualities, with its exceedingly global reach enhanced by evermore advanced information technologies.

This capacity was in its infancy in the era of German critical theory, and only in our own time could a researcher have an experience such as the following: not long after entering the words 'Philip K. Dick' and 'jewellery' into a search engine I began to receive daily, unsolicited messages in my university email inbox from a company selling jewellery whose marketing slogan was 'Jewellery deals for seriously smart people'. Nevertheless, what Dick refers to with his crafted objects embodying either '*wu*' or 'spirit' or, in his later fiction, 'God', is this same quality of experience evoked by Bloch and Adorno, one that is as unavailable to the bloodless abstractions of idealist philosophy as to a present and future world of infinite exchangeability. This quality, which resonates with Bloch's comments about the nature of subjectivity ('What really happened there, then, what we really were there, refuses to coincide with what we can really experience'), is not of some static and identifiable state of being but of being permanently, and irretrievably, out of sync.[16]

Notes

1 Xiaohong Wu, et al., 'Early Pottery at 20,000 Years Ago in Xianrendong Cave, China', *Science*, Vol. 336, No. 6089 (2012), 1696–1700.

2 Aaron Barlow, *How Much Does Chaos Scare You?: Politics, Religion, and Philosophy in the Fiction of Philip K. Dick* (Raleigh, NC: Lulu, 2005).

3 Gregg Rickman, *Philip K. Dick: In His Own Words* (Long Beach, CA: Fragments West, 1984), 146–7.

4 Walter Benjamin, 'The Work of Art in the Age of its Technological Reproducibility', in *The Work of Art in the Age of Its Technological Reproducibility, and Other Writings on Media* (Cambridge, MA: Harvard University Press, 2008), 19–42.

5 Philip K. Dick, *The Man in the High Castle* (1962) (New York: Houghton Mifflin Harcourt, 2011), 185–6.

6 Francis Davis, *The History of the Blues: The Roots, the Music, the People* (Cambridge, MA: Da Capo Press, 2003), 92.

7 Phillip K. Dick, 'Novelty Act', in *The Minority Report and Other Classic Stories by Philip K. Dick* (New York: Citadel Press, 2002), 207.

8 Philip K. Dick, *The Simulacra* (1964) (New York: Houghton Mifflin Harcourt, 2011), 170.

9 Philip K. Dick, *The Three Stigmata of Palmer Eldritch* (1965) (New York: Houghton Mifflin Harcourt, 2011), 71.

10 Philip K. Dick, *Flow My Tears The Policeman Said* (1974) (New York: Houghton Mifflin Harcourt, 2012), 249

11 Dick, *Flow My Tears The Policeman Said*, 198–9.
12 Philip K. Dick, *Galactic Pot-Healer* (1969) (New York: Vintage Books, 1994), 177.
13 Philip K. Dick, *Valis* (1981) (New York: Houghton Mifflin Harcourt, 2011), 14.
14 Ernst Bloch, *Geist der Utopie* (Munich and Leipzig: Dunker, 1918), 14f, quoted in Theodor Adorno, 'The Handle, the Pot and Early Experience', in *Notes to Literature*, Vol. 2. (New York: Columbia University Press, 1992), 211–9.
15 Theodor Adorno, 'The Handle, the Pot and Early Experience', 219.
16 Ernst Bloch, *The Spirit of Utopia* (Stanford: Stanford University Press, 2000), 7.

OSW

outposts and frontiers

Devil in the Dark
(*Star Trek*—Original Series)
Airdate: March 9, 1967
Stardate 3196.1. The Enterprise is in orbit around Janus VI. On the planet below a Federation mining colony is under

conditions and consequences

Hemp and war
The establishment of a colony at Port Jackson in Australia in the 1790s was set against the background of a series of major conflicts in Europe sparked by the French Revolution. These conflicts, following on from the American War of Independence, dominated the final decade of the eighteenth century and extended through to 1815. The significance of these conflicts to the settlement of Australia is usually explained in terms of the United Kingdom's need to find a new home for its growing criminal class following its losses in America. However, historian John Jiggens argues it had more to do with the central role of hemp in maintaining

layers, veins and connections

The succession of scripts, observations and commentary gathered here can be framed by something like an expanded geological diagram, similar to that advanced by Manuel De Landa in *A Thousand Years of Nonlinear History.*[12] With reference to complexity theory and the philosophy of Gilles Deleuze and Félix Guattari, De Landa describes physical and biological systems in economic

attack from an unknown life form.
CHIEF ENGINEER VANDERBERG: That thing has killed fifty of my men.
CAPTAIN KIRK: You've killed thousands of her children.
VANDERBERG: What?
KIRK: Those round silicon nodules that you've been collecting and destroying? They're her eggs. Tell them, Mister Spock.
SPOCK: There have been many generations of Horta on this planet. Every fifty thousand years, the entire race dies, all but one, like this one, but the eggs live. She cares

the maritime power of the empire.[1] *Noting the word canvas comes from the Dutch word for cannabis, Jiggens points out that equipping a first rate man-of-war sailing ship required eighty tons of hemp for sails, rigging, anchor ropes, cargo nets etc., and that these needed to be replaced every three or four years. To produce that much hemp from the long vegetable fibers of* cannabis sativa, *320 acres had to be grown.*

Navel power was crucial to the United Kingdom during the course of the Napoleonic War when the United Kingdom blocked the English Channel in order to restrict French access to Atlantic ports and the Mediterranean. Napoleon attempted to break the blockade by signing a treaty with Czar Alexander in 1807, restricting the UK's access to

and social terms. His approach characterises differentiating flows of matter-energy, organic and inorganic information, force and intensity, across a broad spectrum including rocks, plants, animals, genetic code, language, social, cultural and discursive practices. Through accumulative processes—binding, connecting, folding, thickening, hardening—these flows yield formations across different durations, before dissipating again into transitory singularities or reforming. For De Landa this for them, protects them. And when they hatch, she is the mother to them, thousands of them. This creature here is the mother of her race.

KIRK: The Horta is intelligent, peaceful, mild. She had no objection to sharing this planet with you, till you broke into her nursery and started destroying her eggs. Then she fought back in the only way she knew how, as any mother would fight when her children are in danger.

VANDERBERG: We didn't know. How could we? You mean if these eggs hatch, there'll be thousands of those things crawling around down here?

Russian hemp. The United Kingdom responded by seizing American ships, threatening to confiscate their cargo and press their crews into service in the British navy unless they helped bypass Napoleon's trade restriction under the cover of the supposedly neutral American flag. During this time, hemp, which normally sold for £25 per ton, reached a price of £118 per ton.

Jiggens argues the crisis in hemp supply was a recurrent theme in British strategic thinking during the Georgian era, making hemp production as significant as oil has been for the last century. He suggests that colonising Australia was not primarily motivated by the need to find a replacement prison but by the need for hemp. Numerous schemes to grow hemp were tried in the early years of colonisation: settlers

dynamic movement of forces and constraints, change and stasis is a mixture of coexistent intermingling hierarchies comprising uniform elements and what he terms 'meshworks' or self-consistent aggregates.[13]

These events of formation are the beneficial but also disastrous, and ultimately unavoidable, processes of stratification described by Deleuze and Guattari in terms of a double articulation.[14] 'Borrowing from the linguist Louis Hjelmslev, Deleuze and Guatarri characterised

KIRK: This is where they live. They digest rock, they tunnel for nourishment.
SPOCK: And they are the most inoffensive of creatures. They harbour ill will towards no one.
APPEL: Now look, we have pergium to deliver.
KIRK: Yes, I know. Here's your circulating pump. You've complained this planet is a mineralogical treasure house if you had the equipment to get at it. Gentlemen, the Horta moves through rock the way we move through air, and it leaves tunnels. The greatest natural miners in the universe. It seems to me we could make an agreement,

were offered free seeds and bounties, and convicts were employed in its cultivation and processing. Despite setbacks, hemp production increased. By the turn of the century, new mechanical methods for harvesting and retting allowed hemp to be manufactured much more efficiently. However, this new era of industrialisation also brought about steel cable and steam-powered ships, which rendered much of the hemp industry obsolete. Hemp production went into decline as cotton became easier to produce and petrochemical industries introduced synthetic textiles such as nylon.

Scramble for Africa

In 1884 and 1845, fifteen nations gathered for the Berlin West Africa Conference in order to settle existing territorial

this formulation as adhering to a tetravelent structure, which sees the paired terms content and expression, and substance and form delineate a field within which the two intertwined movements pass. It is through this articulation that Deleuze and Guattari avoid a simple dualist relationship between form and substance, as each operation is doubled such that both content and expression have substance and form. Significantly, substance is understood as 'nothing other than formed matters', a

reach a modus vivendi. They tunnel. You collect and process, and your process operation would be a thousand times more profitable.
VANDERBERG: Sounds alright, if it will work.
SPOCK: Except for one thing. The Horta is badly wounded. It may die.
DOCTOR MCCOY: It won't die. By golly, Jim, I'm beginning to think I can cure a rainy day.
KIRK: Can you help it?
MCCOY: Help it? I cured it.
KIRK: How?

disputes, and lay down the rules for subsequent annexations that resulted in a partitioning of Africa. The gathering was dominated by the United Kingdom, Germany, France and Portugal, and focused on sub-Saharan Africa. Of the nations present, none were African. This gathering followed at least four centuries of imperialism during which countries such as Portugal and the United Kingdom exploited Africa's populations as slaves (some 12 million between the 1440s and 1867), along with its raw materials (especially gold, ivory and rubber).

Although the scramble for territory was driven by imperial rivalries, with the aim of excluding opponents from potentially lucrative regions, it also took place against the backdrop of a worldwide financial crisis. Initiated by the

residue of specific accumulations and codings at work in a particular process of territorialisation and deterritorialisation.[15] These formed matters comprise layers or stratum that are always at least in pairs and open to change, as the substance of expression on one stratum serves as a new substratum for another and so on.

This understanding allows us to observe amid various registers—organic, inorganic, social or economic—specific historical assemblages. Whether the assemblage

MCCOY: Well, I had the ship beam down a hundred pounds of that thermoconcrete. You know, the kind we use to build emergency shelters out of. It's mostly silicone. So I just trowelled it into the wound, and it'll act like a bandage until it heals. Take a look. It's as good as new.
KIRK: Well, Spock, I'm going to have to ask you to get in touch with the Horta again. Tell her our proposition. She and her children can do all the tunnelling they want. Our people will remove the minerals, and each side will leave the other alone. Think she'll go for it?
SPOCK: It seems logical, Captain. The Horta has a very

collapse of the Vienna Stock Exchange in 1873 and marked by subsequent bank failures, this crisis is sometimes referred to as the Long Depression. Numerous factors were at play: France was struggling with war reparations to Germany, while Germany saw unsustainable growth driving booming stock prices as a result of unification and the influx of capital. The US witnessed bank closures—in part due to a tightening of monetary policy in an effort to return to the gold standard after Germany's 1873 demonetisation of silver, but also as a consequence of speculative investments in building railroads, driven by government land grants and subsidies. The period of deflation lasted until 1879 and remains the longest period of contraction in US history. The United Kingdom suffered until 1896, as trade slumped

is mining or slavery, the processes of accumulation, sedimentation and coding operate according to various supple and rigid processes of stratification. For example, De Landa maps the intensification in food production and other energy sources that saw European countries digest the world as vast regions were turned into its supply zones.[16] Through the surplus extracted from the ground and the unpaid labour of slaves, the New World contributed to the transformations underway in eighteenth logical mind. And after close association with humans, I find that curiously refreshing.

Force of Nature
(*Star Trek: The Next Generation*)
Airdate: Nov 15, 1993
Stardate: 47310.2. In the Hekaras Corridor, an unstable region of space, the crew of the Enterprise discover that warp engines are damaging the fabric of space–time.
CHIEF ENGINEER LAFORGE: Yeah. Maybe I was taking the whole thing personally.

and its economy stagnated with little investment in infrastructure. Overall, the period was characterised by falling prices, tariff wars and protectionist policies driven by fierce nationalism. Although the value of trade with Africa was small, during this time of significant economic downturn, the lure of potential wealth from African resources cast imperial expansion as a viable alternative.

Following the Berlin West Africa conference, there was a headlong race between the European nations to extend 'effective occupation' from their respective coastal enclaves to Africa's interior hinterland. Motivated by 'a heady mix of self-interest, racial arrogance, and missionary zeal', the expansion effectively remapped the African continent into fifty different colonies, paying no attention to the

century European urban environments, as much as European colonisation transformed the New World.

Historically, 'land' has been one of the most important mechanisms of capture through which the state exercises monopoly over territory, so as to, amongst other things, control mining rights. Through a refinement of legal understandings, mining rights encode processes of segmentation that have given rise to a peculiar distinction between the soil of the earth and the minerals it contains.

DATA: I do not understand.
LAFORGE: Maybe I was a little threatened. The thought that warp engines might be doing some kind of damage…
RABAL: I don't think we can look at space travel the same way anymore. We're going to have to change.
LAFORGE: I've been in Starfleet for a long time. We depend on warp drive. I just don't know how easy it's going to be to change.
RABAL: It won't be easy at all…
PICARD: You know, Geordi, I spent the better part of my life exploring space. I've charted new worlds, I've

rich diversity of existing cultural or linguistic borders.[2] *Although land remained the legal property of the Africans and occupation was often secured by negotiation and treaty, it was also accompanied by coercion, violence or dubious offers of 'protection'.*[3] *Despite considerable opposition to European forces in some regions, in the face of industrial technology, such as repeating rifles and the Maxim Gun (precursor to the modern-day machine gun), indigenous resistance proved futile. The conquering 'tools of empire' also included 'medicines, steamships, railways, telegraphs, and the organisational capabilities of the industrial state'.*[4] *These had disastrous consequences for large numbers of Africans who lacked a mechanism through which to organise a united resistance; it was not until 1900 that the*

While this codification may be configured differently, it should not be assumed that mechanisms of capture can be simply overcome. Rather, Deleuze and Guattari propose various paths towards triggering transformative energies and forces through which power might operate as life-affirming rather than life-denying.[17]

The geo-logically inspired schema De Landa draws from Deleuze and Guattari presents ways to think about the connections between thought and materiality met dozens of new species. And I believe that these were all valuable ends in themselves. Now it seems that all this while, I was helping to damage the thing that I hold most dear.

Prodigal Daughter
(*Star Trek: Deep Space Nine*)
Airdate: Jan 14, 1999
Stardate 52300 (approx.). On a planet near New Sydney in the Sappora System, the Tigan family discuss recent events at their pergium mining facility.

first Pan-African Conference was held in London.

Struggles continue in Africa over who should profit from its natural resources. The people of Nigeria see little benefit from their petro-chemical industry, which is dominated by multinational corporations such as Royal Dutch Shell and Chevron. In the Nzérékoré region of southeastern Guinea, companies such as Rio Tinto are forging contracts with Chinalco to develop the Simandou iron ore reserve.[5] *While African mineral reserves rank first or second in the world for bauxite, cobalt, diamonds, phosphate rocks, platinum-group metals (PGM), vermiculite, and zirconium, Africa remains the world's poorest inhabited continent, as measured by gross domestic product per capita.*

as movements and flows that take into account non-linguistic expression. To this can be added Deleuze and Guattari's understanding of territory in a geographical sense that extends Friedrich Nietzsche's privileging of milieus over origins, and sees them nominate him as the founder of a geophilosophy.[18] For Deleuze and Guattari, geography emphasizes the irreducibility of contingency and proposes that thinking isn't what takes place in, around or between subjects and objects, but is rather

YANAS: Why was this woman on our payroll?
JANEL: We were returning a favour.
YANAS: To whom?
JANEL: To the Orion Syndicate.
YANAS: And what favour did they do for us?
JANEL: Remember when the Ferengis opened up the Timor Two mine and there was a ten point drop in the price of pergium? Well, that came at a bad moment. We were overextended on some loans, our cash reserves were depleted, and a Jem'Hadar raid destroyed an entire shipment before it reached the refinery on Rigel Four.

Freehold/leasehold

Current freehold property rights in Australia permit the utilisation of surface land, but do not generally allow for the exploitation of mineral resources on or below ground level. The extraction of mineral reserves such as petroleum, natural gas, and precious metals requires a mining lease, a ruling first introduced in the Australian colonies in 1851 during the gold rush. Prior to this date, English common law prevailed, whereby the owner of the land was also entitled to the resources on, above or below the surface: 'to whomsoever the soil belongs, he owns also to the sky and to the depths'.[6] *While common law established a distinction between soil and mineral deposits, it also stated that 'whatever is affixed to the soil belongs to the soil'.*[7] *Exceptions to*

what 'takes place in the relationship of territory and the earth'.[19] In this relationship, earth isn't understood as the primal layer of the world nor the ultimate substrate; the layers of stratums described by geology make evident the contingency of foundations. Rather, earth, ground, land, and territory, as John Protevi writes, 'express manners of occupying terrestrial space by different social machines: the nomad war machine, the territorial tribe, the overcoding State'.[20]

EZRI: So you turned to the Syndicate?
JANEL: They came to me! They offered us a way out and I took it. I did what I had to do. And I don't remember you asking a lot of questions when our cash problems were resolved overnight.
YANAS: Because I trusted you. Obviously it was a mistake.
EZRI: What about Morica?
JANEL: About a month after Bokar arranged the loan, he came to me and said it was time to return the favour. There was a woman who needed a job with a salary, but without any actual work involved. He said she was the

these rights were made for the 'royal metals' of gold and silver, to which the Crown retained absolute possession. In 1840, the British Secretary of State issued a direction to the colony of NSW to include all mineral rights in future grants of Crown lands. However, mining laws of 1851 reversed this decision and English common law was 'progressively superseded in accordance with the policy that the Crown should own all minerals whether in private or public land'.[8] *This continuing policy of public ownership of minerals sets Australia apart from countries such as the US and Canada, where private ownership of mines and minerals is prevalent.*

The legalities governing the exploitation of mineral reserves in Australia relate directly to the initial formative engagement with the land during its annexation by Great

The creative potential of this understanding lies in an experimental engagement with material systems to form divergent consistencies that emphasise a nonlinear dynamic in and between 'natural' and social systems. In place of an image of thought that uncovers or constructs universals, or establishes values, the layering of geophilosophy is constituted by a double becoming, a zone of exchange that refuses to see creativity as something essentially human and therefore non-natural.[21] Amongst widow of one of their associates and they needed to take care of her. I didn't feel like I was in a position to say no. So I started making the payments. No one would've been the wiser if Norvo had altered the payroll records like I asked him.

YANAS: You dragged your little brother into this?

JANEL: You're the one who says there's nothing more important than the company. Well, that's all I was thinking about. The company. You dumped it in my lap and I saved it, so don't start complaining now. If it weren't for me, we would have been finished.

Britain. In regarding the country as terra nullius, *and ignoring all pre-existing social laws, cultural practices and centuries of land management by Indigenous peoples, the land and the wealth embedded within it were automatically vested in the Crown. The concept of* terra nullius *was overturned as a consequence of the second Mabo case in 1992, where legal recognition of common law title to land on the Murray Islands in Torres Strait was successfully argued. The subsequent Native Title Act of 1993 recognises the rights and interests to land held by Indigenous people under their traditional laws and customs, including the right to negotiate access to their land.[9] The changing and at times contentious relationships between Aboriginal communities and mining companies that Native Title has enabled was*

other things, geophilosophy invites a consideration of the limits of territory zones of anomalous dimensions where an outside is encountered. Whether the outside is another race, entity, territory, time, or as Deleuze and Guattari find in a short story by H.P. Lovecraft, 'the ultimate regions of a Continuum inhabited by unnameable waves and unfindable particles', these regions can be characterised by the hard edges of boundaries between fixed states of being.[22] As Protevi and Bonta suggest, a borderline

Homestead
(*Star Trek: Voyager*)
Airdate: May 9, 2001
Stardate 54868.6. In the briefing room on the Starship Voyager negotiations between a Talaxian colony and a mining operation are taking place.
CAPTAIN JANEWAY: Isn't there enough to mine here, without destroying their home?
COMMANDER NOCONA: Their home contains more than thirty percent of the field's ore. Without that asteroid the operation isn't worth the expense.

addressed by Professor Marcia Langton in her 2012 Boyer lecture 'The Quiet Revolution: Indigenous People and the Resources Boom'. Langton challenges assumptions that Aboriginal people are simply 'caretakers of wilderness', arguing for the benefits that resource-based economic development can bring to Indigenous communities largely neglected by mainstream Australia.

The complex relationship between freehold and leasehold rights is also dramatised in the context of coal seam gas extraction rapidly developing in the eastern states of Australia. For example, the Queensland Gas Company currently holds more than 800 agreements with landholders, and is planning to sink around 6,000 new wells across 4,500 square kilometres over the next twenty

is activated by processes of bordering: 'bordering is effected by individuals that reach a zone characterised by a threshold of density beyond which they sense that it is "unsafe" to venture'.[23] It is in this encounter with that which is unrecognisable that Deleuze and Guattari argue we are compelled to think, to pass beyond habits and clichés to negotiate alternate ways of being and, or, experiences of time and space.

NEELIX: Would you be open to some kind of compensation?
NOCONA: All we want are the minerals.
OXILON: And you'd kill us to get them.
NEELIX: Wait. The Talaxians have found a way to produce a lot of geothermal energy. Maybe they could share it with you.
NOCONA: What do you mean, share?
NEELIX: You could convert it into fuel to power your ships.
NOCONA: The energy they generate isn't compatible with our technology.

years.[10] *Farmers with gas reserves on their land are generally unable to restrict mining on their property, and state and federal governments are entitled to sell mining rights to third parties without the consent of the landholder.*[11] *Growing tension between farmers with private freehold and mining companies with leases seeking access to gas reserves below the surface reveal the complexity of ownership rights and highlight the difficulty in taking into account long-term effects, such as the water quality in the Great Artesian Basin.*

JANEWAY: We'd be willing to help you make the modifications.

NOCONA: We have quotas to meet. We don't have time for that.

JANEWAY: Commander, the future of more than five hundred people is at stake here.

Notes

1 John Jiggens, *Sir Joseph Banks and the Question of Hemp, Sea-Power and Empire 1776–1815*, (Clarence Park, SA: John Jiggens, 2012). See also *ABC Radio National*, 'Ockham's Razor—was Australia intended as a hemp colony?', broadcast 9 September 2012.
2 John Parker and Richard Rathbone, *African History: a very short introduction* (Oxford: Oxford University Press, 2007), 96.
3 Parker and Rathbone, *African History*, 91.
4 Parker and Rathbone, *African History*, 97.
5 'Simandou', *Wikipedia*, accessed 6 December 2012, http://en.wikipedia.org/wiki/Simandou. See also AAP, *The Age*, 'Rio Tinto, Chinalco hook up for Africa venture', March 19, 2010. Accessed 6 December 2012, http://www.theage.com.au/business/rio-tinto-chinalco-hook-up-for-africa-venture-20100319-qkay.html.
6 Anne Fitzgerald, *Mining Agreements: negotiated frameworks in the Australian minerals sector*, (Chatswood, NSW: Prospect Media, 2010), 93, http://eprints.qut.edu.au/34063/2/Mining_Agreements_Anne_Fitzgerald.pdf. Accessed 6 December 2012.
7 Fitzgerald, *Mining Agreements*, 93.
8 Ibid, 95.
9 Australian Government Attorney-General's Department, 'Native Title'. http://www.ag.gov.au/LegalSystem/NativeTitle/Pages/default.aspx. Accessed 6 December 2012.
10 Bridget Andersen, 'Landholders to know their rights on CSG', *ABC News*, broadcast 30 September 2011. http://www.abc.net.au/news/2011-09-30/coal-sem-gas-rights-feature/3193850. Accessed 6 December 2012.
11 Samantha Hepburn, 'Coal seam gas expansion:

devastating farmers and the environment', *Right Now: Human rights in Australia*, September 1, 2012: http://www.righnow.org.au/writing-cat/feature/coal-seam-gas-expansion-devestating-farmers-and-the-environment/. Accessed 6 December 2012.

12 Manuel De Landa, *A Thousand Years of Nonlinear History*, (New York: Zone Books, 1997).

13 Ibid, 32.

14 Gilles Deleuze and Félix Guattari, *A Thousand Plateaus*, trans. Brian Massumi (Minneapolis: University of Minnesota Press, 1987), 40.

15 Deleuze and Guattari, *A Thousand Plateaus*, 41.

16 De Landa, *A Thousand Years*, 162.

17 Gilles Deleuze, *Nietzsche and Philosophy*, trans. Hugh Tomlinson (New York: Columbia University Press, 2006), 85.

18 Gilles Deleuze and Félix Guattari, *What is Philosophy?*, trans. Hugh Tomlinson and Graham Burchell, (New York: Columbia University Press, 1994), 102.

19 Deleuze and Guattari, *What is Philosophy?*, 85.

20 John Protevi, 'Earth/Land (Terre)', in *The Deleuze Dictionary*, Adrian Parr (ed.) (Edinburgh: Edinburgh University Press, 2005), 80–1.

21 Mark Bonta and John Protevi, *Deleuze and Geophilosophy: A Guide and Glossary* (Edinburgh: Edinburgh University Press, 2006), 5.

22 Deleuze and Guattari, *A Thousand Plateaus*, 248.

23 Bonta and Protevi, *Deleuze and Geophilosophy*, 65.

Clear light, dark times: Science fiction as fact

Charles Green

1. Robert Heinlein, *Starship Troopers* (1959); Isaac Asimov, *Foundation Trilogy* (1951–53)

During my early teens in the mid- to late-1960s, I eagerly read every science fiction novel I could borrow from the several libraries I belonged to. Isaac Asimov's and Robert Heinlein's novels were at the centre of science fiction's vast worlds. With Arthur C. Clarke (whose stories seemed wooden and whose ideas were clearly leaden even to a hyper-impressionable thirteen-year-old), Heinlein and Asimov were of course the Big Three science fiction writers of the period, as Wikipedia kindly reminds me.[1] If at the time I understood the Ayn Rand-derived libertarian underpinning beneath Heinlein's *Starship Troopers*, then inside that novel's imaginary, hyper-dangerous worlds, Heinlein's (and Rand's) doctrine of extreme self-discipline, coupled with his emphasis on ethical obligation, seemed not only reasonable but infinitely extendable out to the magicians' world I lived in.[2] That labyrinth only seemed to be furnished in its 1960s suburban veneer (in fact, I now understand that my parents and family were highly unusual, not least amongst which was my Moorabbin grandmother, who was as certain that she had reincarnated from ancient Egypt as I was that she was perfectly reasonable). It's commonplace to think that everything seems very big to a small child. It's not so often understood that everything can equally seem very small. Incompletely confined by my surroundings, I felt safe by being able to float over tables and invisibly hide out just below the ceiling, peer through walls and fly across roofs. Then the inevitable happened: I grew up and it was neither socially acceptable to fly nor could I remember being able to do so. Apart from chance meetings with other initiates, it was now not so often that I remembered who I was. That is, until those novels, where I was completely swallowed whole inside Isaac Asimov's *Foundation Trilogy*, which consisted of *Foundation* (1951), *Foundation and Empire* (1952), and *Second Foundation* (1953).[3] The three books recount the collapse and rebirth of a vast interstellar empire in a universe of the future. The further I moved into the trilogy's spiral embrace, the more the world darkened and teenage walls caved in. Of course, the basic trope of Asimov's vast trilogy is a sudden clearing at the centre of the universe; of course, this prefigures film director Andrei Tarkovsky's science fiction masterpiece, *Stalker* (1979). First, Asimov's scenes are described as precise, semi-static tableaux. Second, the characters in his narratives move slowly, like ceremonial images (ceremonial in the precise sense identified by Walter Benjamin) rather than like the heroes and heroines of other books. Finally, his novels suggest that they are a microcosm of a much larger narrative and they could, like the other books and movies in my list, be re-entered at their middle, end or beginning, depending on how orderly my continuous, looped, repetitive re-readings. Asimov's superficially linked trilogy unfolds across a vast, shimmering starry backdrop in relation to which his books' characters choreograph themselves theatrically. I realise now, much later, that the improbable theorist of such an experience of science fiction is Proust, whose reinvention of the modernist novel (a form already then as anachronistic as Asimov's Eisenhower-era-like future) resulted in imaginary worlds ruled by sequences of memory images and madeleines rather than by computers and freeways. As Barthes acutely observes, Proust's work is neither essay nor novel, but a third form, one that uncannily recalls science fiction: 'The structure of this work will be, strictly speaking, rhapsodic, i.e. (etymologically) sewn; moreover, this is a Proustian metaphor: the work is produced like a gown; the rhapsodic text implies an original art, like that of the *couturière*: pieces, fragments are subject to certain correspondences, arrangements, reappearances'.[4] I want to press literary theorist Mieke Bal into equally unlikely service: she frames the same observation slightly differently, explaining that Proust's innovation was his montage and his cinematographic focus. She insists on his serialisation and repetitions, 'by means of a progressive adjustment of the same image, also functions syntagmatically in the production of consecutive images, each of which announces the next'.[5] Asimov's serialisation took the form of repetitive, progressive adjustments, continual re-disclosures, his insistence on flat characters, and a disinterest in personal revelation. The result: an ethnography of types as his characters migrate from world to world. All of this results in something quite different to the conventional science fiction description of gadgets and spaceships—different to the flat-footed scientism that Asimov's books might be mistakenly pegged as exemplifying—and Asimov sets the rhapsodic template for Frank Herbert's great *Dune* books.

2. Philip K. Dick, *The Man in the High Castle* (1963); Alfred Bester, *The Stars My Destination* (1956; also published as *Tiger Tiger*)

Again, a teenager. Now, faced with an insoluble choice. Who do I like more: the Beatles or the Rolling Stones? With the money for only one LP, would I buy the Rolling Stones' *Their Satanic Majesties Request* (1967) or the Beatles' *Sgt. Pepper's Lonely Hearts Club Band* (1967)? Psychedelic music and proto-cyberpunk science fiction emerge around this same time: the late 1960s. Both are essentially very dark—very *noir*—and both had a considerable, subterranean influence on what would become contemporary art. The secret: their *contemporaneity*. Sure, there is something similarly Pop about the fluorescent colours used by British psychedelic design studio Hapshash and the Coloured Coat and the equally fluorescent surfaces of Don Judd's sculptures and Dan Flavin's neon tubes; repetition and form were key, self-justifying and solipsistic. That wasn't so much the locus of their and science fiction's contemporaneity. Philip K. Dick's now-celebrated psychedelic novels move through the most labyrinthine plots without any substantial character development. His figures are self-consciously self-conscious types.[6] Dick renovates Jules Verne's particular nineteenth-century ficto-documentary genre that involves the modeling of imagined worlds. Dick's particular renovation enables him to queer and darken the sentimental idealism that had thus far accompanied science fiction. His successors are contemporary French novelist Michel Houellebecq and British writer China Miéville. In Houellebecq's *Atomised*, a gentle scientist, Michel, explains the significance of the ficto-documentary form: 'It is possible to construct a history which is logically consistent. It cannot be said to be true; simply that it can be sustained without contradiction… You make this hypothesis about real life, rather than the memories of dreams.'[7] Through Michel, Houellebecq argues that an imaginary, modeled world—science fiction—disentangles supposedly entwined thoughts. We can recognise this disentanglement in Philip K. Dick, but at the same time acknowledge that his vision of impersonality and process is not particularly idealistic. Michel is attacking memory's real status and Michel's brother, Bruno, replies that this attack implies the self is an illusion. Houellebecq immediately notes that his character Michel does not know anything about Buddhism and therefore could not answer. We can add that if he did know, he would have been able to reply that the self was not as simple as an illusion as such and prescribe that the reader should re-visit Dick's *The Man in the High Castle*. A post-Dick science fiction masterpiece, *The Matrix* (1999) graphically and brutally shows just this: at the moment that Neo (Keanu Reeves) swallows the reality pill, there is no such natural thing as memory or identity, just binary process and the code.

3. Frank Herbert, *Dune* (1965)

If there can be a complete parallel universe, this book maps it out. Written thirty-five years before Hardt and Negri's post-Marxist tract *Empire* (2000), *Dune* is harder and harsher than *Empire* and predicts its thesis. Both paint the universe in bright, shiny, clear, hard light. At the same time—and necessarily so—*Dune*'s narrative is fragmented, broken and immersive.[8] *Dune* devalues coherence, unity and narrative seamlessness. Hard light comes with sharp edges and therefore also with damage, with the bright sunshine and *noir* unpleasantness we've already emphasised of *Man in the High Castle*. Hard light implies the entropic devolution of story into archive, into database fragmentation, and thence into a very *contemporary* model of cosmological organisation. *Dune* shows us the coincident emergence of body, speech and mind but not of corporeality nor, even less, of dysfunctional pathology. This is quite exhilarating. It might be plausibly argued, then, that *Dune* is a quasi-Buddhist demolition of the concept of the sublime: the latter is nothing but a category error. This might seem an appropriate pathway to describe the disorientation and decorporealisation of *Dune*'s view of vast social phenomena, and thus we would be grounding the book on a negation. But it would be a misinterpretation, given that we have also pointed to the shifting relativity of flux-like experience, and to the constant mental chatter and ceaseless motion depicted in *Dune*. A further mental image underlies the book. It is connected with the flickering of Herbert's imagist writing, which gradually hints at an underlying image that is so metaphorically loaded, so overdetermined, that it is almost disqualified before it is sighted: the explosion. The image is almost omnipresent in science fiction, contemporary art, art cinema and popular cinema, not to mention news photographs, during the later 1960s. Explosions might seem at first to be the opposite of social theory or psychedelia, but play a videotape of an explosion backwards and you see a model world created. Review an explosion in slow motion and you see a master image fragment into facets, as in the final sequence of Antonioni's *Zabriskie Point* (1970), in which a sleek, architect-designed, modernist residence in the desert explodes in slow motion to the white-noise crescendo of Pink Floyd's early psychedelic rock composition, 'Careful with That Axe, Eugene' (1969). The live half of Pink Floyd's great double album, *Ummagumma* (1969), which includes 'Careful with That Axe, Eugene', could be *Dune*'s soundtrack (and would be much better than anything in David Lynch's unfortunate film adaption of the novel). *Dune* is *Zabriskie Point*'s prequel. *Dune* is a dispersed, kaleidoscopic scatter-piece, in which uncontained, semi-autonomous histories and collective memories tumble through centuries as their angelic Benjaminian debris breaks worlds apart. The point is less that a millenarian social explosion—which is what *Dune* is about—is sexy because it is dangerous than that an explosion is coherent, since its parts move fast. This is to say that such an explosion is hard to see or grasp and impossible to hold together. It is unified since it has a shape, at least in the science fiction eye, as did the slowed-down, beautiful explosion that ended *Zabriskie Point*, and as did the gathering cacophony of chanting, staccato voices in Paul's pre-birth memories in *Dune*. The only way that such a world view of destruction, matrix, and interpenetrating sight could be represented is through the representation of the invisible beyond the individual life. This representation would have to both assert and undermine normal representational practice, which is exactly what *Dune*'s environmental narrative manages, disfiguring its chief characters whilst opening them (and us) to global configurations of sheer force.

4. Carlos Castaneda, *The Eagle's Gift* (1981)

A BBC television documentary screened in grainy black and white in the early 1960s walks the viewer up the Kulu Valley in the Indian Himalayas and I watch, astounded and alert with the fierce desire to go there; this may, after all, be one of the places the young child flew over. A decade later I am reading Frank Herbert's *Dune* series—overblown and operatic in its later iterations—in tandem with Carlos Castaneda's great ficto-documentary books. Under the latter's influence I am rather foolishly walking in pitch blackness across sandstone bluffs in the Grampians and the Flinders Ranges at night, waiting for hours in such places as works of art that must remain undocumented and which were not to be told to anyone. A decade further on again, in 1984, I walk for most of the year in the Himalayas, hauling Castaneda's recently published two books across Ladakh in my pack as I ascend and descend high mountain passes. For many of my generation, the veracity of Castaneda's astonishing stories is irrelevant. It is clear that he intended them as a disguise that posited imaginative power and extravagance as true. That was a psychedelic, navigational cocktail, already familiar from science fiction. Like the first three *Dune* books, Castaneda's nine linked volumes testified to the failure of the self as either a symbolic or a permanent entity, advocating instead a lived experience of micro-time and the renewal of perception. Castaneda presented, quite simply, one of the most breathtaking, extended displays of fireworks I had seen in a long time. Operatic and revelatory in mood compared with *The Teachings of Don Juan: A Yaqui Way of Knowledge* (1968), the author's later book, *The Eagle's Gift* (1981), expanded the depressive pseudo-objectivity of the former book's anthropological reportage into a much more subjective and enveloping environmental experience that was also strategically stuttered, looped and fragmented. Castaneda turned the depiction of a shaman's mentorship into the superimposed juxtaposition of networked times, spaces and narratives. This broken narrative cannot be emphasised too much. Castaneda's book was a metaphoric and metonymic network of images mimicking the fragmented but meaningful movement of the author towards memory recovery. His broken memories produce the illusion that the workings of obliterated, unrecovered memory govern the world. This does not mean that a surrealist visual unconscious governs the world, but that erased memory collects pathos.

5. Andrei Tarkovsky, *Stalker* (1979)

At the start of the 1980s, one night, I suddenly discover Andrei Tarkovsky's great film, *Stalker*.[9] We turn the television idly on: as it turns out, SBS's late night movie is already a few minutes underway. No credits, no television program, we have no idea what we are looking at but we know, increasingly emotional, that this agonisingly slow science fiction film is indelibly changing our sensibilities. About Tarkovsky, Ingmar Bergman famously said, 'Suddenly, I found myself standing at the door of a room the keys of which had, until then, never been given to me. It was a room I had always wanted to enter and where he was moving freely and fully at ease.'[10] Watching *Stalker* for the first time, I am once again walking in a world that exists in the further recesses of a mind where layers of childhood recollection, science fiction and desire coexist. More recently, I remember that it was almost an accident, but certainly due to my awkwardness in acquiring new languages, that I wrote a PhD in art history instead of in screen studies with Tarkovsky as my subject. Nevertheless, it's clear that this profoundly anachronistic film director remains an underground cult amongst contemporary artists. As is well known and endlessly discussed, *Stalker* is composed of small, telling pauses nested within long camera takes. This is not unlike both Hitchcock's and David Lynch's use of close-ups: the registration of a multitude of details or clues gives way to a critical reflection upon the conditions of viewing—a panoramic spectatorship akin to minimalism—and then to an inspection-mode self-consciousness, a sense-heightened version of catching and collecting. Analogously, Miwon Kwon had noted the unexpected attributes of minimalism in connection with sculptural installation: 'Minimalism's effort to expand the viewer's field of vision, which was equated with the expansion of the viewer's critical consciousness of the art-viewing experience, was predicated on certain formal strategies or interdictions that disallowed intimacy'.[11] *Stalker* could be understood in the same way: the limitlessness, fragmentation and intimate detail meant that revelation never definitely appears. There isn't a punch line; his wandering scientist, writer and guide do not arrive. *Stalker*'s narrative structure does not move beyond the simplest plot nor is there any genuine character development. British novelist Geoff Dyer describes *Stalker*'s frustrating power in deliberately pedantic detail in his startling book, *Zona* (2012).[12] We will merely summarise *Stalker*'s fascination to artists: from a virtual experience of a film made up of stills, recollection images are extracted. What this means is that cinema is a first-order experience and still images are a second-order experience. They are, whether paintings or photographs, a special case of cinema held in a virtual space of recollection, pointing to a recollected past. A single image derives from a virtual recollection of a panorama unfolding in time. So, a work of art is a still, ceremonial image. In ceremonial images, people do not blink, nor do they have an autonomous existence; they are recalled as formulae rather than people.

Conclusion

So far, the idea that science fiction is non-fiction has been framed obliquely through the equation that science fiction is ficto-documentary. Narrative is pretty much a decoy, as is cathartic resolution and allegory. It is a mistake to pathologise Paul Atreides or Carlos Castaneda, and an error to see the planet Dune or the Mexican high plateau as the backdrop to each author's symptoms.[13] Art is not therapy and identity is fantasy. When I was assembling the book that accompanied an exhibition, *World rush_4 artists: Doug Aitken, Eija-Liisa Ahtila, Lee Bul and Sarah Sze* (National Gallery of Victoria, Melbourne, 2003), I asked Mieke Bal if she would write about Eija-Liisa Ahtila, knowing full well that she would explain that the Finnish artist's videos are not at all 'about' fantasy or psychosis, but only take those experiences to do something else altogether. Bal wrote that 'This keen detailing of space–time specificity, along with the disturbing melting of walls and the severance of sound from image, is a first indication that the possibility of storytelling itself is at stake'.[14] At stake as well, Bal added, is the adequacy or inadequacy of philosophical and theoretical interpretation of visual images. Empathy for a character is the least important element in the face of our struggle to work out a point of view in a field of superficially incoherent surface incident. This is continually defeated for, like Ahtila's young woman in her multi-channel video, *The House* (2002), Castaneda's Carlos and Herbert's Paul Atreides are continually suspended: in time, in space, in fate. To move forward, both Carlos and Paul must constantly concentrate on peripheral vision, as must we. This results in their decorporealisation and not their embodiment.

I have written before that writers often assume that intensely affective sensations automatically confirm the most familiar mode of embodiment—that of inhabiting the body—and criticised this as lazy thinking.[15] Other experiences more appropriately describe the sensation of reading *Dune* or watching *Stalker*. We are spectralised. We are turned into phantoms. We walk through walls. We become invisible and we fly across shimmering spaces and times. This is the edge of the Eagle's gift.

Notes

1 See paragraph two of the Wikipedia entry on Isaac Asimov; 'Isaac Asimiov', *Wikipedia*: http://en.wikipedia.org/wiki/Asimov. Accessed 25 December 2012.

2 For the writer's biography and plot outlines, see 'Robert A. Heinlein', *Wikipedia*: http://en.wikipedia.org/wiki/Robert_A._Heinlein. Accessed 25 December 2012.

3 For the writer's biography and plot outlines, see 'Isaac Asimov', *Wikipedia*: http://en.wikipedia.org/wiki/Isaac_Asimov. Accessed 25 December 2012.

4 Roland Barthes, 'Longtemps, je me suis couché de bonne heure', in *The Rustle of Language*, trans. Richard Howard (New York: Hill and Wang, 1986), 281. For a famous instance of Proust's image of stitching, see Marcel Proust, *Time Regained* (1927), trans. Andreas Mayor (London: Chatto & Windus, 1970), 454, where Proust writes: 'These "paperies", as Françoise called the pages of my writing, it was my habit to stick together with paste, and sometimes in this process they became torn. But Françoise then would be able to come to my help, by consolidating them just as she stitched patches onto the worn parts of her dresses or as, on the kitchen window, while waiting for the glazier as I was waiting for the printer,

she used to paste a piece of newspaper where the glass had been broken.'

5 Mieke Bal, *The Mottled Screen: Reading Proust Visually* (Stanford: Stanford University Press, 1997), 213.

6 For the writer's biography and plot outlines, see 'Philip K. Dick', *Wikipedia*: http://en.wikipedia.org/wiki/Philip_K._Dick. Accessed 25 December 2012.

7 Michel Houellebecq, *Atomised* (1999), trans. Frank Wynne (London: Vintage, 2001), 76. Later in the book, Michel continues, 'Back in his kitchen, he realized that belief in the notions of reason and free will, which are the natural foundations of democracy, probably resulted from a confusion between the concepts of freedom and unpredictability. The turbulence of a river flowing around the supporting pillar of a bridge is structurally unpredictable, but no one would think to describe it as being *free*'. Houellebecq, *Atomised*, 270, emphasis in the original.

8 For the writer's biography and plot outlines, see 'Dune', *Wikipedia*: http://en.wikipedia.org/wiki/Dune_(novel). Accessed 25 December 2012.

9 For Tarkovsky's biography and plot outlines, see 'Andrei Tarkovsky', *Wikipedia*: http://en.wikipedia.org/wiki/Andrei_Tarkovsky. Accessed 26 December 2012.

10 Ingmar Bergman, quoted in Peter Culshaw, 'Andrei Tarkovsky — "a mystic and a fighter"', *The Telegraph* (London), 1 December 2007, http://www.telegraph.co.uk/culture/film/starsandstories/3669621/Andrei-Tarkovsky-a-mystic-and-a-fighter.html. Accessed 26 December 2012.

11 Miwon Kwon, 'The Other Otherness: the Art of Do-Ho Suh', in Lisa G. Corrin (ed.), *Do-Ho Suh*, exh. cat. (London: Serpentine Gallery, 2002), 9–25, 11.

12 Geoff Dyer, *Zona* (Melbourne: Text Publishing, 2012).

13 The mood that pervades *Dune* fits theorist Elizabeth Grosz's description of autoscopy: 'The subject's ego is no longer centered in its own body, and the body feels as if it has been taken over or controlled by outside forces'. Elizabeth Grosz, *Volatile Bodies: Towards a Corporeal Feminism* (Sydney: Allen and Unwin, 1994), 43.

14 Mieke Bal, 'What if… ? Exploring "unnaturality"', in Charles Green (ed.), *World rush_4 artists: Doug Aitken, Eija-Liisa Ahtila, Lee Bul and Sarah Sze*, exh. cat. (Melbourne: National Gallery of Victoria, 2003), 30–7, 34. The next sentences paraphrase this section of Bal's argument.

15 Charles Green, *The Third Hand: Artist Collaborations from Conceptualism to Postmodernism* (Minneapolis: University of Minnesota Press, 2001); Charles Green, 'Group Soul: Who Owns the Artist Fusion?', *Third Text*, Vol. 18, No. 71 (November 2004), 595–608.

Exinterior: On Stanislaw Lem's *Fiasco*

Helen Johnson

> tho a man were admitted into Heaven to view the wonderful Fabrick of the World, and the Beauty of the Stars, yet what would otherwise be Rapture and Extasie, would be but a melancholy Amazement if he had not a Friend to communicate it to.[1]
> —Christiaan Huygens, 1698

Stanislaw Lem's *Fiasco* narrates a journey to another civilised planet in an attempt to make contact. Despite some degree of good intention, the outcome proves disastrous. *Fiasco* might be understood as a spatialisation of what, in philosophical terms, constitutes an attempt to exceed the limits of human subjectivity. At the same time, it is a topical allegory of the specific geopolitical situation in which Lem had found himself.

Lem wrote *Fiasco* in 1986, at a stage in his life when most of his writing was philosophical. He accepted an advance, the first in his career, to write the novel. It was written in East Berlin, Lem having fled Poland along with around 700,000 others in the economic aftermath of Polish Martial Law, introduced in 1981 as a means of crushing political opposition. At numerous points Lem uses the speculative space of *Fiasco* to critique the tortuous bureaucratic workings of the People's Republic of Poland, then a satellite state of the Soviet Union. At one point in the story, the commander-in-chief of a station on Titan comments 'Look at the name of the mine: Grail. Except that heaven has turned out to be damned expensive. The whole thing could have been set up better. The bookkeeping is a nightmare. Payments for those who die are hefty, but less money than it would take to reduce the danger. That's about all I have to say.'[2] This might be read as an oblique reference to the massacre of nine miners that took place at Wujek Coal Mine under Polish Martial Law in 1981 as the culmination of a strike-breaking action.

The first stage of *Fiasco* describes the plight of the astronaut Parvis. In attempting to cross the inhospitable terrain of Titan in a gigantic strider in search of his former supervisor Pirx,[3] Parvis finds himself trapped in his inadequately designed transport and forced to activate an emergency cryogenic capsule. Even in the most technologically elaborate, advanced futures that Lem fashions, processes are constantly being disrupted due to human folly, intentions stymied by convoluted bureaucratic processes: 'Into this concatenation of oversight, poorly conceived economising measures, haste, shipping delays, and ordinary foul-ups—typical of people everywhere and therefore in space as well—went one unfortunate strider after another'.[4]

Having crawled up between the strider's legs into its control room like a parasite entering its host, Parvis is thence shoved violently into a cryogenic capsule and snap-frozen. He has no guarantee of survival, since reanimation from cryonic stasis has not yet been technologically developed.[5] We barely get to know Parvis before he is frozen, at which point we leap forward a century to find his capsule retrieved from the wastes of Titan, along with several others, by a vessel lately embarked on a voyage to make contact with another life-supporting planet. Due to human error (again) only one of the salvaged bodies can be restored to life, pieced together from bits of all the others. Age, damage and technological incompatibility mean the individuals' identities cannot be fully determined. The future Lem fashions in *Fiasco* is one in which genetics exist but DNA is not applied for identification purposes; it is instead a society of heightened forensics. Government funding of space travel is unlimited. There is no such thing as anti-psychotic drugs, and all psychological issues are addressed interpersonally. Terms such as depression, fatalism and claustrophobia have been rendered obsolete. There is no concept of a shortage of resources (presumably since humans are mining other planets).

We find ourselves meeting a newly resurrected protagonist who may be Parvis or may be Pirx, the commander for whom he was searching. Having lost the ability to remember names, our man is as unsure of his identity as we are, so the book's central character is, before anything else, a nameless, split subject, his context erased by distance and time. In his new life, the resurrected man assumes the name Tempe.[6] In a bid to rehabilitate the broken pilot, the ship Euridice—whose object manifestation takes the form of a shaggy-headed, animated bust of Socrates—is conjured. 'If you will permit a small philosophical digression', Euridice comments, 'only things exist, and their relations. To be a man is to be a particular thing, it does not matter that it is a living thing. To be a brother or a son—that is a relation.'[7]

Fiasco is littered with references to myth, legend and literature, beginning with the parallel between Parvis and Parsifal, who quested for the Holy Grail.[8] Parvis becomes stranded in a region of Titan dubbed 'Birnam Wood' for its tendency to shift and migrate. He is retrieved and reanimated by the ship Euridice, named for its intended role in a sidereal shift to another dimension. The Euridice deposits the Hermes, a smaller vessel, at the event horizon through which it will travel sidereally to another galaxy. From this constellation of mythological references emerges an essentially biblical narrative in which the humans, putting themselves in the position of a deity in relation to another planet, enact a Sodom and Gomorrah story that is ultimately shown to be a projection of humanity's own existential wretchedness, rather than an astute reading of an alien civilization. 'Was the Universe nothing but a very large pie, and a civilization a child trying to consume the pie as quickly as possible?'[9]

The characters in *Fiasco* are not crafted to produce empathy in the reader, but to serve as ethical placeholders: the man without identity, the unhinged commander, the priest. We are made privy to very few aspects of their personal lives, but instead are offered a mode of characterisation that sits between the claustrophobic, quotidian banality of their existence aboard the vessel and their philosophical musings about the mission. One might find a model for this mode of characterisation in Erich Auerbach's *Odysseus' Scar*.[10] Auerbach writes:

> with the [Old Testament stories], the perpetually smouldering jealousy and the connection between the domestic and the spiritual, between the paternal blessing and the divine blessing, lead to daily life being permeated with the stuff of conflict, often with poison. The sublime influence of God here reaches so deeply into the everyday that the two realms of the sublime and the everyday are not only actually unseparated but basically inseparable.[11]

Though Lem was a self-professed atheist, in applying Auerbach's conception to *Fiasco* we can see again its biblical underpinnings, not only in terms of its narrative form but in its spatio-temporal conditioning. The humans in Lem's story are not only trapped in a space of the domestic inseparable from the sublime, but the root of poison in the situation lies in their failed attempts to play God to another planet, an overwhelming position of power whose stakes bleed into all quotidian interactions aboard the Hermes. The humans are locked in a sublime moment of their own making: though they are in some sense inhabiting the space of the classical sublime, they are incapable of apprehending it experientially, of processing it. The limits of human subjectivity are reinforced in the very attempt to go beyond them: 'Sidereal operations, as phenomena of astronomical proportions, cannot be for the observer—despite the power liberated in them—an experience as profoundly moving as a flood or a typhoon'.[12] As a freestanding phenomenon, 'the sublime' is a construct; it is a function of subjectivity, a billowing out. It makes sense then that post-anthropocentric thought should seek to do away with the sublime altogether. The danger is that we lose the sense of our real limits whilst believing we are dismantling them.

The 'new aesthetics', a movement oriented towards the integration of digital and technological perception into art, is a case in point.[13] With a focus on cognitive mapping, it claims to be geared toward the apprehension of the technological sublime, as though the sublime were a condition of high technology to be overcome, rather than a persistent experiential possibility. Proponents of the 'new aesthetic' speak of the digital *augmentation* of reality, positioning this against traditional media as seeking to represent reality, and in so doing to take a point of distance from it. I would argue that this is the point at which the 'new aesthetics', and the project of moving thought beyond anthropocentrism generally, disavows criticality. What we will arrive at if we follow this trajectory is, in Lem's words, 'not a society but an enormous collection of individuals'.[14]

In this regard *Fiasco* can be read as a defence of anthropocentric thought, or perhaps a warning against the belief that it can be exceeded. *Fiasco* draws upon the common binary between man and computer as a means of opening a space for thought about the ethics of seeking to step outside human subjectivity. Lem, it seems, understands humanity as a limited species, and presents the human-instigated extra-terrestrial encounter as a 'bull in a china shop' scenario.

> One cannot experience a star as one does a stone or diamond...But this same rule, making it impossible to experience immensity, operates in human affairs. One can feel compassion for the agony of an individual, of a family, but the extermination of thousands or millions of beings is a numerical abstraction whose existential content cannot be absorbed.[15]

The humans, too timid to make a landing on the planet that they have travelled so far to visit, sit in their ship for months, speculating on the nature of the inhabitants below. A large proportion of *Fiasco* is made up of these interminable speculations. The crew are obsessed with what form the alien society might take, envisaging a range of complex state-of-war scenarios to account for the planet's reticence to communicate. Their conviction that the planet must be in a state of global war leads them logically to consider what acts of assertion might goad the planet's intelligent inhabitants into giving a response. As they speculate, Lem's characters have pretensions towards thinking outside anthropocentrism, but in so doing can only project human structures of being onto the unknown: 'a civilization, in a series of costly crises, would fluctuate demographically. It could decline and regenerate itself many times, paying for this self-destructive inertia with billions of lives. The establishing of interstellar contact would not rank high on its list of priorities.'[16] The outcome is a sequence of large-scale, clumsy acts of destruction, a production of the experiential sublime. It is worth considering Lem's analysis of anthropocentric projection in relation to recent space missions. Recently, NASA satellites Ebb and Flo, which since 2011 have been orbiting the moon and mapping its gravity and surface, came to the end of their mission and were duly retired. By design they collided, within a short interval of one another, with a mountain on the moon's surface: a sort of mythopoetic termination for post-9/11 America.

Attempting to think beyond the limits of human subjectivity moves thought beyond ethics. The Hermes's priest Arago comments: 'In my eschatology there is no such thing as a lesser evil. With each slain being an entire world dies. For that reason arithmetic provides no measure for ethics. Irreversible evil cannot be measured.'[17] Whilst the optimist might believe that post-anthropocentric thought constitutes an expansion of empathy beyond human existence, hopefully extending to the environment in general, the pessimist might counter with an argument that post-anthropocentrism, and its attendant attempts to disavow human subjectivity, negates the possibility of empathy by refusing to accept human agency as it pertains to the world we both inhabit and produce. Lem shows us what it might mean for humanity to 'get out of itself': it turns violently back onto itself. 'There are physicists', Lauger explained, 'who claim to understand this the same way they understand what stones and cupboards are. What they understand, in fact, is only that a theory agrees with the experimental results, with measurements. Physics, my friend, is a narrow path drawn across a gulf that the human imagination cannot grasp.'[18]

The mainframe computer on board the Hermes—its acronym DEUS, Latin for 'God'—occupies the position of middle-manager that has been instrumentalised by communist and capitalist bureaucracies alike. As both facilitator and policy-maker, DEUS is 'at one and the same time subordinate and superior to the crew; it was to execute orders, yet supervise the mental condition of those who gave the orders. Thus, it held the rank of both tool and overseer.'[19] Amusingly, DEUS uses the term 'nondiscursive dismantling' for destruction by brute force, echoing the sort of institutional vernacular often deployed for sliding unpalatable policy into effect; one thinks of the Royal Melbourne Institute of Technology's recent introduction of a 'Behavioural Capability Framework' for its staff which, basically speaking, made them contractually obliged to appear happy and positive at all times in the workplace.[20]

Scenographically, *Fiasco* slips between two modes: internal spaces of vessels and space stations rendered quotidian and banal for their inhabitants, though remaining uncomfortable and humiliating spaces due to their variable gravity; and exterior, alien landscapes, the conditions of which are invariably insurmountable, revealing repeatedly the ineptitude of human engineering for intergalactic application. Concrete foundations crack and collapse, striders tumble in unexpected terrains and spill forth their hydraulics, emergency cryogenic capsules fracture the skull in the process of freezing. Lem presents us with a space travel that, in spite of ideal funding conditions and seemingly unlimited material resources, is reduced to the ad-hoc and the jerrybuilt in the face of contingency. As such it might be thought of as illustrating a failure to enact the transcendental subject. Humanity, generally speaking, is deficient in reflexivity about its own inadequacies. This is a leitmotif of *Fiasco*. Bristling with mythic referents, it is as though the overseers of the voyage have armoured its components with a carapace of ancient stories in order to broach the future. Stumbling towards the unknown, mythology becomes a talisman for Lem's characters.

Philosopher Quentin Meillassoux shares with Lem the project of contemplating being beyond human thought, though their respective projects are embedded in very different lines of intention. Lem takes us towards an unimaginable future; Meillassoux takes us towards an unimaginable past. In the face of the unknown, archaeology becomes an oracle for Meillassoux, who presumes to think the absolute beyond absolute being through his conception of the arche-fossil, as outlined in *After Finitude* (2008).[21] Lem wants to show us the futility of presuming to exceed our own subjectivity.

We might also consider this question of inward and outward as it pertains to artists—inner reflection as against the expanded field. It is natural that these positions (of subjectivity and the 'artist's hand' against pure form in the service of pure idea) should tumble in the dust together. The problem lies in believing that one might constitute an absolute solution that negates the other, for it is the dialectical opposition that enables growth, that necessitates putting oneself at stake. Art is already outside ontology.

Meillassoux writes, 'This is the enigma which we must confront: *mathematics' ability to discourse about the great outdoors; to discourse about a past where both humanity and life are absent*'.[22] Lem's characters head into Meillassoux's 'great outdoors':

> It was only in places where eternal, still death reigned, where neither the sieves nor the mills of natural selection were at work, shaping every creature to fit the rigors of survival, that an amazing realm opened up—of compositions of matter that did not imitate anything, that were not controlled by anything, and that went beyond the framework of the human imagination.[23]

For Meillassoux, thought has a new frontier, a realm we have not inhabited where the conceptual hunting is still good. He argues that we need to extract ourselves from our solipsism. I would argue that, rather, we need to collectively become capable of recognising our solipsism, and integrating it into a complexity that is not ourselves. In seeking thought beyond anthropocentrism, we can forget that we remain in many ways an enigma unto ourselves. Lem's position is opposed to Meillassoux's insofar as Lem narrativises the material conditions under which human beings might seek to stage a move beyond their own subjectivity, with the result of escalating levels of disaster and destruction, even genocide, wrought upon a misapprehended alien populace. As Meillassoux has written: 'The unthinkable can only draw us back to our inability to think otherwise, rather than to the absolute impossibility of things being wholly otherwise'.[24]

Notes

1 Christiaan Huygens, *Cosmotheoros*, trans. unknown (London: Timothy Childe, 1698), 4, as quoted in Frédérique Aït-Touati, *Fictions of the Cosmos*, trans. Susan Emanuel (Chicago: University of Chicago Press, 2011), 117.

2 Stanislaw Lem, *Fiasco*, trans. Michael Kandel (Florida: Harcourt Brace Jovanovich, 1987), 12.

3 Pirx the Pilot had previously been the subject of a series of speculative novels by Lem.

4 Lem, *Fiasco*, 42.

5 Interestingly, in the same year that *Fiasco* was written, Robert Mosley released a book entitled *Disney's World* in which he argued for the plausibility of the urban legend that Walt Disney's body had been cryonically frozen at death in the hope of future reanimation.

6 Named after a canyon in Greece between Mount Olympus and Mount Ossa, and with the obvious reference to time.

7 Lem, *Fiasco*, 86. Perhaps the most disturbing aspect of *Fiasco* is that there is not a single female character in the entire book. One wonders how the story might have changed if there had been female crew members.

8 Also close to the Latin *Parvus*, meaning peacock.

9 Lem, *Fiasco*, 125.

10 Erich Auerbach, 'Chapter 1: Odysseus' Scar', in *Mimesis* (New Jersey: Princeton University Press, 1953), 6–24.
11 Auerbach, *Mimesis*, 19.
12 Lem, *Fiasco*, 223.
13 As discussed in Nick Srnicek's paper 'Navigating Neoliberalism: Political Aesthetics in an Age of Crisis', presented at *The Matter of Contradiction: Ungrounding the Object*, Vassivière, France, 8–9 September 2012.
14 Lem, *Fiasco*, 224.
15 Lem, *Fiasco*, 223.
16 Lem, *Fiasco*, 91.
17 Lem, *Fiasco*, 254.
18 Lem, *Fiasco*, 115.
19 Lem, *Fiasco*, 86.
20 More information on the policy can be found in this article: 'RMIT Academics really not happy about having to be happy at work', *The Age*, 27 March 2012, http://www.theage.com.au/national/education/rmit-academics-really-not-happy-about-having-to-be-happy-at-work-20120326-1vuob.html. Accessed 15 January 2013.
21 Quentin Meillassoux, *After Finitude: An Essay on the Necessity of Contingency*, trans. Ray Brassier (London: Continuum, 2008).
22 Meillassoux, *After Finitude*, 26. Emphasis in the original.
23 Lem, *Fiasco*, 28.
24 Meillassoux, *After Finitude*, 44.

Tempo Kolossal

Damiano Bertoli

The ancient Roman harbour of Ostia now exists as a duality: simultaneously an inland village of immaculately preserved ruins—defined as Ostia Antica—and Ostia Lido, a nearby Fascist-era settlement of municipal architecture which fronts a sprawl of low-income housing, and hosts middle-class Roman holiday makers in its role as a beach resort in warmer months. As a topographical narrative, Ostia Lido marks the retreat of the Tyrrhenian Sea from antiquity to modern times, straddling the mouth of the Tiber River, which continues through to central Rome. As a location, its 'event memory' is historically and thematically linked with the life, and subsequent death, of the Italian poet and director Pier Paolo Pasolini. Sometime in 2006, a friend accompanied me on a visit to locate the site of Pasolini's notorious murder, stopping along the way to introduce me to the famed archaeological site at Ostia Antica. Clean and bristling with the school-excursion positivity and funding which Italy reserves for the extended restoration fantasy of its *beni culturali* (a program which collects and recycles endless tourist dollars while contemporary art receives little government support), its past is activated and alive, an immersive and interactive tracing of daily life in ancient Rome.

Whilst Ostia Antica is clearly signposted and impossible to miss, the site of Pasolini's death is difficult to locate, and after several frustrated hours we were unable to find this monument dedicated to the most significant artist and public intellectual in twentieth-century Italy. In the years since, I've realised through researching the area that we had walked around, toward and almost directly into, yet skilfully managed to never actually arrive at the nominal enclosure which houses this neglected Modern memorial. I've also come to realise this 'failure' as an experience that—devoid of the tokenism and perfunctory ritual of tourism—inadvertently traced a context for Pasolini's activities, a way of inhabiting his 'geography'. This deferral, a narrative of failed connectivity, enabled a continued desire for a missing 'object'; an amalgam of memory and actual experience, past and present, documentary and cinema, which revealed a more complicated idea of Pasolini's context, one of ambiguous provenance and parameters, neither fact nor fiction, but consistent with his articulation of spatial, social and temporal peripheries.

Pasolini died where he played, in the liminal urban 'non-spaces' that featured in his poems, novels and early films. Around his monument are weeds, sky, scattered garbage and endless metres of cyclone fencing: the kind of space that doesn't announce itself as public or private and is usable by everyone and no one. In films such as *La Ricotta* (1963) and *Uccellaci e Uccellini* (*The Hawks and the Sparrows*, 1966), Pasolini uses these spaces where industrial sprawl begins to take a grip on the pastoral utopianism of pre-modern Italy as sites where ideology is examined and contested, and suggests that the sub-proletariat which lives there belongs to a prehistoric tradition 'in the limbo of a mythic past projected into a modern present'.[1] In his later films these spaces became less populated, evolving into wastelands representing deep time or primal psychological states.

Pasolini shares this relationship to abandoned and unpopulated spaces as potential sites of social and archaeological value with Robert Smithson, and their contemporaneous investigations into the location of time and movement within ruins, both ancient and industrial, share similarities in form and historical span. Where Pasolini used the shanty towns encircling modern Rome as both context and sanctified protagonist, establishing a visual and iconographic relationship between characterisations of urban poverty and the imagery and narratives of Renaissance and Mannerist painting (the locations themselves becoming sanctified protagonists in his films), Smithson extracted meaning from the materiality of disused industrial machinery and abandoned architecture in outlying American suburbia, defining them through poetic conjecture as monuments which participated in the flow of geological and anthropological time. Parallels between Smithson and Pasolini's methodology and style also proliferate in their shared use of quotation, their deployment of hand-held tracking shots through fetishised landscapes, and their explicit, rhythmic use of the edit to move around and through time, a tactic that privileges the fragment over continuity and realism. Regarded equally as artists and writers, Pasolini and Smithson negotiate the moving image as a product and generator of language, and both adopt a dry, notational style which situates them between late Beat-era tone poetry and the aesthetic of conceptual art, grounding their speculations as 'documents'.

The filmed documentation of Smithson's earthworks in particular is positioned as an extended dialogue between research and poetry. *Ashphalt Rundown* (1969), filmed in the outskirts of Rome, and *Spiral Jetty* (1970) contextualise the works as both an intervention in and a dialogue with the landscape. The discursive, fragmented structure of Smithson's film work bears a resemblance to Pasolini's late '60s films *Teorema* (1968) and *Porcile* (1969), which are punctuated with extended desert scenes, and especially to Pasolini's 'meta-cinema', a series of documentaries made by and of the director as he visited potential locations for his films. Shot in Palestine, India, and Tanzania, these film essays depict Pasolini interacting with and assessing the 'suitability' of these pre-industrial landscapes based largely on the effects of modernisation they had incurred and their capacity as readable signifiers of the 'ancient'.

This framing of landscape as simultaneously archaic and contemporary, as an historically ambiguous descriptor of time and space, places Pasolini and Smithson within the collective energy of the late 1960s, and specifically within a broader tendency to explore representations of space and its relationship to temporality. The inner space of transcendental meditation and psychedelia, the colonisation of the lunar landscape, the appropriation of the American desert as both a refuge for radicals and fringe dwellers and as a site for alternative culture and earth art contributed to an awareness of the 'desert' as an arena for literary and cinematic narratives of collapsed and expanded 'time', such as science fiction and the road movie.

While the concept of time travel as elaborated in popular science fiction of the '50s and '60s is explicit throughout Smithson's writing and in the material rhetoric of his sculptural work, Pasolini sublimated this idea through the narrative of art history and myth. His relationship to the modernisation of society, counterculture, and the acceleration of 'popular' form was antagonistic, and reflected Italy's wider relationship to Pop in the post-war era. Whereas mainstream screen culture adopted 'Americanised' form and content wholesale, filmmakers and artists such as the Arte Povera group transfigured or even classicised the contemporary, and Pasolini shared with them an 'oppositional impulse to find models for a non-commodified aesthetic'.[2] Rather than a reflection of Pop, or a framed citation affirming its temporary and accessible allure, Arte Povera used Pop as an operative form that recognised and resisted the industrialisation of urban post-boom Italian centres through its use of archaic structures and primitive materials. This stylistic and symbolic association with the 'peasant resistance as a model for the renunciation of consumerism'[3] and its implied connection to a pre-industrial ideal connects these artists to the vernacular of Pasolini's 'modernism'. As an educated European 'bourgeois' schooled in art and letters, Pasolini subsumed the idea of time travel into a definitive historical continuum, as if to illustrate its existence as an integral component of what constituted the modern existential 'subject'. Significantly, Pasolini's 'time' usually travelled backward rather than forward, and his subjects encapsulated the sum of their inheritance with little speculation of, or projection into the future (in *La Ricotta*, Pasolini, speaking through the body of Orson Welles, describes himself through a quote from one of his own poems as 'a force from the past—more modern than all the moderns').

Whilst outside the defined parameters of science fiction in its intention and visuality, a fluid and complex temporality motivated much of Pasolini's work. This movement through time is established rhetorically, by representing the connectedness of images and archetypes through montage, proximity and overlap. Absorbing units of quotation from art and history into an elaborate form of collage, Pasolini superimposed references and realities, flattening and fixing them into a singular image. In his writings Pasolini used the term 'contamination' to describe this method, challenging the concept of the authorial voice as pure. In *Il Vangelo Secondo Matteo* (*The Gospel According to Matthew*, 1964), this method shapes his depiction of Christ's life, a text usually seen as fixed with regard to interpretive possibilities. Pasolini presents an image of Christ in the style of a contemporary social agitator who sides with the proletariat, mirroring the ideological conflict between Christianity and Marxism that defined Pasolini's, and modern Italy's, political context. This analogue between biblical and modern time is enhanced by a visual treatment which combines the reverential epic with documentary style, the camera often at a distance from the protagonists, integrating them into their physical and social contexts and casting their activities as commonplace and quotidian. *The Gospel*'s 'literal depiction of the supernatural'[4] in particular gave a credibility to the idea of Christ performing miracles, reminiscent of early science fiction movies and their capacity to create wonderment by visualising the 'impossible'.

The pastiche is extended into the figural realm through an idiosyncratic cross-identification of typologies: Herod's army are 'dressed as Knights Templar, some as fascist thugs, and some as soldiers from a Paolo Uccello canvas. Each term is mirrored in others, the historical and ideological truth of the collage resting in its internal analogies, the repetition of likenesses'.[5] Throughout *The Gospel*'s soundtrack this layering of analogues reinforces the tone of several movements in the narrative—a Resistance hymn supports Christ's oration, Bach, Mozart and Negro spirituals play during moments of celebration and hope, and 'in a particularly complex moment the music evokes overlying strands of both film and history: we see Herod's massacre of Jewish infants while hearing the Prokofiev music Eisenstein used in *Alexander Nevsky* to accompany scenes of a battle on the ice in which Russian soldiers defend their homeland'.[6] Rather than identifying the image and text of biblical narrative as a predetermined historical object, Pasolini projects 2000 years of theology, politics and representation back onto the story of Christ's life, reconstructing it texturally through a montage of discontinuous signifiers from the future.

In Pasolini's later films, his method of moving time shifted from an additive approach where associated forms are superimposed upon a master text, to a synthesised unity, where multiple histories are compressed into a deterministic whole. In *Salò o le 120 Giornate di Sodoma* (*Salò or The 120 Days of Sodom*, 1975), Sade's index of systematic perversion written while imprisoned in the

Bastille in 1785 is transposed to the Fascist Republic of Salò. Rather than moving back and forth between the two, the narrative describes both continuously, and an 'essential bibliography' which the director inserts into the opening credits references modern writing on Sade—leaving the viewer under no illusion that its analysis reflected a contemporary context—Pasolini designed Salò as an allegory of the late-capitalist consumerism which he saw as a destructive and dominating cultural discourse in post-boom Italy.

Articulating the rationalised mania of Sade through a sophisticated sequence of referencing and *mise en scène*, Salò is a rhythmic and reflexive construct 'where everything is mathematically composed, geometrically balanced, endowed with a precise function and meaning. Using metaphors drawn, significantly, from the inorganic world, Pasolini noted that he wanted Salò to be as exact and perfect as a "crystal", to have the "precision" of unreality.'[7] Salò becomes a temporal knot which enables eighteenth-century France and 1940s Italy to exist as an integrated parallel. Visual, musical and literary quotations and references are layered and embedded in discursive reprise, generating a metonymic/metaphoric 'language' that connects Salò, via the refined erudition of Borges, to the metaphysical, 'continental' edge of science-fiction, where time is refracted and multiplied, past and present collapsed into a dense historical web.

An extension of the director's aversion to naturalism, Pasolini's narratives describe a definite and legible shape, largely through a clear rhythmic montage reinforced by mannered characterisations and constructed speech. In his later work in particular, a bounded, circumscribed, and often utopian world is often 'spoken' into being. As 'figures of worlds'[8] rather than illusions of reality, these films then evoke a structural and linguistic similarity to science fiction as proposed or visualised hypotheses, an illustrated parable or 'a type of non-fictional fiction, evidently made up and false, yet whose falsity is there to express a truth'.[9] As with much sci-fi narrative, the 'parabolic' defines Pasolini's cinema, particularly the 'myth' films (*Edipo Re*, *Medea*, 1969) and is likewise used to articulate humanity's ontological anxiety with regards to origin and being, promoting 'a historical, even ahistorical solution to the trauma of entry into history'.[10]

In *Edipo Re* (*Oedipus Rex*), ancient myth is re-examined through a 'profound temporal lapsus'.[11] The 'body' of the narrative — situated within 'original' antiquity — is framed by a prologue set in 1922 Bologna, and an epilogue set in present-day (late-'60s) Bologna. The montage or edit is the device that defines the movement and the form of this exchange between times. Through abrupt cuts and ruptures, narrative objects are pushed backwards and forwards through historical time, establishing temporal relations between archaic and modern forms. Motifs, gestures and biographical details are mirrored across the films' three segments, and, as in *Porcile*, where a contemporary fable is abruptly transferred to a mediaeval context and back again, this exchange suggests a singular theme occupying two historical moments, a Borgesian tale where one segment could be a dream of the other.

As a seamless mash of interwoven texts, *Salò* represents Pasolini's most integrated example of historical counterpoint, whereas *Edipo Re*, through the potential of montage to shift and relocate units of time *as event*, and present them as a constellation, engages three narratives simultaneously, refracting and reflecting each other. The Greek myth of Oedipus is interpreted directly and with little deviation from its original text, providing an armature over which Pasolini 're-projects psycho-analysis'.[12] As the 'fundamental operation' in *Edipo Re*,[13] this re-telling of Freud, much as the history of Christianity articulates the life of Christ in *The Gospel*, serves to retrospectively inform the myth—the future is contained within the past—while it also provides a structural connection to the third text. In the film's prologue, Pasolini inhabits the story of Oedipus as a partial self-portrait; 'a metaphoric—and therefore mythicised—autobiography'.[14] Through this stylised characterisation of Pasolini's infancy at the film's beginning, and his subsequent appearance as the High Priest of Thebes in the mythic central narrative, the director 'locates himself at the centre of a transformative and figural interaction between past and present'.[15]

Rather than take the subject, and viewer, through and toward another time by way of travel in physical form—with its associated exteriority and displacement—*Edipo Re* brings time to and through the subject, complicating the collectivity of myth and psychoanalysis by describing these systems through the mechanism of an applied autobiography. As method and intuition, Pasolini approaches the idea of movement through time as a symptom of desire, a function or potentiality borne from the condition of 'subjectivity' as innate and integral to the human subject. As a process, this event—time travelling through the subject, rather than the subject travelling through time—is enabled through the fundamental technic of cinema, the edit and its relativity to the fluid continuum of film in time, and in turn, the way this continuum forms an analogue with human consciousness. In Pasolini's film 'language', the literal depiction of time travel through the apparatus of science, via portal, vessel, or subatomic transport, is replaced by the representation of myth, dream and history as a simultaneous reality, the paradigm of time travel enacted within the form and the content of the work. By describing 'time travel' through the subject, Pasolini's cinema presents it as an experiential, conceptual possibility of mind, as an innate urge or drive for the human mind to travel across what is lacking within it as a historical and existential subject, and the dispersal of the human 'unit' beyond its singular autonomous present—toward its past and what came before, and simultaneously toward its future.

Notes

1 Pei-Suin Ng, 'Poetry of Squalor: Exploring the *Borgata* in Pier Paolo Pasolini's *Accatone*', *Opticon1826*, 2 (2007), 3: http://dx.doi.org/10.5334/opt.020706. Accessed 15 July 2013.

2 Luca Caminati, *Cinema as Happening: Pasolini's Primitivism and the Sixties Italian Art Scene* (Milano: Postmedia Books, 2010), 45.

3 See Nicholas Cullinan, 'From Vietnam to Fiat-nam: The Politics of Arte Povera', *October*, No. 124 (Summer 2008), 8–30.

4 Naomi Greene, *Pier Paolo Pasolini: Cinema as Heresy* (Princeton: Princeton University Press, 1990), 73.

5 Patrick Rumble, *Allegories of Contamination, Pier Paolo Pasolini's Trilogy of Life* (Toronto: University of Toronto Press, 1996).

6 7 Sam Rohdie, *The Passion of Pier Paolo Pasolini* (London: BFI & Indiana University Press, 1995), 47.

7 Greene, *Pier Paolo Pasolini*, 76.

8 Greene, *Pier Paolo Pasolini*, 198.

9 Rohdie, *The Passion of Pier Paolo Pasolini*, 113.

10 Rohdie, *The Passion of Pier Paolo Pasolini*, 3.

11 Robert S.C. Gordon, *Pasolini: Forms of Subjectivity* (Oxford: Clarendon Press, 1996), 213.

12 Angelo Restivo, *The Cinema of Economic Miracles* (Durham: Duke University Press, 2002), 140.

13 Oswald Stack, *Pasolini on Pasolini: Interviews with Oswald Stack* (Bloomington: Indiana University Press, 1969), 120.

14 Stack, *Pasolini on Pasolini*, 120.

15 Gordon, *Pasolini: Forms of Subjectivity*, 200.

I do not come from your planet

Philip Brophy

[*Clearly define your character by type so the reader will be able to relate it to real life experience.*]

You are an artist. At your art school were some older staff—frumpy women who still wear Cyndi Lauper glasses, and stodgy bearded oafs dressed as if they work outdoors. If the police asked you to pick them out in a line-up, you'd have difficulty sighting them because they were never there much. They were out on 'professional practice', even though they had exhibited maybe twice in the last decade. In Richmond. You were mostly taught by sessional staff who weren't much older than you.

You went to art school because you didn't know any better. Your parents supported your choice. They were 'cool' with the idea. They subscribed to Arts Hub and knew that art was part of the culture industry. Friends of your parents who worked somewhere in the bowels of Arts Victoria wised them up to this at a BBQ. The main reason you went to Art School though is because you were a teenage narcissist. (Your other friends were in edgy indie bands. Duos actually, formed after seeing LCD Soundsystem and Sigur Ros live, and somehow melding the two.)

At fifteen, this was kinda OK, but you weren't savvy to the fact that now everyone is a narcissist, so really you're not that special. You specialised in installation art (duh) without realising that no matter how much you were told about relational aesthetics, you weren't doing much else but creating pretty clutter or cluttered prettiness (same diff) like chic boutique design concepts for franchises at refurbished airports.

Oh, yeah: relational aesthetics. You did some theory when you were at art school. Some of it stuck with you.

Some of it you liked, but of course you had no idea of how to relate it to what you were doing. But you had some friends doing a curatorial course at a real university. (Your art school 'became' a university—which is as dumb as saying Peter Carey is a world-class author.) Actually, they were a lot sharper than anyone in your class. They were smarter, savvier and weren't as slack as you and your grungy friends. Maybe that's why 'curators' are the new 'artists'. But you haven't worked that out yet. That comes later.

[*Introduce a momentarily disorientating shift in time so as to elaborate a dramatic change in your character.*]

You've been exhibiting for some time now. You are mostly known for your quotative video work based on scenes from Tarkovsky's *Stalker* (1979). You haven't watched many movies. They're all too narrative for you. You prefer to read anything by Don Delillo. (It helps you understand reviews of your work that start by discussing a scene from a Don Delillo novel.) But *Stalker* 'resonated' with you. That's what one curatorial essay said, and you figured it was good, even though it's a meaningless phrase.

The great thing about *Stalker* is—well, actually, you never watched it all the way through. But you're pretty sure that over five years, you've watched enough excerpts on ubuweb to get what's going on. Plus it's the only film that everyone in contemporary art seems to know, so you figured it's good to stick with it. It's European (Russian, to boot); it presages the nuclear fission meltdown at Chernobyl in 1986; and it has lots of 'art-cinema' extended-takes of real-life toxic areas near chemical plants in Estonia. It really made you think about toxic responsibility and one's relation to the planet. (A quote from another curatorial essay.)

But just as you might have got stuck in a creative rut, the nuclear meltdown at Fukushima happened. Nuclear gold. It was in Japan; it was exotic enough to not worry about the 24,000 dead (who died from the *tsunami*, not the nuclear meltdown); and it was rated seven on the Nuclear Incident chart just like Chernobyl. It was like science fiction, but for real. You watched a *Four Corners* report on it that told you all about it. They didn't interview a single Japanese person, but they did interview three heads of anti-nuclear organisations in Australia. It finished with an American economist specialising in Asia who compared the workers undertaking the clean-up in the Dainichi NPR at Fukushima to 'kamikaze' fighters. That was real dramatic and appealed to you. Yeah, nuclear energy still is bad shit. Best of all, a slew of people are now scared about it because they have children or are on IVF programmes trying. You're not being cynical though. You figure that maybe you'd like to have kids soon enough. You are genuinely concerned about the future of the planet. (You said that in an interview.)

And so you make your most 'edgy' work: you restage scenes from *Stalker* with a bunch of Japanese backpackers in Australia who answered an internet ad you posted for your new 'art project'. You told people they represented a 'community' of young people in Japan opposed to their country's nuclear policies. (Right on, man.) You haven't been to Japan but you do know some good Japanese restaurants in Melbourne. And you read Peter Carey's book on Japan which you found very informative. You especially liked the bit where he questioned a master sword-maker on the ethics of making instruments designed to kill human beings. It felt real 'interventionist'. You've filed that away as an idea for a future 'art project'.

This new work was a smash for you. Everyone loved the title: *Fukushima Is The New Chernobyl*. It's been in a trail of national and international group exhibitions with themes dealing with how an artist responsibly engages with the future of society. You met lots of cool artists from

Poland, Dubai, the US and Russia—some of whom you first met online signing petitions to have Ai Wei released from Chinese prison. You all make similar work critiquing global power structures. You often think back at your foolish friends in bands trying to get lower rung slots on *The Big Day Out*. You were right all along: art was the new rock. They read books on Oasis; you're friends with people who've been Turner-shortlisted.

[*Introduce a death of some kind to make the story feel momentous and powerful.*]

But you'll never get Turner-shortlisted. I killed you about two years ago. I stumbled into your *Fukushima* video in San Francisco. I was writing an article for *Frieze* on the post-3/11 situation in Japan and thought I'd check out your work.

I spent three months in Tokyo just after the Great Tohoku Earthquake and the resulting *tsunami*. I had contacted *The Monthly* back in Melbourne about doing an article on Japan after I had read a slew of lazy, ill-informed, knee-jerk, humanist drivel from Australia's 'intelligentsia' waffling on about global issues, international responsibility and how nuclear energy still is bad shit. Plus they were shitting themselves that somehow Australia would one day go nuclear, and here was their proactive chance to make a stand.

The Monthly declined my proposal saying their next issue already had a 'mini-symposium on Japan'. I read it online while in Japan. One article was an economist waffling on about how important China is in the new global economy (duh) and how Australia needed to be savvy about connecting to its emerging and converging industries. It occasionally mentioned Japan, only in terms of how Australia should decide carefully whether to be aligned with Japan in case we offend China, our utopian cash cow to exploit as if we're a colonial power. It was one of those laughably obsequious 'Canberra white paper' screeds *The Monthly* trades in. Actually, your dad wrote it. The other article was a whining poetic text about how 'dreadful' nuclear devastation is (duh) and—well, actually the article made no sense. It was written by your mother, who has made a career from writing 'historical novels set in the rich past of traditional Japan'. She's like James A. Michener in drag. I guess she has real 'insight' into 'the Japanese' even though she doesn't know what the letters 'AKB48' stand for.

I made a note to kill your parents when I got back to Australia. They both teach at Melbourne University, so all I have to do is wait until they do another tedious panel at the Wheeler Centre ('Books. Writing. Ideas.') and gun them down on stage.

Your death wasn't so spectacular. But I wasn't planning it, so it kinda lacked a sense of theatre. You were on a panel a week after the opening. There was a guy from a university over there who was the main speaker. I couldn't believe the name of his department: 'Global Cities Research Institute'. The only word missing was 'Ethics'. He cited how important Tarkovsky's *Stalker* was; the whole panel nodded in unsubstantiated agreement. It sounded like everyone had memorised passages from Alvin Toffler's *Future Shock*. Their collective Green Scare has replaced the Red Scare from half a century ago.

At question time, I pointed out there was no connection whatsoever between Chernobyl and Fukushima, save for the imaginary fear in the minds of ill-informed liberals whose notion of nuclear energy ramifications is on par with Reagan-era Hollywood movies like *War Games*. (That's the Matthew Broderick one—not the turgidly righteous one directed by Peter Walker.) Responding to how this guy—typical of the ethical 'international community' of the time—admonished the Japanese for using nuclear energy, I said that if there's one nation in the world who has the right to decide what they want to do with nuclear energy, it surely has to be the only nation in the world that disproves the neurotic myth that nothing exists beyond the 'nuclear holocaust': Japan, where wheat grew at ground zero in Hiroshima one month after the A-bomb blast.

I guess I shouldn't have been so shocked by how the panel and the audience ridiculed my comments. Americans—like Australians—still respond to the Japanese with bad hang-ups because someone in their family past was involved in WWII in the Pacific. I keep forgetting that Anzac Day is still a big deal in Australia, and that while we're still nothing more than a dumb British colony farming lamb in a desert; our deeper ties with America come from us both being attacked by the Japanese back then.

After the panel finished I was waiting for a bus and you were nearby with some friends. They looked like curators, actually. All dressed in greys and black, wearing '90s designer glasses like the people you see waiting in transit at Helsinki airport. You were laughing loudly. Now, I know you probably had already forgotten about me, but the tone and pitch of your voice really irritated me. I walked up to you and stared at your face. Everyone went quiet.

You didn't look like an art student anymore. You looked like a sessional staff member working at an art school somewhere. You looked so Anglo it was frightening. A real Aussie. Your face was like a flag. Your nose an Anzac Shrine, ungainly sticking out like a heritage-listed edifice, kept erect for no good reason. Your hair a vineyard designed by an architect and run by a development group comprised of lawyers and doctors who hung indigenous paintings in their office foyers. Your eyes looked like Coffin Bay oysters. Your cornea looked like folds of Kraft cheddar cheese slices. Your skin was a desert of Canberra white papers, slightly cream in hue due to the recycled paper. You smelt like *The Body Shop*.

But I hadn't walked up to you. I had run into you full-on, thrusting a Japanese short sword into your heart. In that second, the dumb look on your face seemed to go into an extended still shot—just like those scenes in *Stalker* you so loved. When you restaged that shot for your *Fukushima* video, you filmed Uluru in real time as the sun set. Me? I felt like I was restaging the famous photo of Yamaguchi Otoya assassinating Japanese Socialist Party politician Asanuma Inejrio on live TV. I think I got a hard-on. As your eyes glazed over, I thought of those blades of wheat growing in Hiroshima. I bet you were gluten intolerant.

Your parents are on a panel next week at The Wheeler Centre. They've written a book about 'their son' which is being launched at the Writers' Festival. The panel is on violence in society. I've marked the date in my calendar.

Australia: An alternat(or) future

Brendan Lee

ANNIE: You've been reading too much Science Fiction.
BALLARD: Reading what?[1]
— *The Time Guardian*, 1987

Unlike most popular science fiction, an Australian filmic future has its feet firmly set in a blue-collar reality that doesn't seem fantastical or far-fetched. If we are to believe the sensationalist media of our day, an Australia of the future will be a drought-ridden dustbowl—a degraded, non-functional desert of urban decay brought on by governments and corporations hell-bent on raising the price of energy and fuel. Just like the signpost pointing to Anarchy and Bedlam at the start of *Mad Max* (1979), that dystopia may be just a few years from now. Dystopian futures are neither a new concept nor unique to the worlds created by George Miller and Terry Hayes in their *Mad Max* series of films. However, what Australia offers to the genre of speculative fiction is a distinctive vision of the future in which a dystopian convict past and a recent, blue-collar history of energy booms and busts come together to construct a future reliant on the means of survival or escape. The role of the car and its associated energy resources in this conjunction is central.

In *The Fatal Shore*, Robert Hughes's description of Van Diemen's Land is every bit as bleak as that of *The Road Warrior* (1981). Hughes outlines the evolution of the bushranger as a product of necessity and opportunism. As the gun replaced the plough as the primary means of survival, 'settlers tended to neglect the long-range pursuits of farming and instead concentrated on killing whatever they could'.[2] The resulting extermination of edible wildlife forced convicts and aboriginals to compete for food:

'Hunger had put guns in the hands of convicts—and this had never been allowed to happen in New South Wales. It soon created a fringe class of armed, uncontrollable bushmen, most of whom regarded aborigines as vermin… Very soon these mountain men of Van Diemen's Land shed whatever vestiges of obedience they might have felt to the system. They became the first bushrangers.'[3]

The Van Diemen's Land of Australia's convict past is the same world portrayed in the post-apocalyptic future of the *Mad Max* trilogy and a fair share of the Ozploitation films of the 1970s and '80s. The exploitation film *Turkey Shoot* (1982) depicts a future where totalitarian rule is the way of life (and death), and where breaking the order of things puts you at the whim of the state. Roger Ward's role as Fifi McCaffey in *Mad Max* and Chief Guard Ritter in *Turkey Shoot* are one and the same character—only a few years apart. Fifi McCaffey believed in heroes upholding the law, where Ritter had discarded civility to exert the rule of the gun—as premised in *Mad Max*.

Comparisons between the futuristic vision of *Mad Max* and the anarchic past of Van Diemen's Land can also be found in the film's original novelisation, which explicitly attributes society's demise to restricted access to the basic essentials of life. 'A few years from now', Armalite gangs control the roads beyond the urban sprawl, commandeering anything of value. Fed up with having to hire armed escorts to provide security for road trains from the pirates, the powerful National Retail Corporation prohibits the transportation of goods on the highways. The cost of consumer items skyrockets, forcing the Central Bureaucracy to buckle under public pressure. Breaker Squads are established to keep the roads clear at any cost. An oil embargo and war in the Middle East give the gangs a thirst for the black gold to power their means of survival. With no fuel, no food and no stable government, Australian society is freed from the burden of civility only to disintegrate into chaos, violence and even cannibalism. In *The Road Warrior*, everyone lived in fear. Max's world existed out on a stretch of Transcontinental One, a world reverting back to the days of bushrangers, opportunistic piracy and the survival of the fittest.[4]

In the original screenplay for *The Road Warrior*, the opening scene portrays Pappagallo—the future leader of the oil-refining compound—as the Chief Executive of a giant corporation named Seven Sisters Petroleum. Below the company's crest is the byline 'Fuelling the future'. Pappagallo leaves his office with a pile of maps and two books: *The Whole Earth Catalog* and *Teach Yourself Solar Energy*. This is quite possibly the most telling of any form of speculative fiction from the 1980s. Self-sufficiency would be the key to survival and a means to escape the self-destructive elements of society. The message is reinforced through the character named Pig Killer in *Mad Max 3: Beyond Thunderdome* (1985). The trading post known as Bartertown is powered by methane, and 'methane comes from pig shit'.[5] Energy in *Beyond Thunderdome* is power. Killing a pig deprives the town of its one main commodity, compromising the fragile position it holds in the badlands.

This is a realm of little hope, where weapons and machinery do little to stem the tide of violence or save society from an encroaching waterless wasteland. Whereas Max doesn't fight against or for anything except himself, the futures of James Cameron or Ridley Scott rely upon a battle of wits to survive against the consequences of uncontrollable corporate greed. Miller's world is one where fuel is scarce and corporations more so, leading to a culture of brutal self-sufficiency and survival at all costs—as was the case in Van Diemen's Land.

It isn't a far stretch of the imagination to conclude that the events between *Mad Max* and *The Road Warrior* stem from the same timeline as those depicted in Neville

Shute's 1958 book *On the Beach* and both of the film adaptations.[6] The post-World War III Melbourne of *On The Beach* is also one of depleted fuel reserves. A radioactive cloud of cobalt fallout moves south across the planet, wiping out all life in its path. As the last major port to be affected, the state of Victoria is the drawcard for all those with enough fuel to make the voyage across the Pacific. One vessel, the nuclear-powered submarine USS Scorpion, escapes Melbourne to search for signs of life up and down Australia's east coast but finds none. In desperation, the submarine journeys to Seattle chasing a bogus radio signal. On their return, the crew spend their dying days drinking themselves into a stupor at end-of-the-world parties, finally taking government-issue cyanide pills to end it all.[7]

Like the tanker and school bus hauling gasoline in *The Road Warrior* or the methane-powered train in *Beyond Thunderdome*, the nuclear-powered submarine in *On The Beach* is a vehicle for escape, a symbol of freedom and potential within a hostile Australian landscape. This is a world in which horses once again pull trams, and streets are illuminated by candlelight. Children have become so accustomed to quiet streets that they freely play on the road without fear of being run down. Taking advantage of the situation, the character John Osborne uses his naval connections to milk a supply of ethanol from an aircraft carrier, which he uses to fuel his preferred mode of transport — a Ferrari. 'For God's sake don't go and kill anybody', his friend Peter advises. 'They're all going to be dead in a couple of months' time anyway', John responds. John takes the car out onto Elizabeth Street at fifty miles an hour and then up Lonsdale Street at an average of seventy-five, skidding around trams and through crowds shocked at the sight of a car on the road.

Alex Proyas's *Spirits of the Air, Gremlins of the Clouds* (1988) is similarly set in an isolated outback future where the only way to survive is to flee. Without power or contemporary technology, a pair of religious survivors eventually takes to the air in a plane they've been attempting to finish before they go bonkers. But where do they go? Do they end up in Tomorrow-morrow Land like the children from the crack in the earth in *Beyond Thunderdome*, only to revert back to living off the corpse of the old world?

The message is clear: those with wheels will have the ability to escape from whatever threat the future holds—whether it's cobalt fallout, Smegma Bikies or the hungry hordes—as Australian speculative fiction depends upon the nation's fascination with and fervent reliance on the automobile to define itself. *Mad Max*'s black-on-black Interceptor tapped into an undercurrent of nationhood, anxieties and desires that informed the everyday lives of Australians,[8] as embodied in the Bathurst races of street legal vehicles in the 1970s and '80s. Ironically, the Interceptor was born (in part) from the scare campaign raged by the *Herald Sun* newspaper against the muscle of the Ford GT-HO Phase III that spelled the death of the Phase IV—a car that would win all future James Hardie 1000 races at Bathurst and inevitably kill hundreds of youthful Peter Brock imitators if it was ever released.

At Bathurst (for one weekend a year) the lawlessness on Mount Panorama demonstrated a reality that the *Mad Max* future forewarned. The 'Bull Pit'—a cleared area consumed by dust in the heat and mud in the wet—was the worst example of a male-only space; here, cars were sacrificed and anything that could be blown up, set on fire or launched into the air (preferably all three), were. Links to the haunting images of the marauding assault on Pappagallo's oil refinery compound in *The Road Warrior* are not that unrealistic, and—for any unwilling witness of 'The Hill'—the first thing they'd be looking to do was get as far away as possible and return to civilisation.

Is the post-apocalyptic, fallout-heavy desert of an Australian speculative future setting the scene for what is to come? If we are to take the films Australia has produced as a guideline or roadmap, we aren't in for many surprises. The convict past of Van Diemen's Land will haunt us as men drive until the last drop of fuel is exhausted, eat until there's nothing left to eat, and then turn on each other for whatever else is left. The fortunate ones with a means to escape will inevitably flee to the expanding deserts and just wait until the vermin have inherited the earth—wondering where it all went so terribly wrong. The rest of us will have watched them leave, indulged in end-of-the-world parties and dropped the government-issue cyanide pills, hoping we made the right choice.

Notes

1 *The Time Guardian*, dir. Brian Hannant, prod. Hemdale Film, Australia, 1987.

2 Robert Hughes, *The Fatal Shore* (Australia: Pan Books, 1987), 126.

3 Hughes, *The Fatal Shore*, 126.

4 Terry Hayes, George Miller, and B. Hannant, *Mad Max 2* (Australia: Progress Publications, 1981), 22–3.

5 *Mad Max 3: Beyond Thunderdome*, dir. George Miller, prod. Kennedy Miller Entertainment, Warner Bros., Australia, 1985.

6 Neville Shute, *On The Beach* (London: William Heinmanne Ltd), 1958.

7 Similarly, Ray Bosely's *Smoke 'em if you got 'em* (1988)—a celebration of Australian pub culture—ends with a final gig within an underground bunker in Melbourne as everyone dies of post-nuclear radiation poisoning, band included.

8 Adrian Martin, *The Mad Max Movies* (Australia: Currency Press, 2003), 5–6.

Fabulation in the contact zone: Aboriginal art and Australian science fiction

Darren Jorgensen

The most reproduced work of art from Australia may be a photograph of Wandjina rock paintings from the northwest of the continent. For the Ngarinyin, Wororra and Wunambul people who live in this region, now known as the Kimberley, the Wandjina brought the earth to life with rain before embedding themselves into the rock. They appear with haloed faces and shoulders, staring with giant eyes and no mouths from caves and escarpments. A photograph of these beings was published in Erich von Däniken's 1970 bestseller *Return to the Stars*, as part of a tapestry of evidence for a theory that aliens had been in touch with ancient civilisations around the world.[1] Däniken thought that the Wandjinas' haloed heads commemorated the sun from which they descended. Ironically enough, Däniken's theory was closer to the truth of the Wandjina than many other interpretations of them. Generations of writers before Däniken, mostly far from the Kimberley itself and reliant on secondhand drawings and photographs, speculated that the Wandjinas had been painted by everyone but the local indigenous people, comparing them to the art of Europeans, Indians, Japanese and Malays.[2] In fact, the Wandjina are star beings who come from the Milky Way, arriving from the far reaches of the galaxy to put in place the law that the Ngarinyin, Wororra and Wunambul still follow today.[3]

The history of misinterpreting Wandjina rock art was inaugurated by the explorer George Grey's descriptions and drawings after his expedition into the northwest in the 1830s. Grey believed the images were too 'skilful' a representation to have been made by local indigenous people, so imagined that they had been made by a race long lost in space and time.[4] In moving from Däniken's theory to Grey's diary, we shift from one subgenre of science fiction to another, from the 'lost race' story to the alien encounter. The experience of Aboriginal art inspired Däniken and Grey to write science-fictional scenarios to explain what they could not explain. In their history of Australian science fiction, Russell Blackford, Van Ikin and Sean McMullen trace the legacy of Grey's description of the Wandjina upon the lost race novel in nineteenth-century Australia.[5] In this popular subgenre of science fiction, Grey's account of the Wandjina becomes mixed up with both the fate of the lost explorer Ludwig Leichardt, and fantasies about finding the ancient country of Lemuria. Aboriginal art plays a key role in feeding this fantasy, as arrows, painted hands and even the figurative art painted onto Uluru becomes evidence of such a civilisation.[6] In these novels, heroic explorers discover gold, princesses and an inland sea in the unexplored reaches of the continent. Aboriginal people are sidelined and forgotten as lost riches are discovered hidden in the desert.

These early Australian novels have little to recommend them today, being the product of nineteenth-century attitudes toward indigenous people. Yet the confluence of Däniken's theory of alien visitation and Wandjina theology offers a way of constructing a speculative common ground between indigenous and non-indigenous cosmologies. At a public talk in 2012, the Martu filmmaker Curtis Taylor was asked about extra-sensory perception among Aboriginal people.[7] In answer, Taylor explained the Martu concept of *kapukurri*, in which people meet each other in dreams. Here the science fiction of one culture turns out to be the science fact of another. Such reversals take place in both directions: the first encounters of remote desert people with bulldozers, cattle and helicopters were subsequently explained as the science of invading whitefellas. These moments of recognition between cultures are all too rare, however, and for the most part, the history of race relations in Australia has been one of wilful disregard and misunderstanding.

The most famous representation of Aboriginal people in a science fiction novel takes place in H.G. Wells's *War of the Worlds*, first published in 1898. Wells took the English invasion narrative of the late 1800s, one that imagined Britain's defeat by France or Germany, and turned it into science fiction by creating an enemy from beyond the Earth.[8] At the time of Wells's writing, it was presumed in England that the Tasmanian Aboriginal people had been wiped out by the colonisers. Wells compares their extinction with that of the plight of the English who are under Martian attack.[9] Although the Martians wielded a heat ray weapon of great sophistication, their victory is portrayed not merely as a result of technological superiority, but a consequence of Darwinian laws of survival. Next to the Martians, humans are given the status of 'monkeys and lemurs'.[10] Next to the English, the Tasmanians take up the same place in a Darwinian hierarchy. Wells was horrified by what the English had done in the name of 'civilisation', and used the science fiction narrative to make a moral point. His character in *War of the Worlds* concludes that 'the English cannot claim to be such apostles of mercy as to complain if the Martians warred in the same spirit?'[11] This is the spirit of English imperialism.

The idea that Australian Aboriginal people were extinct or were becoming extinct underpinned not only the science fiction of the nineteenth century, but also early cultural collecting practices in Australia at the time. Anthropologists and other enthusiasts raced to assemble evidence from what was thought to be a dying people. In 1998, contemporary anthropologist Howard Morphy began his book *Aboriginal Art* with an account of the anthropologist Baldwin Spencer commissioning a bark painting in Arnhem Land in 1913.[12] This is an early image of the trade in art between white and indigenous Australians, one that Morphy uses to introduce a narrative of cross-cultural exchange. Yet Australian art historian Ian McLean points out that Spencer was collecting from what he thought to be a dying race.[13] While assembling an impressive collection of Aboriginal art, Spencer was also collecting Australian impressionist paintings by such luminaries as Arthur Streeton. It is as if he was collecting what he imagined to be the past and future of Australia, the remnants of one society and the beginnings of another. This scenario also played into the hands of Aboriginal people, who saw the fetish for Aboriginal culture among the whites as a way of striking bargains with the invaders.

In his explorer's journal, George Grey reveals that Europeans were not the only tellers of science-fictional tales. Investigating a cave somewhere in the York district of the southwest of Australia, Grey tells us that the Aboriginal stories about the cave were largely inventions:

> These legends nearly all agreed in one point, that originally the moon, who was a man, had lived there; but beyond this there was nothing common to them all, for every narrator indulged his own powers of invention to the greatest possible degree, scarcely ever relating the same story twice, but, on each occasion, inventing a new tradition; and the amount of marvels and wonders, which he unfolded in this revelation were exactly proportioned to the quantity of food which I promised to give him. I once or twice charged them with attempting to impose upon my credulity, and, far from denying the charge, they only laughed, and said 'that was a very good thing which they told me, and that the Djanga (white men) liked it very much'.[14]

Aboriginal people manipulated the wilful misunderstanding of the invaders, creating a contact zone of fabulation. This is not so much a moral science fiction, as in that of Wells, but one that belongs to the genre of fantastic parody as represented by Swift and Voltaire.

The contact zone can be understood as a kind of speculative opportunity, and its legacy is everywhere even in contemporary science fiction. The lost race story, for example, remains a part of science fiction even as the era of exploration recedes further into the past. The most successful contemporary Australian science fiction writer is Greg Egan. His 1997 novel *Diaspora*, although relying on hard science about disembodied intelligence and interstellar travel, carries with it the narrative structure of a nineteenth-century search for lost races in unexplored regions.[15] Here the lost race is not located in the interior of Australia, but in deep space and time. Egan's immortal characters live in virtual spaces of their own making. Having abandoned their bodies, they explore the cosmos as technological supermen embedded within nanobots that cross the stars. Most of this novel is set in this nanospace that allows for any number of possible lives. By the end of the novel, the hero Yatima is following the trail left by an unknown intelligence, across light years and millennia.

At the conclusion of *Diaspora*, Yatima discovers that the alien trail he thinks he has been following is actually an immense, galaxy-long sculpture that looks like a four-legged creature. The intelligence itself has disappeared, leaving behind a monument to itself, or at least to its former self. Yatima's journey reveals a work of art created within a fictional universe, a speculation within a speculation, all the more obtuse because it was created by a creature that remains unknown. Yet this attempt to imagine an alien sculpture of near infinite scale is also an exercise in banality, as it returns to the shape of what appears to be a biological, terrestrial creature. In reaching the limits of the cosmos, Egan's hero finds only the finitude of its biological origins. Egan here recalls a Darwinian model of evolution, but he is also describing an interstellar sculpture, one of the largest works of art in science fiction's brief history. The work of art imagined within a fantastic novel pushes the coherence of a world reduction to its limit, because art is not imagined to be a reduction but an expansion of the imagination. Works of art imagined within SF worlds test the capacity of a writer against their own fictional extrapolations, their own capacity to create imaginary consistency. Perhaps the most successful attempt to create a work of art within a science fiction text is J.G. Ballard's 1975 story 'Cloud Sculptors of Coral D', about an isolated settlement of glider pilots who launch themselves from towers of coral to carve the clouds.[16] From fluffy white cumulus to life-threatening storm fronts, the nimbus are transformed by the gliders into ephemeral sculptures, conjuring images of presidents, seahorses, lizards or exotic birds in the sky. It is a new kind of art, both fantastic and yet strangely conceivable.

In older anthropological scholarship, works of Aboriginal art often play this same role of mediating the possible with the fantastic. The cosmogonies and cosmologies of remote Aboriginal people, their allusions to the metaphysics of the Dreaming, are tied to interpretations of artwork that open onto this Dreaming. The work of art is explicable within the world that anthropologists are creating in their texts, while also opening out onto the more spiritual dimensions of Aboriginal life. In the deserts of Australia, anthropologists prized the tjurunga above all else as that which gave them the secrets of this esoteric life, while also holding these secrets within themselves. Whitefellas sought out these sacred carvings in stone and wood, regarding them as the keys to indigenous knowledge. Herbert Spencer's collaborator and the postmaster of Alice Springs, Frank Gillen, appreciated the value of these artworks not only to collectors around the world, but to indigenous people of central Australia. In the late 1800s and early 1900s, when collectors, including amateurs, anthropologists and missionaries, were buying, stealing and conning tjurunga from desert people, Gillen wrote of their significance that 'to realise this one has to go with bush natives to their sacred storehouses and watch them reverently handling their treasures. It impressed me far more than anything else I had ever witnessed.'[17] For 'outsiders', such artefacts may be perceived as science-fictional, as they represent the conflation of the poetic with the reason of an alternative society. For the Arrente and other language groups of Central Australia, however, tjurunga mean much more than this, being immersed in the fabric of existence and that of the world around them.

Such disjunctions are also at the core of the beginnings of the trade in Aboriginal art in Central Australia. In her book on the early history of the Papunya Tula movement that kicked off the market for desert painting, Vivien Johnson tells the story of Aboriginal men who had been asked to rake sand outside the house of the superintendent of the community.[18] The superintendent flew the British flag and was boss of this government settlement in the desert, where desert people from the surrounding stretches of country were crowded together. Johnson explains the superintendent's frustration with getting this task done, as different men appeared every day, and raked the sand in circles. What he did not understand was that these were the circles of classical desert iconography that remained invisible to a colonial order whose cosmologies did not include the Dreaming. Such invisibilities, of one cosmology, culture or religion to another, populate the history of relations between coloniser and colonised in

Australia. Such encounters are science-fictional scenarios, as one people's science is another's fantasy.

For some SF authors, one way of balancing the disjunctions between indigenous and non-indigenous world views is to empower Aboriginal characters through endowment of high-end technologies. The Australian writer Terry Dowling's 1990 collection of interconnected stories, *Rynosseros*, envisages a future Australia ruled by 'Ab'O' princes, criss-crossed by sand ships and populated by artificial intelligences.[19] He also imagines, in this far future, science fictional works of art painted by so-called 'mirage divers' who peer into the desert waiting for visions of fantastic cities. The punch line of this part of *Rynosseros* is that they are seeing the same city, and that this city is recognised not only by the descendants of colonial Australia but by the Ab'O nations that rule the interior of the continent.[20] Dowling's interest in imagining the autonomy of technologically sophisticated tribes of Aboriginal peoples is tied here to a reconciliation fantasy. Such a technologically empowered image of Aboriginality also turns up Egan's debut genre novel, *Quarantine* (1992). In this brilliant story of an alien quarantine of human beings and the intricacies of quantum physics, an independent nation called the 'Tribal Confederation of Arnhem Land' exercises its autonomy by selling land to create New Hong Kong.[21] Such autonomous visions for Aboriginal societies are not restricted to Australian writers. In British writer Stephen Baxter's *Manifold: Space* (2000), an Aboriginal community migrate to Triton, a moon orbiting the planet Neptune.[22] As far-fetched as some of these visions may be, they at least acknowledge the autonomy of Aboriginal societies. Dowling and Egan turn the representation of Aboriginal societies from conquered peoples to canny and technologically empowered political groups.

American scholar Brian Attebury positions Dowling's

work as a part of a 'Hopeful Moment' in SF representations of Aboriginal people. Attebury's 2005 essay 'Aboriginality in Science Fiction' expanded the scant research on Australian SF with a punchy exposé of its racial politics.[23] The 'Hopeful Moment' spans from the 1950s to the 1980s—a period roughly coinciding with the legacy of Albert Namatjira—before giving way to what Attebury calls 'The Troubled Now', a postcolonial era spurred by a movement toward racial equality. As indigenous writers and non-indigenous writers alike navigated the political difficulty of representing Aboriginality, Dowling's future Australia met the brunt of postcolonial concerns about the appropriation of Aboriginal culture.[24] Attebury's genealogy also mirrors the history of the reception of Aboriginal artists, whose works first confronted European explorers, missionaries and pastoralists in what Attebury calls the 'Bad Old Days'. This is the time in which Grey's descriptions of his discoveries in the northwest had an impact upon SF writers of the nineteenth century, and in which Aboriginal artworks were seen as alien constructions that gave up little of their indigenous meanings. Attebury's 'Troubled Now' could well describe the status of Aboriginal art during the commercial boom of the 1980s and '90s, when its reception was vexed by a national Australian consciousness in crisis about how to come to terms with the identity of Aboriginal people.

Representations of Aboriginality within science fiction rely largely upon the imaging of Aboriginal culture, rather than any direct experience of it. Dowling relies on such popular conceptions of Aboriginality as the Dreamtime, the singing of kurdaitcha men and tribal identities.[25] Such conceptions are already science fiction for Dowling, who uses them to build a coherent future world. Yet they are also mistranslations, misunderstandings of Aboriginal world views that remain beyond the scope of his fantasy. While such simplifications represent one means by which Aboriginal cultures are translated into science fiction, a second lies at the level of narrative. The lost race fantasy, for example, is underscored by assumptions of Aboriginal extinction, as Aboriginal people are either invisible or marginalised by narratives of discovery set in the Australian interior. The lost race story is not confined to science fiction. Marlo Morgan's bestselling *Mutant Message Down Under* (1990), for instance, is the fable of an American traveller who meets an Aboriginal tribe somewhere out of Broome, and was presented as fact to its millions of American and European readers.[26] The tribe that Morgan travels with have decided to allow themselves to become extinct: the novel manages to deliver both the discovery of a lost race and Aboriginal extinction in one story arc.

The lost race narrative is also at work in Egan's *Diaspora*, played out in a universe populated by infinitely differentiated virtual beings, whose capacity to recreate themselves produces an array of consciousness. Experiments in cognitive, virtual mathematics lead many of these disembodied minds into abysses of their own difference. Although works of art—figured in the text as installations in virtual space—are the sites at which minds come together, they often only serve to magnify differences, as each mind experiences the works differently and in isolation. While the pretence around works of art is that they bring people together, in Egan's novel art is a marker of separation, revealing only the vast distances between beings.

The history of Australian science fiction and Aboriginal art testifies to this space of difference. Even the most hopeful fictions and shared fascinations expose the rifts between cultures. It is precisely at this site of encounter, this intersection, that the cognition of science fiction is helpful in tracing the lines between imagination and truth, revealing the ways in which one is caught up in the other. While Attebury describes only the most recent period of Australian science fiction as the 'Troubled Now', the term could well characterise the breadth of Australian colonial history, as it grapples with an ongoing alien encounter.

Notes

1 Erich von Däniken, *Return to the Stars: Evidence for the Impossible*, trans. Michael Heron (London: Souvenir Press, 1970).
2 Ian McNiven and Lynette Russell, '"Strange Paintings" and "Mystery Races": Kimberley rock art, diffusionism and colonialist constructions of Australia's Aboriginal past', *Antiquity*, 71 (1997), 801–9.
3 David Mowaljarlai and Jutta Malnic, *Yorro Yorro: Everything Standing Up Alive: Spirit of the Kimberley* (Broome: Magabala Books, 2001).
4 George Grey, *Journals of Two Expeditions of Discovery in North-West and Western Australia, during the years 1837, 38 and 39, under the Authority of Her Majesty's Government*, *Vol. 1* (London: T. and W. Boone, 1841), 214–5, 261–4.
5 Russell Blackford, Van Ikin and Sean McMullen, *Strange Constellations: a History of Australian Science Fiction* (Westport, Connecticut: Greenwood Press, 1999), 10–3.
6 Blackford, Ikin and McMullen, *Strange Constellations*, 13–4.
7 Curtis Taylor spoke as a part of 'We don't need a map: public talk and gallery tour', (Perth: Fremantle Arts Centre, 16 January 2012).
8 For an account of the way Wells transforms these invasion narratives, see Bernard Bergonzi, *The Early H.G. Wells: a Study of the Scientific Romances* (Manchester: Manchester University Press, 1969), 135.

9 H.G. Wells, *War of the Worlds* (1898) (Wisconsin: Golden, 1964), 13.
10 Wells, *War of the Worlds*, 13.
11 Wells, *War of the Worlds*, 13.
12 Howard Morphy, *Aboriginal Art* (London: Phaidon Press, 1998), xvi.
13 Ian McLean, *White Aborigines: Identity Politics in Australian Art* (Cambridge: Cambridge University Press, 1998), 67.
14 Grey, *Journals of Two Expeditions of Discovery in North-West and Western Australia*, 261.
15 Greg Egan, *Diaspora* (London: Orion, 1997).
16 J.G. Ballard, 'The Cloud Sculptors of Coral D', in *Vermillion Sands* (London: Panther, 1975), 11–30.
17 Frank Gillen quoted in *First Australians*, Episode 4: 'There is no other law', dir. Rachel Perkins, ABC Australia, 2008.
18 Vivien Johnson, *Once Upon a Time in Papunya* (Sydney: University of New South Wales Press, 2010), 296.
19 Terry Dowling, *Rynosseros* (Adelaide: Aphelion, 1990).
20 Dowling, *Rynosseros*, 183–5.
21 Greg Egan, *Quarantine* (London: Millennium, 1992), 35.
22 Stephen Baxter, *Manifold: Space* (London: Voyager, 2000).
23 Brian Attebury, 'Aboriginality in Science Fiction', *Science Fiction Studies*, 32 (2005), 385–405.
24 Blackford, Ikin and McMullen, *Strange Constellations*, 166.
25 Dowling, *Rynosseros*, 121.
26 Marlo Morgan, *Mutant Message Down Under* (New York: HarperCollins, 1994).

Loop

Chronox

Sound is pressure waves oscillating through a substance. The lower the sound, the longer the wave. The louder the sound, the deeper the wave. To record sound is to transcribe these waves to another medium such as a hard drive, tape, or disc. These objects are not in themselves a record of sound. Only upon playback are we re-introduced to the sound that has gone before. Like a time machine, these devices allow us to travel back to past events and experience them again.

In 1877, Thomas Edison produced a prototype of the first device that could reproduce recorded sound, patented as the phonograph. The cylindrical objects that served as containers for the sound were engraved with a continuous line that progressed around the outer surface of the cylinder from one side to another on a sheet of tin foil. Earlier recording technology could record only, or was intended only as visual transcribers of sound, such as Édouard-Léon Scott de Martinville's phonautograph, which traced soot onto paper.[1]

Soon after, Emile Berliner produced the gramophone, utilising lateral cuts onto discs moving from the outside edge in a spiral formation.[2] Over the next half-century several companies advanced the technology, most significantly Alexander Graham Bell's Volta Laboratory. Their graphophones featured a number of experimental models. One used a jet of compressed air focussed through a point of glass. Another design used a cylinder and the tip of a fountain pen, laying down iron-rich ink which could be rendered magnetic and read by a device sensitive to the magnetic fluctuations. In 1886, the Volta Lab patented a device that utilised neither cylinder nor disc, rather a strip of wax-covered paper tape that passed mechanically through a playback head from one reel to another. Here is the mother of the tape recorder, nearly forty years prior to the first practical model demonstrated by German company AEG in 1935.

The irregularities of the various systems, the proliferation of radio and the economic downturn during the Great Depression meant that it wasn't until the 1940s when recorded sound media was commonplace in the home, at least in the West. Around this time, shellac 78s were replaced by 33-rpm long-playing records and 45-rpm singles. Recording fidelity and durability were hugely improved on the media itself, which could now contain over twenty minutes of sound per side of an LP. Advances in playback technology meant frequency response was widened, noise levels were reduced and amplification levels were increased.

Throughout these rapid shifts in audio technology, there was one constant that could always be relied upon—malfunction. When a stylus skates over dust or a scratch, one might hear a pop or a crackle, but when in the right place, a bridge is created where the stylus will jump back in time to the groove that preceded it, at precisely the same point with each revolution. More often than not, it will stay there, repeating over and over until you pick up the tonearm and move it along in time. This phenomenon was so familiar it birthed the phrase, 'you sound like a broken record'.

With the 'broken record', we are introduced to the idea of the exactly repeating time segment, involuntarily recurring ad infinitum. When one transposes this anomaly in recorded media-time to the lived experience of time itself, we arrive at an entirely new perception of time as malleable, susceptible to manipulation and to unpredictable malfunctions. Two early manifestations of

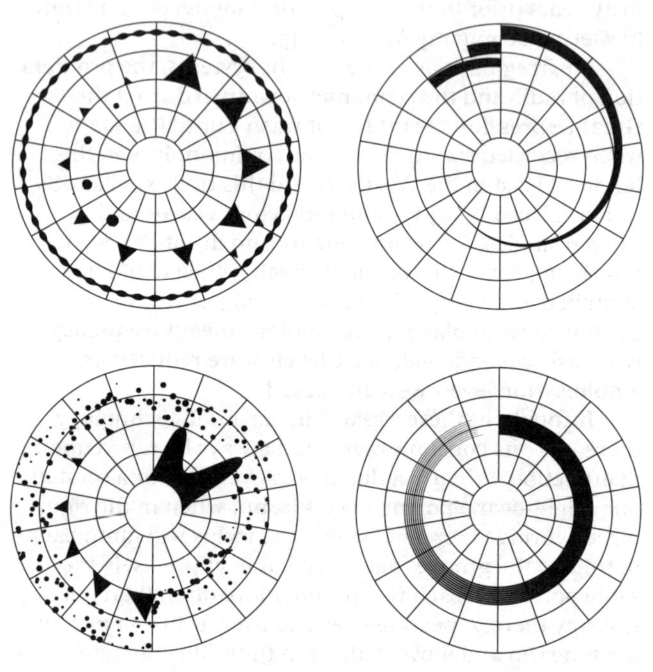

Chronox, *Loop Scores*, 2012

this new vision of time emerged in two contemporaneous but disparate threads of mid-century culture: sci-fi pulp fiction and early tape music.

The audio loop's closest analog in science fiction is a trope referred to today as The Groundhog Day Loop. Named after the 1993 film, the form first emerged in the early 1940s in sci-fi pulp fiction stories such as Ross Rocklynne's 'Time Wants a Skeleton' and Malcolm Jameson's 'Doubled and Redoubled', both published in 1941. A Groundhog Day Loop can be described as a plot 'in which the character is caught in a time loop, doomed to repeat a period of time (often exactly one day) over and over, until something is corrected. Usually, only one character or group of characters realizes what's going on—everyone and everything else undergoes a complete Snap Back, and if not interfered with will do the exact same things every time, right down to dialogue.'[3]

For anyone who has heard a broken record, the connections between this plot device and the audio loop are clear. The loop forms not a perfect circle but a sudden jump back to an earlier point in time. The protagonist, standing in for the audience/ listener, is aware of the loop and experiences the loop as the sole outside observer. The loop repeats into infinity until the protagonist finds the cause and corrects it. She must lift the tonearm to restore the linear flow of time.

In addition to grappling with the philosophical implications of this effect, practitioners also aestheticised the loop, highlighting the innate properties of the structures and the unique experience to be drawn from them.[4] Loop-based tape music—and more specifically Process or Systems music—acts as 'a compositional process and a sounding music that are one and the same thing'.[5] The tape loop provides a structure or system which is applied to raw audio material.

Similarly, the science-fiction time-loop narrative is a

highly visible structural device that generates the story as it runs. The time loop is set up with duration and cycles, loaded with character and setting, and set off. This basic set of conditions is the seed for all time-loop narratives. In both cases, the looping structure results in a number of parallel experiences for the audience. Relentless repetition provides strong rhythms, the gradual abstraction of mundane phenomena, and seemingly small or inconsequential details slowly coming into focus. Unexpected variations in the loop occur as a result of knowledge the protagonist accumulates through these repetitions, and through fluctuations in audio looping technology and phasing.

Notes

1 In 2008, Scott's soot on paper graphic recording was converted into a playable form. See *First Sounds*, http://www.firstsounds.org/about/. Accessed 4 May 2013.

2 For a history of the phonograph and graphophone, see Leslie J. Newville, *Development of the Phonograph at Alexander Graham Bell's Volta Laboratory*, Project Gutenberg E-Book, available at http://www.gutenberg.org/files/30112/30112-h/30112-h.htm. Accessed 22 April 2013.

3 See '*Groundhog Day* Loop', *TV Tropes*, http://tvtropes.org/pmwiki/pmwiki.php/Main/GroundhogDayLoop. Accessed 4 May 2013.

4 Michael Peters, 'The Birth of Loop: A Short History of Looping Music', *Looper's Delight*, http://www.loopers-delight.com/history/Loophist.html. Accessed 22 April 2013.

5 Steve Reich, 'Music as a Gradual Process (1968)', in Paul Hillier (ed.), *Writings about Music, 1965–2000*, (Oxford and New York: Oxford University Press, 2002), 35.

'The only true science is science fiction', or: On the cause of the differences between *science* fiction and science *fiction* as originating in the divagations of letters

Justin Clemens

The nature of mathematical language, once it is sufficiently isolated in terms of its requirements of pure demonstration, is such that everything that is put forward there—not so much in the spoken commentary as in the very handling of letters—assumes that if one of the letters doesn't stand up, all the others, due to their arrangement, not only constitute nothing of any validity but disperse.[1]
—Jacques Lacan

For me, the only true science is science fiction.[2]
—Jacques Lacan

0

Thesis: true science *is* science fiction. But don't feel relieved about this: the fictions of science are not the fictions of art and literature. They are constituted utterly differently—in their methods, technologies, institutions, personnel and objects—and the fictions of science are not amenable to the sorts of contestations beloved of humanistic types. To take them as such is to mistake them as debatable, relative and partial, to reduce their politics to the politics that we feel comfortable about, and hence to treat them as if we, the people, had anything scientifically relevant to say about the sciences, say, of climatology or quantum physics. But we don't. Yet we do, too, because the effects of science are ubiquitous, patent and unavoidable, constantly trickling down into the routines of everyday life, affecting us at the core of our being and our non-being. Science fiction is historically the genre which has taken this non-relation—between *science* fiction and science *fiction*, that is, between modern science as a specialised practice of technologised knowledge and the speculative literary reconstruction of the former's social effects—as primary, and sought to elaborate its consequences. Fiction against fiction, then, a war of incommensurable kinds of fiction, one, the scientific, singularly self-involved in its own processes, the other, the artistic-literary, singularly desperate to intervene in the processes of the first, and, to that end, always susceptible to fudging the absolute distinction between them. The ultimate cause of this war is not, I believe, simply in the differing efficacies of the magnificent visions of the universe that both *science* fiction and science *fiction* have projected, but in the most humble and the most minimal of locales: in the mere mark, in the letter itself.

1

The Renaissance announced itself as a rupture-and-return: a rupture with the culture of its immediate environment, and a return to the ancients. This is why, despite the corrosive rhetorical blandishments of academic relativists and revisionists, it's false to consider the epoch under the empty-headed and bombastic neologism of 'The Early Modern'. Certainly, the Renaissance may not have been as radical a rupture as it felt itself to be, nor necessarily in the ways that it thought—but its very announcement and self-presentation in the form of such a 'rebirth' was itself new. Moreover, in thinking of itself so, it made itself so, precisely because its epistemic fervour was thereby invested in recovery-and-rescue missions of all kinds: locating, retrieving, transcribing, editing, translating, republishing and commenting-on dusty manuscripts from the accursed depths of noble libraries and monastic scriptoria. The recurrent philosophical anxieties about temporality arise again like a metamorphic phoenix: fallen, historical time must now be considered as a sequence of emergence-decline-rediscovery; the intense attentiveness to sacred texts must be extended far beyond all previous limits. The recurrent problems of recovery find another ideal: to return to the greatness of the past over and against the diminished activities of the present. The recurrent injunctions of knowledge take up a new literary mode: philology as primary philosophy.

2

If you don't get the absolute centrality of the Renaissance injunction for rupture-and-return, linked to its bizarre self-image and to its almost-violent innovations in philology, then you also won't get something essential about the sense of scientific modernity proper—at least that promulgated in the emblematic form of its great *buccinator*, Lord Francis Bacon, Baron Verulam and Viscount St Albans, one-time Lord Chancellor of England eventually cashiered for corruption, and distant ancestor of the scabrous twentieth-century Irish painter. A *buccinator*—the word is Bacon's own, an instance of his magisterial self-irony—is a trumpeter or herald, that is, a minor but indispensable servitor of law, whose instrument announces the proclamations of the monarch. What, then, did Bacon announce? As Lorraine Daston and Katherine Park put it:

> Sir Francis Bacon, Lord Chancellor of England under James I and prolific writer on topics ranging from the common law to friendship to horticulture, mapped between 1605 and 1620 a program for the reform of natural history and natural philosophy that reverberated loudly throughout the seventeenth and eighteenth centuries. Although almost no one adopted in its entirety his plan for a 'Great

> Instauration', or new beginning in natural philosophy, almost everyone — Descartes, Boyle, Leibniz, Hooke, Huygens, Newton — incorporated fragments of his vision into their own work.[3]

Bacon's program for a 'Great Instauration' was not just a program of reform, however, but something much more revolutionary. If the Renaissance had established itself as a 'rupture-and-return', Bacon's vision was of a 'rupture-with-the-rupture'. Why? Because Bacon's program of natural philosophy was precisely directed *against* the Renaissance celebration of the genius of the classical world. For Bacon, the Greek and Roman authors could be just as confused and as stupid as any Scholastic, and it was therefore unforgivably foolish to take their works as authoritative simply because of their age. Age has nothing to do with wisdom. We need, rather, to 'put nature to the question' as Bacon notoriously asserts (in such a way that many scholars have suspected he was suggesting the torture of Mother Nature), to suspend our assent to all untried propositions, to blind inheritance, to scholastic disputations and logic-chopping, to grand theorising of all kinds — and to turn towards experience and experiment as providing the only acceptable bases for useful knowledge.

3

In presenting his new program as a rupture-with-the-rupture, a doubled-rupture or rupture-squared, Bacon sought to transform the topics, means, institutions, and personnel engaged in the pursuit of knowledge. As Steven Gaukroger asserts: 'Bacon's was the first systematic, comprehensive attempt to transform the early-modern philosopher from someone whose primary concern is with how to live morally into someone whose primary concern is with the understanding of and reshaping of natural processes. And his was the first systematic, comprehensive attempt to transform the epistemological activity of the philosopher from something essentially individual to something essentially communal.'[4] In fact—and Bacon is, not coincidentally, one of the first people to make facts, as well as the phrase 'matter of fact', crucial to the practice of science—it's crucial to underline the new temporalisation that Bacon installs at the heart of knowledge. The Renaissance returned to the very old as an assault on the present; Bacon thought knowledge was worthless if it wasn't new, or at least, newly-refounded. Bacon is therefore a Time Lord, the father of a new experience of time, of a new binding of knowledge to power to time. The new is the true for Bacon or, more precisely, only the new has a chance of being true. All of a sudden, knowledge has a different status. Knowledge is now at once more absolute than ever before (for when the program is instituted, all scholars must agree on the veridical status of verified facts) *and* radically conditional (what now counts 'as true' is on notice, always on the verge of being supplemented, modified, or even overturned). As Steven Shapin and Simon Schaffer note, this means that 'rejected knowledge is not knowledge at all, but error'.[5] Though artists may not appreciate this attribution, it is actually Bacon—an anti-artist of a particularly virulent kind—who is the real herald of avant-gardism. Moreover, and this should also be underlined, avant-gardism, in the full sense of radical irreversible communally-engaged novelty, therefore begins in science, not in the fine arts, and, indeed, is directly opposed to the practice of such arts. In Bacon's wake, what we would now call the arts can be, at best, rhetorical accompaniments to knowledge, but produce nothing true themselves.

4

Bacon is also at the origin of the phrase 'knowledge is

power': as such, his ideal of science must also be given its full *technological* motivation and import. As he very famously puts it in *Novum Organum*: the 'arts of printing, gunpowder and the nautical compass...have changed the whole aspect and state of things throughout the world'.[6] Moreover, when Bacon speaks of 'power' in Latin, I believe he almost invariably uses the words '*potestas*' or '*potentia*' (e.g., '*scientia potestas est*'); he is followed in this by his one-time secretary and renegade political thinker Thomas Hobbes, who also thinks of knowledge as directed towards power. This problematic of power is of central interest for a number of reasons, not all of them obvious. First of all—and, as a great lawyer, Bacon was well aware of the fact—*potestas* was traditionally opposed to *auctoritas*, functional operations to the force of law. As Giorgio Agamben has argued, '*auctoritas* can assert itself only in the validation or suspension of *potestas*'.[7] If this is the case, one can see immediately that, in regards to nature, Bacon, the 'perfect monarchist', was subjecting human beings, including all temporal powers, to the authorising and exceptional power of God; as such, man, as Bacon also says, must become *minister and interpreter* of nature. Expressly *not* author or authority, man will gain power over nature only through a proper administration of God's works. Nature itself must be subject to due process, to a communally-undertaken technico-legal process, if she is truly to give up her secrets. As Carolyn Merchant has argued, against the idealising grandiosity of much scientistic self-satisfaction: 'Bacon's concept of the contained, controlled experiment arose out of three influences: the juridical tradition, the idea of nature in bonds (Prometheus), and the idea of extracting the secrets of nature'.[8] The scientist is God's functionary, who puts the world on trial in accordance with the injunction to know and practice His laws.

5

In a sequence of famous studies, such as 'The Question Concerning Technology', 'The Age of the World Picture', and 'Science and Reflection', Martin Heidegger returned again and again to this fateful historical moment. Heidegger makes some extraordinary claims, including: all modes of thinking begin with language; technology is not just a means, but a way of revealing; the essence of technology is nothing technological; that modern technology treats nature as a 'standing-reserve'; and that the essence of such technology is 'enframing' (*Ge-stell*). In Heidegger's words:

> Modern science's way of representing pursues and entraps nature as a calculable coherence of forces. Modern physics is not experimental physics because it applies apparatus to the questioning of nature. Rather the reverse is true. Because physics, indeed already as pure theory, sets nature up to exhibit itself as a coherence of forces calculable in advance, it therefore orders its experiments precisely for the purpose of asking whether and how nature reports itself when set up in this way.[9]

For Heidegger, the 'supreme danger' raised by such a mode of revealing has two primary consequences. First, it means that all of nature gets sucked up into a resource to be exploited without limit, including human beings themselves; second, it perverts the sense of Being into an absolute-ordering-without-outside. As Heidegger further, famously, proposes: it is not in modern science or even in philosophy, but in the sayings of the great poets that Being can more fulsomely be discerned in a destitute time.

6

There are elements of Heidegger's analysis that remain

convincing, not least in his account of the extraordinary destructiveness of modern technology, its rapacious transformation of the natural world, and its liquidation of all objects. But is Heidegger entirely correct in his diagnosis? The distinction between poetry and mathematics as paradigmatic rival modes of apprehension of the real, which hinges on their radically different treatments of language, is surely a consequence of the emergence of the new sciences in the seventeenth century, which goes far beyond its ancient Pythagorean–Platonic roots. As Jean-Claude Milner reminds us, modern science differs from ancient science in a number of key ways, not least because it has an integral relationship to technology. But science and technology are not the same thing, and we could suggest that the ways in which their possible linkages are rearticulated is one of the primary ideological modes of modernity. In fact, both Bacon and Heidegger are limited by their clear obsessions with technology, however differently they conceive of it; this limitation further blinds them to the powers and independence of another discourse altogether, that of mathematics. But to return to mathematics—or, as Milner emphasises, to mathematical *writing*—is to notice another aspect of the scientific revolution as rupture-with-the-rupture.[10] For 'writing', it turns out, is not quite 'language', even in the radical sense that Heidegger gives it, to the extent we can discern a dynamic tension *within* modern science itself.

7

Galileo's declarations are certainly the most famous of the relevant documents:

> Philosophy is written in this grand book—I mean the universe—which stands continually open to our gaze, but it cannot be understood unless one first learns to comprehend the language and interpret the charac-

> ters in which it is written. It is written in the language of mathematics, and its characters are triangles, circles, and other geometrical figures, without which it is humanly impossible to understand a single word of it; without these, one is wondering about in a dark labyrinth.[11]

Milner's gloss is decisive here:

> let us take another look at this formula. For [Alexandre] Koyré, the important word is mathematics. For me, the important word is letters. In my opinion, what defines Galilean science is this literalization. He believed that for physics and, to a larger extent, for the natural sciences, the most straightforward literalization is mathematical literalization…what concerns him, however, is not mathematics and its status, but rather what he calls the book of the universe. In his attempt to decipher it, he considered he was incorporating it within a much larger movement, which had started in the realm of the arts and letters. I base my case on a few clues. First of all, thanks to philology, Galileo took seriously the renaissance of Greek and Latin studies; in fact, he believed that philology should serve as the model for physics much as philology was at that moment the pioneer in the deciphering and correction of written texts.[12]

What could also be pointed out here is that, if philology is at the origin of science, the *origin* is not always a *cause*. Galileo will be instrumental in developing an altogether different function for letters, one which no longer bears on the comparative integrity of texts and their meaning, but which ensures a transition between the indubitability of abstract mathematical demonstration and the contingency of worldly events.

8

Milner's analysis picks up on two quite different scholarly traditions: the first emphasises the relationship between Protestantism and the new sciences; the second emphasises the relationship between Renaissance art and the new sciences.[13] Ernst Cassirer—not, coincidentally, a long-term adversary of Heidegger—has provided an extraordinary account of the latter relationship. Cassirer notes of Leonardo da Vinci, that: 'In a manner that is characteristic and determinative of the total intellectual picture of the Renaissance, the logic of mathematics goes hand in hand with the theory of art. Only out of this union, out of this alliance, does the new concept of the "necessity" of nature emerge. Mathematics and art now agree upon the same fundamental requirement: the requirement of "form".'[14] Indeed, Galileo bases his mathematicised physical work upon Leonardo's model, which is thus the former's conceptual precondition… with one key difference. Whereas Leonardo still thinks of the integral unity of mathematics and the arts, Galileo will relegate his great precursor to the shadow worlds of fiction and fable, severed from the necessity delivered by mathematical physics. There is no question that Galileo begins to attend to the book of the world with the same sorts of attention as the humanists had previously attended to books and, above all, to the supposed Book of Books that is the Christian Bible. But he simultaneously makes a cut whose implications are absolute and immediate. Here, Milner enables us to see where Cassirer's account is lacking: the latter fails to mark the new and radical differentiation between (perceptual) *form* and (mathematical) *formalisation* that is introduced by Galileo and his comrades in the new sciences.[15] If Luther and the other Protestants had emphasised the 'literal meaning' of Scripture in their radical hermeneutics, they opened up a diet of worms regarding just what this literality might be.[16] Their irresolvable difficulties, however, were *de facto* resolved by the new science, which sorted out precisely how the literal could be decided: the literal is an *operation* performed with letters, not the un-veiling of any *meaning*. Humanistic and Protestant philology was *hermeneutic*; scientific philology involves the combination and permutations of letters *without any meaning at all*.[17]

9

Between the Scylla and Charybdis of Bacon and Galileo, where does this leave us? If we pass over the salient details so crucial to the history and development of the new sciences—the invention of the telescope, the various experiments with falling bodies, the unprecedentedly detailed observations of the heavens, the Keplerian orbital ellipses, the practical immanentisation of mathematics, and so on and on—we can pinpoint a few particular developments, as well as some more paradigmatic features of the new science. First, and generally speaking, despite all of its agents continuing to share vocabularies, references, attitudes, methods and objects with their pre-scientific predecessors, at the same time that they are disagreeing violently with their putatively scientific colleagues, we can still assign an epistemological break to the new sciences. The key to understanding this is at least triple: that an epistemological break takes place (perhaps despite the implications of the word 'break'), not suddenly, but as an ongoing practice of separation whose actual lineaments and ultimate limits are unavailable to the participants themselves; moreover, that the very confusion and dissension of the participants is nonetheless organised around specific new opacities; that the 'unity' of the new sciences is thereby inspired and directed not by unification, clarity or distinctness as such, but by immanent torsions in the emergent field.[18] As everybody agrees, a new method or *novum organum* is required—even if nobody can agree about what that might be.[19]

10

What, then, are the determining torsions in the new sciences? As I have been suggesting, they are above all due to the double twist of the new, contorted relationship between experiment and mathematics. 'Experiment' here is no longer the simple observation of natural phenomena, familiar to scholars from antiquity. Rather, an experiment now means the technological establishment of an artificial environment—that is, an explicitly non-natural, local space—in order to isolate a particular trait to be investigated. This renders every experiment a fiction, but a fiction of a particular kind, a fiction which is a *material space of purified repetition*. That these spaces can potentially and in principle be set up anywhere, presumes that the laws they are directed to investigating are everywhere: 'space' in general is no longer hierarchised or striated, regionalised in one way or another (as was the Aristotelian cosmos), but genuinely universal, and precisely insofar as it is susceptible to the fictional exceptions of experiment. Observation and experiment in science become inextricably intricated with each other, and the former a function of the latter. The moon and stars become subject to the same laws as earth. In these experimental spaces, then, traits can be studied in themselves. But the essentially en-framing techniques of experiment are not, as we have seen, enough on their own to constitute modern science; these technologies must somehow be meshed with theory, whose paradigm is mathematics in all of its indubitable, abstract and rigorous glory. The tension between concrete and abstract, particular and general, technique and theory, is at its greatest.

11

But acknowledging this tension enables us to give a strict definition of modern scientific formalisation: *those combinations of letters which can simultaneously articulate the necessary consistency of pure mathematics with the contingency of experimental repetition*. Such formalisation *historically* requires, as I have said, the humanist philological isolation of letters as its precondition, but departs entirely from that philological enterprise insofar as the letters themselves no longer make up words and are no longer directed towards making sense. Rather, as marks that link spatial fiction to abstract demonstration, they are detached from any human inheritance in order that they might become referential inscriptions of inhuman necessity. Even more paradoxically, such necessity is drawn from the new contingency of the universe: everything that happens may also be able not to have happened. The universe is infinite; there is nothing outside it; whatever happens is contingent, but governed necessarily by universal laws; matter can be experimented upon because it is not out to fool us. 'God is tricky, but he isn't mean', as Einstein hilariously put it.[20] Truth changes its status: no longer for all time, but only for a short time, until it is disproven or falsified. Such truth is at once more absolute and more transient than before, ever-ready to be *falsified* by *discoveries* but no longer *contested* by the *debates* of scholars. As Alexandre Koyré puts it in the title of his famous book: we have moved from the closed, finite world of the classical cosmos to the infinite universe of the moderns.[21]

12

So: the Renaissance and the Reformation developed forms of philology that became a necessary condition of the new sciences. Yet the new sciences exceeded these conditions, not simply by adding something—but, paradoxically, by subtracting something, by purifying. They purified letters of their sense, indeed, of any human grammar whatsoever. But what happens to art and literature under this dispensation? In a word, as Douglas Bush puts it: 'In the world of the new philosophy, a mechanistic and deterministic world inhabited by mechanistic and egotistic beings, there was little room for imagination and intuition, for spiritual struggle and mystical contemplation. Even if poets did not accept the new creed, they could not help breathing a different air.'[22] Indeed, those identifying with the new sciences immediately and explicitly start to scorn poetry. The motto for the Royal Society is '*nullius in verba*'; asked about his opinion of the value of poetry, Isaac Newton himself remarked: 'I'll tell you that of Barrow;—he said, that poetry was a kind of ingenious nonsense'; Boileau lamented that Descartes had slit the throat of poetry. This literally must be understood literally: in the sciences, letters are simply the operational trace of a bond between technically-supported repetitions and mathematical abstraction; in the arts, letters appear at once as themselves (*as* perceptible forms) and as pregnant with inherited meanings (mythical, historical, accidental) for which those forms are merely the conveyancers. What, under such unpropitious circumstances, is an artist or writer to do?

13

All modern art and literature become belated fictions of belatedness, jets of generic singularities.[23] Hence the tendency for modern fiction to develop as a speculative realism: fiction is observational (experimental), but it is not so much a formalisation (the inscription of a bond between repetition and consistency) as a form (the apparition or non-sense of sense). What is later institutionalised in the modern academy as the humanistic disciplines will now forever be structurally *behind* the sciences, belated and derivative, but therefore straining all the more strenuously to be new, and essaying to do this in a radically self-reflexive way. Therefore and thereafter the fictions of art tend to become practices of observing observations, practices of observational speculation about the speculation that it is not (real science and its effects); art-fictions propose or purport to ground themselves in what the grounded cannot think. According to the new humanists, science and technology cannot think the abysses of time.[24] If modern fantasy, for example, clearly repurposes medieval romance, it can only do so because the new sciences—which so often have to go unmentioned in fantasy texts proper—have disrupted the status of fiction itself. Magical elements, utterly crucial to fantasy, thereby become the privileged generic symptoms of an ambivalence towards modern science's technology: the acceptably hypocritical and mystified return of high-tech in a resolutely med-tech world. Post-Galilean Merlin becomes a *de facto* military scientist, there to supplement the lances and swords of the ladies and the lords with his special esoteric knowledge of supernatural powers. But science fiction and speculative fiction also attempt the same 'repression' by other means, above all, by simulating acquiescence to—and often even affirmation of—the non-negotiability of modern science. Space-war, temporal paradoxes, technological inventiveness—science *fiction* acts as if it could shape the *science* fictions whose exigencies are shaping it. Hence the paradox that I see at the heart of the genre of science fiction. As a genre, science *fiction* is a form of fantasmatic philological belatedness that melancholically laments its secondariness vis-à-vis *science* fiction proper by pretending that it can overleap its rival, a secondariness that was once indeed primary, and which once, long, long ago in a Gutenberg Galaxy far, far away, unknowingly incubated its own grave-digging mother. Science *fiction*, as bizarre a creature as any of the many memorable aliens it spawns, nonetheless survives, precisely because it was birthed from and as its own death.

Notes

1. Jacques Lacan, *Encore: The Seminar of Jacques Lacan, Book XX: On Feminine Sexuality, The Limits of Love and Knowledge, 1972–1973*, trans. B. Fink (New York: Norton & Norton, 1999), 128.
2. Jacques Lacan and E. Granzotto, 'Il ne peut pas y avoir de crise de la psychoanalyse', *Magazine littéraire*, No. 428 (2004), 28.
3. Lorraine Daston and Katherine Park, *Wonders and the Order of Nature, 1150–1750* (New York: Zone Books, 2001), 220.
4. Stephen Gaukroger, *Francis Bacon and the Transformation of Early-Modern Philosophy* (Cambridge: CUP, 2001), 5.
5. Steven Shapin and Simon Schaffer, *Leviathan and the Air-Pump: Hobbes, Boyle, and the Experimental Life* (Princeton: Princeton University Press, 1985), 11.
6. Francis Bacon, Book 1, 129.2, *Novum Organum*, trans. J. Bennett, available online: http://www.earlymoderntexts.com/f_bacon.html. Accessed 25 April 2013.
7. Giorgio Agamben, *State of Exception*, trans. K. Attell (Chicago: University of Chicago Press, 2005), 86.
8. Carolyn Merchant, '"The Violence of Impediments": Francis Bacon and the Origins of Experimentation', *Isis*, No. 99 (2008), 750. Brian Vickers has objected to this position: 'reputations of philosophers… rise and fall irrationally, like the movements of stock markets. Perhaps no major figure has been subject to so many fluctuations as Francis Bacon. The moving spirits in the early Royal Society idolised him, Voltaire and Diderot lauded him, Blake damned him. Macaulay and De Maistre annihilated him, Whewell

and Spedding resuscitated him, and so on', 'Francis Bacon, Feminist Historiography, and the Dominion of Nature', *JHI*, Vol. 69, No. 1 (2008), 117. Vickers proceeds to criticise two recent 'essays' in feminist historiography, by Katharine Park and Carolyn Merchant that allegedly condemn Bacon, damning Park's concept of a feminist historiography of science as 'fuelled by what sociologists call *ressentiment*', 119. Against the feminist 'hostile interpretation of a few of [Bacon's] metaphors', Vickers protests that 'in Latin *natura* is a feminine noun, a gender it retains in modern European languages', 122. He continues: 'But nature is not a woman; fortune is not a woman, nor is justice. You cannot "torture" nature, since she is not a percipient being able to experience pain', 123. I believe these remarks show just how little Vickers's erudition contributes to any understanding of the pertinent texts, not least because Merchant's account is anything but 'hostile', and because anybody who doesn't understand that the contingencies of grammatical gender are themselves well-heaped rhetorical fodder for the early-modern speculators themselves has simply missed the point.

9 Martin Heidegger, *The Question Concerning Technology and Other Essays*, trans. with intro. William Lovitt (New York: Harper and Row, 1977), 21.

10 See Jean-Claude Milner, Ann Banfield and Daniel Heller-Roazen, 'Interview with Jean-Claude Milner', *S*, No. 3 (2010), 4–21, but, above all, his *L'Oeuvre Claire: Lacan, la science, la philosophie* (Paris: Seuil, 1995).

11 Galilei Galileo, *The Assayer* (*Il Saggiatore*, 1623), in *The Controversy on the Comets of 1618*, trans. Stillman Drake and C.D. O'Malley (Philadelphia: University of Pennsylvania Press, 1960), 184. See also: 'My opinions were contradicted without the least regard for the fact that what I had set forth was supported and proved by

geometrical demonstrations, and such is the strength of men's passions that they failed to notice that the contradiction of geometry is the bald denial of truth', Galileo, *The Assayer*, 164.

12 Milner *et al.*, 'Interview', 4–5.

13 For the first of these, see especially the work of Peter Harrison, e.g., *The Bible, Protestantism, and the Rise of Natural Science* (Cambridge: Cambridge University Press, 1998), as well as the essays in Kevin Killeen and Peter Forshaw (eds), *The Word and the World: Biblical Exegesis and Early Modern Science* (Houndmills: Palgrave, 2007) and Peter Dear, *Discipline & Experience: The Mathematical Way in the Scientific Revolution* (Chicago and London: Chicago University Press, 1995); Peter Dear (ed.), *The Literary Structure of Scientific Argument* (Philadelphia: University of Pennsylvania, 1991) and *The Scientific Enterprise in Early Modern Europe* (Chicago and London: University of Chicago Press, 1997).

14 Ernst Cassirer, *The Individual and the Cosmos in Renaissance Philosophy*, trans. Mario Domandi (New York: Harper, 1964), 152. As Cassirer goes onto add: 'Leonardo's vision of nature proved to be a methodologically necessary transition point, for it was artistic "vision" that first championed the rights of scientific abstraction and paved the way for it', 158. For two other major accounts in a broadly Germanic tradition of science-critique, see Hannah Arendt, *The Human Condition*, second edition (Chicago and London: University of Chicago Press, 1958); Hans Blumenberg, *The Genesis of the Copernican World*, trans. Robert M. Wallace (Cambridge, MA and London: MIT Press, 1987).

15 As Jacob Klein puts it, in what is perhaps one of the greatest books ever written about the history of mathematics, 'The creation of a formal math-

ematical language was of decisive significance for the constitution of modern mathematical physics. If the mathematical presentation is regarded as a mere device, preferred only because the insights of natural science can be expressed by "symbols" in the simplest and most exact manner possible, the meaning of the symbolism as well as of the special methods of the physical disciplines in general will be misunderstood', *Greek Mathematical Thought and the Origin of Algebra*, trans. Eva Brann (Cambridge, MA: MIT Press, 1968), 3.

16 The Diet of Worms was a theological assembly convened in 1521 to deal with Martin Luther, who evaded the consequences of his condemnation by hiding out in Wartburg Castle, where he continued his translation of the Bible into German—an exemplarily philologically-enhanced translation exercise which, as Walter Benjamin has underlined, transformed the German language itself. In a famous scene from *The Tragedy of Hamlet, Prince of Denmark*, the eponymous protagonist engages in an impertinent exchange with the King: 'Not where he eats, but where he is eaten: a certain convocation of worms are e'en at him. Your worm is your only emperor for diet: we fat all creatures else to fat us, and we fat ourselves for maggots: your fat king and your lean beggar is but variable service, two dishes, but to one table', 4.2.21–24.

17 The independence of science from 'meaning' is precisely why Bacon and almost every great figure of the new sciences felt it completely acceptable to write in the vernacular: Bacon in English, Galileo in Italian, Descartes in French, etc. And, second, that this independence of truth from language is itself self-consciously proposed as part of the publicity wing of the new science program. As Bacon writes, scholars

'whose conceits are beyond popular opinions, have a double labour; the one to make themselves conceived, and the other to prove and demonstrate; so that it is of necessity with them to have recourse to similitudes and translations to express themselves', *The Advancement of Learning*, 3: 406–7. But the truth is, of course, independent of these *translations*.

18 This is precisely where so many of the histories of the emergence of modern science start to confuse self-consciousness with agency with historical development with multiplicity. The actual emergence of the new science is of course marked, indeed constituted, by manifold rival enterprises, not all terribly clear or distinct or accurate, any of which may easily never have happened, and which can't be given any teleology. Unfortunately, these features don't vitiate the attribution of a break, nor of a new episteme to the period: on the contrary, they show that the key aspects of the break must be *reconstructed* from the *non-evident* points of dissension, from the new opacities and undecidabilities that are at stake. In fact, the errors, false turns, failures and seemingly-incomprehensible arguments are integral to such a reconstruction.

19 So Jacob Klein notes that 'modern mathematics… turns its attention first and last to method as such. It determines its objects by reflecting on the way in which these objects become accessible through a general method', Klein, *Greek Mathematical Thought and the Origin of Algebra*, 123. Or, as Yirmiyahu Yovel puts it in a more general frame, 'From Bacon and Galileo through Descartes to Locke and Kant, modern philosophers have given logical priority to the study of method', Yirmiyahu Yovel, *Spinoza and Other Heretics: The Adventures of Immanence* (Princeton: Princeton University Press, 1989), 35.

20 Or, as Lacan puts it, with reference to Descartes: 'The reference to a nondeceiving god, the one accepted principle, is based on results obtained by science… It need hardly be said that matter does not cheat, that it has no intention of crushing our experiments or blowing up our machines. This sometimes happens, but only when we have made a mistake. It's out of the question that it, matter, should deceive us. This step is not at all obvious. Nothing less than the Judaeo-Christian tradition was required for it to be taken with such assurance', Jacques Lacan, *The Psychoses: The Seminar of Jacques Lacan, Book III 1955–1956*, trans. Russell Grigg (New York: Norton, 1993), 64–5.

21 See Alexandre Koyré, *From the Closed World to the Infinite Universe* (Baltimore and London: The Johns Hopkins Press, 1957), as well as his *The Astronomical Revolution: Copernicus-Kepler-Borelli*, trans. Robert Edwin Witton Maddison (London: Methuen, 1973), *Études d'histoire de la pensée philosophique* (Paris: Gallimard, 1971) and *Galileo Studies*, trans. John Mepham (Sussex: The Harvester Press, 1978).

22 Douglas Bush, *Science and English Poetry: A Historical Sketch, 1590–1950* (New York: Oxford University Press, 1950), 43. So, despite the uncircumventable confusions, some of the consequences of their new science are pretty clear to Bacon, Galileo, Descartes and others, whether or not they felt compelled to polemicise in its favour or tried to avoid undue publicity. Bluntly, this means that rhetoric, logic and grammar — the classical *trivium* — are excluded from the avant-garde of knowledge, which, indeed, is genuinely an avant-garde for the first time.

23 As Harold Bloom has argued, in an analysis inadvertently relevant to the present context: '*fantasy, as a belated version of romance, promises an absolute freedom from belatedness, from the anxieties of literary*

influence and origination, yet this promise is shadowed always by a psychic over-determination in the form itself of fantasy, that puts the stance of freedom into severe question. What promises to be the least anxious of literary modes becomes the most anxious, and this anxiety specifically relates to anterior powers, that is, to what we might call the genealogy of the imagination. The cosmos of fantasy, of the pleasure/pain principle, is revealed in the shape of nightmare, and not of hallucinatory wish-fulfillment.' *Agon: Towards a Theory of Revisionism* (Oxford: Oxford University Press, 1982), 206, emphasis in the original.

24 Two remarks of Foucault's (although one might add that his timing is a little off here, given the foreignness to him of both scientific and English sources): 1) 'In the nineteenth century, philosophy was to reside in the gap between history and History, between events and the Origin, between evolution and the first rending open of the source, between oblivion and the Return. It will be Metaphysics, therefore, only in so far as it is Memory, and it will necessarily lead thought back to the question of knowing what it means for thought to have a history... It is enough to recognise here a philosophy deprived of a certain metaphysics because it has been separated off from the space of order, yet doomed to Time, to its flux and its returns, because it is trapped in the mode of being of History.' Michel Foucault, *The Order of Things* (New York: Pantheon Books, 1970), 219–20; 2) 'At the moment when a considered politics of spaces was starting to develop, at the end of the eighteenth century, the new achievements in theoretical and experimental physics dislodged philosophy from its ancient right to speak of the world, the cosmos, finite or infinite space. This double investment of space by political technology and scientific practice reduced philosophy to the field

of a problematic of time. Since Kant, what is to be thought by the philosopher is time. Hegel, Bergson, Heidegger. Along with this goes a correlative devaluation of space, which stands on the side of understanding, the analytical, the conceptual, the dead, the fixed, the inert.' Michel Foucault, *Power/Knowledge: Selected Interviews 1972–1977*, Colin Gordon (ed.), (New York: Pantheon Books, 1980), 149–50.

L'object sonore undead: Resonant objects in the work of Philip K. Dick and J.G. Ballard

Nathan Gray

The following essay was originally presented as an audio recording to an audience at the 2012 Melbourne Art Fair.

Hi, this is the voice of Nathan Gray. I'm sorry that my body couldn't be here, but I'm elsewhere. I felt it might be appropriate to deliver my talk today via an audio recording because the two short stories I wanted to talk about—'The Preserving Machine' (1953) by Philip K. Dick, and 'The Sound-Sweep' (1960) by J.G. Ballard—both concern sound recording, and I've found them particularly helpful in my practice as an artist who makes work that is largely about sound.

'The Preserving Machine' and 'The Sound-Sweep' are two early examples of what would become the respective authors' signature styles and themes. Both of them are horror stories of a sort that revolve around encoding or infusing objects with sound and fanciful recording techniques.

'The Preserving Machine' has PKD's signature shallow characters and sketchy plot. After reading almost all of his works, I've started to think that this flatness is part of PKD's agenda. It's a kind of intentional implausibility which allows the reader never to fully suspend their disbelief. So in a body of work which almost always deals with layers of reality being stripped away, the narrative is usually right on the surface: visible and always obviously fiction.

'The Preserving Machine' deals with the consequences of an imagined technology designed to preserve music from the horrors of war and cultural collapse. The protagonist Doc Labyrinth decides that in order to protect the fragile art of music, it should be encoded in living creatures capable of defending themselves; he imagines a mole burrowing out of the rubble of a collapsed museum.

The machine he invents creates animals out of musical scores. The character of the animals embodies some of the flavour of the music, with Bach fugues becoming a series of beetles, and Wagner a sinister hyena-like creature. The animals are released into the woods behind his house and when Doc Labyrinth goes to see them they have fed on each other and adapted. When he reverses the process on one of the creatures he finds that the music produced (as sheet music to be played on a piano) is 'distorted, diabolical, without sense or meaning, except perhaps, an alien, disconcerting meaning that should never have been there'.[1]

The evolution of music through the means of its preservation can be read as a prediction about the way technological recording would rapidly come to mutate music: first through the tape manipulations of Musique Concrète (a French movement that experimented with tape collage), then the sampler and the laptop. The horror that the protagonists feel is a conservative reaction to these new 'mutated' sounds.

We can take the idea of animal music and play it backwards or forwards. First, if we rewind it back into history we can imagine how music was initially built by humans imitating animal sounds. If we play it forwards we can see how music descended from high classical values into punk animality and avant-garde emptiness. The horror of the story comes from the destruction of those classical traditions by the means that were intended to preserve them.

At the time PKD wrote the story he was working in a classical music store, but he would later embrace, successively: psychedelic rock, punk rock and the avant-garde compositions of Karlheinz Stockhausen. So there's something a bit less conservative about this story than it would initially appear.

I like to think about the fact that this story was published a year after John Cage's silent piece *4'33"* premiered, and that the lack of sense or meaning in the music is an avant-garde emptiness, like the dice games of the Cubists, and all the other artists who have gone after them who have tried to strip away meaning to open up a space that would provide more fertile ground than one created intentionally.

PKD and Cage would both later use the I-Ching to generate chance to empty out or open up their works and provide experiences outside of their own tastes. For both of them this was a strategy to generate novelties, but with Cage it was also a strategy to empower the listener not the composer as final arbiter of the work's meaning.

The key to the foreboding that the characters feel when hearing the transformed music replayed is, I think, not that it is just meaningless, but that if there is a meaning at all it is 'alien and disconcerting'. The music has not only become stripped of meaning as would happen with the music of Cage and his successors, but this void has become re-inhabited by something whose meaning we are no longer privy to. Maybe this is why so much art provokes such strong reactions from people who are outside its dialogues: where artists see a void other people see a meaning that is not intended for them to decipher.

The final scene of the story features a giant beetle, itself generated by the preserving machine, building a mud structure, scuttling inside and shutting us out—art turning its back on us.

I want to contrast the idea of the preservation of sound in 'The Preserving Machine' to Ballard's 'The Sound-Sweep', which is about noise pollution and its elimination. Ballard often returned to sound as a theme, but his story 'The Sound-Sweep' lays out some of the elements that would continue for the rest of his career: the themes of society in decay, tragedy and mental illness are all there. It was published in 1963 and it's a far more complicated plot than 'The Preserving Machine', dealing with a world in which sound residues left in objects have been found to cause mental and even physical illness in the objects' owners.

This is a really great idea: low levels of sound are left in solid surfaces and slowly trickle out of them over time, giving the inhabitants of the spaces emotional flashbacks, which over time cause disease. It's a way to look at the traumatic nature of spaces and their histories. Uncontrolled sound as pathology.

There's been plenty of sound art studies on the way space alters sound, most famously Alvin Lucier's composition *I'm Sitting in a Room* in which he recorded and replayed a spoken phrase and then re-recorded and replayed the phrase over and over until it became a gushing hiss of unintelligible sound. But 'The Sound-Sweep' talks about how sound alters spaces and people. Then it extrapolates a series of industries built on this discovery. Ballard is the opposite of Phillip K. Dick in the way that he takes outrageous ideas and integrates them seamlessly into the world of low-level commerce, making them almost mundane.

One of these dependent industries is the Sonovac business. Sonovacs are vacuum cleaners that collect sound residues. The best operators of these have exquisitely sensitive hearing, like Manon, the main character who is also mute. The sound residues are taken to a constantly howling sonic dump on the edge of town, next to where Manon lives.

This idea of noise pollution and its positive partner, soundscape preservation, have been championed in the work of R. Murray Schafer, who is dedicated to listening, sound walking and field recording in order to appreciate and document the soundscapes of his native Vancouver. This is a global movement now, with field recording ever increasing in popularity and local artists like Dale Gorfinkel running sound walks in Melbourne.

Ballard's invented device, the Sonovac, is like a microphone that swallows all the sound that it hears, it's a sound pollution eater. There is always the dual question with the concepts of noise pollution and sound preservation of precisely what is noise pollution, and what is the sound to be preserved? The story prescribes properties to sound that many noise artists would love to have: the power to induce actual psychosis. The line 'Noise, noise, noise—the greatest single disease-vector of civilization', sounds like it comes from a press release for some diabolical noise act.[2]

In the story, after the discovery of the dangerous nature of sound, music has had to undergo a series of transformations in order to make it safe. First it is moved beyond the audible range and out into inaudible frequencies, where it is able to be experienced in a manner closer to pure emotion. Then it is condensed and concentrated so that long pieces of music could be experienced in seconds without losing any of their emotional impact.

Ultrasonic music provides 'a direct neural link between the sound stream and the auditory lobes, generating an apparently source-less sensation of harmony, rhythm, cadence and melody uncontaminated by the noise, vibration and danger of audible music'.[3]

This disembodiment from time and conscious perception seems like another step in an increasingly bodiless form, first being divorced from instruments and musicians by recording, then being divorced from physical objects like records and CDs by digital formats, and eventually being separated from files on individual computers by the cloud.

Pierre Schaeffer, one of the pioneers of Musique Concrète, identified a new phenomenon when the invention of radio, tape records and phonograph untethered sound from its sources. He termed the new disembodied sounds *objet sonore* or 'resonant objects'. These were objects in their own right, without form and divorced from the means of their generation, and it's the resonant object from which the horror in each of these stories emanates.

But this original disembodiment, that of the separation of a sound from its means of generation, the person speaking or the instrument playing, is not the root of the anxiety. The departure of the spirit and its continuation after the body aren't necessarily the stuff of horror but the unexpected return of this spirit in a different body, the act of possession—this is well within horror's remit.

In 'The Sound-Sweep' and 'The Preserving Machine', physical objects become inhabited by sound. The bodiless *objet sonore* possesses spaces and animals, places where they have no business being, and this jarring causes a sense of foreboding in the characters to the point of madness, a madness caused by the death of meaning and the possession by a random, malignant, avant-garde spirit.

Ballard and Dick have made noise itself the villain in these pieces and, given the avant-garde's association with noise going all the way back to the Futurists, it may seem that they are firmly anti-modern. But they write in a mode that delights in these horrors, lingering on the gory details of music eviscerated. Like much of the writing around the noise and experimental music genres that borrow horror's adjectives, they share this delight in violence done to tradition.

Notes

1 Phillip K. Dick, 'The Preserving Machine' (1953), in *The Preserving Machine and Other Stories* (London: Pan Books, 1969).

2 J.G. Ballard, 'The Sound-Sweep' (1960), in *The Complete Short Stories* (London: Flamingo, 2001), 154.

3 J.G. Ballard, 'The Sound-Sweep', 149.

Tales of the fourth dimension

Amelia Barikin

> …I shall never sleep calmly again when I think of the horrors that lurk ceaselessly behind life in time and in space, and of those unhallowed blasphemies from elder stars which dream beneath the sea…[1]
> —H.P. Lovecraft, 'The Call of Cthulhu', 1928

March, 1925. Captain Gustaf Johansen's two-masted sailing ship has run aground on a strange and unknown island somewhere in the southern Pacific Ocean. Scrambling across the muddy shore, the crew encounter an alien city, a mind-bending vision of 'cosmic majesty' that appears as a conglomeration of 'vast angles and stone surfaces—surfaces too great to belong to any thing right or proper for this earth, and impious with horrible images and hieroglyphs'.[2] Colossal pillars and gigantic stone blocks tower over the oozing, greenish wasteland. Great monoliths soar above slimy subterranean vaults.

More than the scale or material oddity of the place, it is the sheer and total weirdness of its *geometry* that ultimately strikes terror into the hearts of the sailors. Angles that seem initially to be concave appear on second glance as convex; the position of the sky and the sea are queerly indeterminate and somehow interchangeable; it cannot be decided whether the giant sea-soaked sculptures jutted about the landscape stand as horizontal or perpendicular to the ground. But it is not until Johansen's men come across the door—a portal of darkness so vast it seems acres-wide—that the full extent of the horror is revealed:

> Then, very softly and slowly, the acre-great panel began to give inward…In this phantasy of prismatic distortion it moved anomalously in a diagonal way,

> so that all rules of matter and perspective seemed upset… Everyone listened, and everyone was listening still when It lumbered slobberingly into sight and gropingly squeezed Its gelatinous green immensity through the black doorway into the tainted outside air of that poison city of madness.[3]

Visualised by H.P. Lovecraft as a monstrous assault on the human senses, the non-Euclidean landscape is an unthinkably 'abnormal' realm, 'loathsomely redolent of spheres and dimensions apart from ours': the sublime product of an alien mind.[4]

Art and The New Geometries

In 1928, the year Lovecraft first published his short story 'The Call of Cthulhu', literary and artistic interest in this kind of aberrant geometry had reached its zenith. References to non-Euclidean space had been paired in the popular imagination with the existence of the Fourth Dimension as early as the late 1800s, crystallised in both the science fictions of writers like H.G. Wells and the scientific papers of mathematicians such as Bernhard Reimann, Henri Poincaré, and Gottfried Wilhelm Leibniz. The notion of a space unbounded by Euclid's postulates on right angles and parallel lines was the subject of heated debate amongst English, American and European scientific communities, and the topic attracted significant interest from poets, writers and artists alike (including Apollinaire, Malevich, and Duchamp).

In England, E.A. Abbott's novel *Flatland: A Romance of Many Dimensions* was met with near-instant popular success upon its publication in 1884; in Paris in 1909, Matisse and Charles Camoin were discussing the Fourth Dimension in their letters; in 1912, Albert Gliezes and Jean Metzinger published their influential treatise *Du Cubisme*, in which Reimann's theories of non-Euclidean geometry were explicitly positioned as a way to understand Cubist pictorial space.[5] By the 1920s in America, the idea of the Fourth Dimension was firmly integrated in the pop imaginary, in part due to the editorial efforts of pulp magazines such as *Marvel Tales* and *Weird Tales* (in which Lovecraft frequently published), and to the regular coverage of the subject in magazines such as *Harper's Weekly*, *Scientific American* and *The Popular Science Monthly*.[6]

Significantly, in Lovecraft's works the non-Euclidean bending of space and time was designed not as an *escape* from the materiality of the cosmos, but as a means to highlight the limitations of human thought when confronted with the infinite permutations of the unknown. 'I choose weird stories', Lovecraft explained,

> because they suit my inclinations best—one of my strongest and most persistent wishes being to achieve, momentarily, the illusion of some strange suspension or violation of the galling limitations of time, space, and the natural law which for ever imprison us and frustrate our curiosity about the infinite cosmic spaces beyond the radius of our sight and analysis.[7]

Rather than negating the laws that govern human understanding of space and time, Lovecraft viewed the uniformity of the material universe as a front for a concealed, higher order of reality. The point was to reveal the artifice of humanity's imperfect conceptions of the cosmos so as to access the chaos of a 'shadow-haunted *Outside*'.[8]

From the gulfs of space to the wells of night

It is this tension between the frame and its content—a tension between the tactile utility of materialist knowledge and the amorphous workings of an unimaginable realm—that provides the most explicit link between the stories of H.P. Lovecraft and the sculptures, maquettes, collages and spatial installations of Roy Ananda. In Ananda's world, gridded and locked spaces give way to visions of star-studded galaxies; a Rubik's Cube is emblazoned with images of deep space; tentacled monstrosities are frozen in hyper-geometrical frames. Forms and images develop provisionally, through processes of physical accretion, while the gallery acts as a kind of experimental laboratory for the making of a world teetering on the brink of collapse (as Ananda has said, 'A lot of what I do is only a very slightly more grown up version of cubby-building or model making; the exhibition is clearly an exercise in world-building').[9]

While Ananda has admitted that his works are, in part, an 'unashamedly extended fan letter to Lovecraft', the Lovecraftian influence serves 'less as subject matter and more as an organising principle' for his spatial and sculptural manipulations.[10] The motif of the grid appears particularly prominent, functioning as a reminder of the bounded arena from which visions of the unbounded must necessarily unfold. Modularity, too, develops specific connotations through Ananda's science-fictional approach. The modular structure of his mutable shelving units plays on the enduring modularity of Lovecraft's legacy: a reference to the way in which Lovecraft's 'mythos' continues to be adapted and re-animated by innumerable fans, artists, gamers and writers to suit their own contemporary contexts. As Ananda writes, 'The inventory of bizarre entities, nightmarish locales, alien artefacts and forbidden tomes that constitutes the Cthulhu Mythos grows ever larger… [the mythology serves] as a conditioner for my preferred sculptural strategies: the spatial manipulation of the drawn or printed image; subtle interventions on found objects; and the use of mutable, modular structures, held just shy of their point of collapse'.[11] Subject to change and rearrangement, these works hinge on the creation of provisional spaces in which collections of material objects are brought into a fragile and momentary alliance.

Alien archaeology: new old things

In November 1931, Lovecraft attended a lecture by Willem de Sitter, the Dutch astronomer whose research into the phenomenon of dark matter was subsequently co-published with Albert Einstein.[12] The lecture made a strong impression on Lovecraft, and he referred directly to Sitter's ideas on the expansion of the universe and the curvature of space–time in his story 'The Dreams in the Witch House' (1932). This tale was marked with the same kind of non-representable spaces and complex, alien geometries seen in 'The Call of Cthulhu'. Importantly, however, despite Lovecraft's familiarity with the scientific discourse surrounding the 'new geometries', his most frequent tool for *visualising* the Fourth Dimension was not mathematics or science, but the language of formalist art history, filtered through the prose of his favourite writer, Edgar Allen Poe.

Astonishing works of art appear throughout Lovecraft's stories, primarily as evidence of alien civilisations much older and stranger than humankind might possibly imagine ('They had come from the stars, and had brought Their images with Them').[13] Bas-reliefs, clay idols, jewellery, architectural constructions and sculpted carvings provide material proof of the existence of the 'shadow-haunted *Outside*'. At times likened by Lovecraft to the planar distortions of Futurism and Cubism, the bizarre objects are also attributed to dream knowledge, their designs apparently prompted by alien transmissions (...I made it last night in a dream of strange cities; and dreams are older than Brooding Tyre, or the Contemplative Sphinx, or the garden-girdled Babylon').[14]

Although Lovecraft designates some of the artworks

in his tales as ancient, most are newly created, handmade by humans under the influence of alien aesthetics. As such it is their iconography, rather than their age or historical value, which is the source of their greatest fascination. The ability to create 'new old things'—newly crafted objects that somehow channel the essence of deep time to capture something of extra-human knowledge—is a similarly recurrent element in Ananda's practice. This is a way of inventing ancient histories so as to envisage potential futures, a form of inverted entropy in which faked relics or reversed ruins are gifted with a mysterious totemic power—the kind of power normally bestowed only by the passing of time. Sidestepping a history of art marked by serial progression and gradual innovation, Ananda's Lovecraftian assemblages manifest as shock arrivals from an alien time zone: the archaeological remnants of some weird, alternate present.

Notes

1 H.P. Lovecraft, 'The Call of Cthulhu' (1928), in S.T. Joshi (ed.), *The Call of Cthulhu and Other Weird Stories* (London and New York: Penguin, 2002), 164.
2 Lovecraft, 'The Call of Cthulhu', 165.
3 Lovecraft, 'The Call of Cthulhu', 166–7.
4 Lovecraft, 'The Call of Cthulhu', 167.
5 Albert Gleizes and Jean Metzinger, *Du Cubisme* (Paris: Eugène Figuière, 1912).
6 See Linda Dalrymple Henderson, *The Fourth Dimension and Non-Euclidean Geometry in Modern Art* (New Jersey: Princeton University Press, 1983).
7 Lovecraft, as cited in S.T. Joshi (ed.), 'Introduction', *The Call of Cthulhu and Other Weird Stories*, xv.
8 Lovecraft, *The Call of Cthulhu and Other Weird Stories*, xvi.
9 Roy Ananda, conversation with the author, April 2013.
10 Roy Ananda, conversation with the author, April 2013.

11 Roy Ananda, *R'lyeh Maquettes*, artist's statement (Melbourne: Dianne Tanzer Gallery + Projects, 2012).
12 Lovecraft, letter to Miss Elizabeth Toldridge, 3 December 1931, reprinted in *The H.P. Lovecraft Archive*: http://www.hplovecraft.com/life/interest/astrnmy.aspx. Accessed 22 April 2013.
13 Lovecraft, 'The Call of Cthulhu', 163.
14 Lovecraft, 'The Call of Cthulhu', 143.

This text was originally published by CACSA, Adelaide, in 2012 and is reprinted here with permission.

Copy-world: *Mobilis in mobile*

Patrick Pound

Artists, good, bad and indifferent, say that their work is about representation. That is, that their work isn't simply representational, but that it deliberately tackles the very idea of representation. Well it would, wouldn't it?

One of the attractions of the sci-fi genre is that it likes to unpack the limits of representation. From Verne to Ballard, the world, and how we think of it, and how we can describe it, is put to the test.

My favourite limit-case of representation can be found in Jules Verne's *Twenty Thousand Leagues Under the Sea* (1870, 1873).[1] In that story, Captain Nemo abandons the world and escapes to the confines of a submarine. Like some scientific dropout-cum-cult leader and vengeful terrorist, he lives in his submarine, the 'Nautilus', and cruises the watery underworld. His submarine is a perfect replica of the world. It has a library and a museum. So Nemo's microcosm is itself filled with copies of the world. It might even have an aquarium—a perfect copy of his submarine world in microcosm.

For years I've held Nemo's submarine aquarium as an exemplary, poetic and amusing limit-case of representation. On re-reading Verne recently, I realised its existence might just be a wilful projection of my own. In the 1956 Heritage Press version of *Twenty Thousand Leagues Under the Sea*, translated by Mercier Lewis, the description we are given of this section of the 'museum' is as follows: 'Under elegant glass cases, fixed by copper rivets, were classed and labeled the most precious productions of the sea which had ever been presented to the eye of a naturalist'.[2] There then follows an encyclopaedic list of specimens including zoöphytes, polypi and echinoderms. The list doesn't seem to include any aquatic examples that can be definitely identified as still living things. No 'aquarium' proper is actually mentioned. We are told that '[c]honcological treasures' and 'the rarest marine plants, which, although dried up' can be studied 'behind the glasses'.[3] Later, outside the confines of the vessel, describing walking in the underwater forest, the narrator declares: 'I saw there (but not dried up, as our specimens of the *Nautilus* are) pavonari spread like a fan as if to catch the breeze; scarlet ceramies, whose laminaries extended their edible shoots of fern-shaped nereocysti, which grow to a height of fifteen feet; clusters of acetabuli, whose stems increase in size upward; and numbers of other marine plants, all devoid of flowers!'[4]

In one of Edward A. Wilson's marvellous illustrations in this edition, the fantastic viewing platform with its huge glass picture window effectively turns the ocean itself into an 'immense vast aquarium'.[5] Throughout the novel the viewing platform is a key to the staging of the world as a model. Verne is all-encompassing. The underwater world is depicted as a model to be viewed, a series of tableaux, a museum, an aquarium, or even a photograph. Verne describes a scene of a shipwreck with corpses tied up on deck as: 'taken as it were from life and photographed in its last moments'.[6] Verne's novel summons up the idea of *everythingness*. At one stage a character opines: 'I think, then, with no offence to master, that a happy year would be one in which we could see everything'.[7] The submarine is a floating catalogue.

For all of this, there doesn't seem to be an aquarium on board. However, in the 1957 Heritage Press edition of Verne's sequel, *The Mysterious Island* (a marvellous Robinsonade that inspired the television series *Lost*), Nemo's submarine makes a final appearance. Its interior is again lavishly described, and again sets off a sort of archive envy. Here, in the original English translation of W.H.G. Kingston, the word 'aquarium' is employed.[8]

The text mentions: 'the aquarium, in which bloomed the most wonderful productions of the sea—marine plants, zoophytes, chaplets of pearls of inestimable value; and, finally, his eyes rested on this device, inscribed over the pediment of the museum—the motto of the 'Nautilus'—*Mobilis in mobile*'.[9] The word 'bloomed' also leans towards living things.

So, it seems fair to have thought that there might have been a submarine aquarium in both stories. Writing and reading are forms of conjuring and re-conjuring. However, I don't think Verne meant to conjure up a water-filled aquarium full of living aquatic specimens after all. Reading is always something of an act of 'translation'. (Even the translation of the original title *Vingt mille lieues sous les mers* is problematic. Surely it should be *Seas* plural. That way, the travel would be through the seven seas as intended, and eliminate any possible confusion with the depths at which the submarine plunged.) I'm just another reader, and I'm certainly no expert on Verne. Anyway, whether Verne meant it or not, the submarine aquarium remains the favourite image that I pictured in these two novels, and I'm grateful to have found it there.

Like the terrarium, the wave pool, and the refugee camp, it's a world in miniature. Captain Nemo's submarine (with or without its aquarium) holds the idea I want to discuss. For me, that aquarium is a benchmark of representational possibilities. Nemo's submarine is a fantastic double. For me, it's also a model of what art might be. It captures the contest between art and life. It neatly holds the idea of the copy-world the way a peach holds the sun. It anticipates Borges's story *On Rigor in Science* (1964) where the city is copied in an exact map one-to-one, overlaying the physical world, and suitably, falling apart underfoot.[10] It also echoes James Holiday's beautiful and melancholy chart of the Ocean—a completely empty chart in Lewis Carroll's *The Hunting of the Snark: an Agony in Eight Fits* (1876).[11]

A long time ago I made installations for the Australian Centre of Photography (ACP) in Sydney, and the Centre for Contemporary Photography (CCP) in Melbourne, and the first Auckland Triennial. These rooms were filled with scrapbook pages of an imaginary character that was collecting images of copy-worlds from World Fairs to fish tanks. On trying to explain the world and having failed, my character had been reduced to collecting it.

These days, I try to lessen the art of intervention and simply let things speak for themselves. In Geraldine Barlow's 'Liquid Archive' exhibition at the Monash University Museum of Art (MUMA) in 2012, I arranged a vast set of objects, each of which holds an idea of air. I called it *The Museum of Air*. My *Museum of Air* attempts to reassign meaning to insignificant marginal things: to resuscitate them. I go for things that are neither cool, nor kitsch. I want them to be neutral—to have no real cultural purchase. I bought nearly all of these things on eBay, and mostly from overseas. Together they make up a constellation. They are found to converse.

I also want to upset the false need for *things* to be fixed in their meaning. I want them to behave more like words—to give them more flexibility and put them back to work. Perhaps this is the last breath of these recently redundant things. It's a dictionary of things, shuffled so as to conjure up a meaningful network. The museum is like a flip book of *things*. From an asthma inhaler to a bicycle pump, from a Spanish fan to a draft excluder, each thing contains an idea of air. Some are clearer than others. A battery-powered 'breathing' dog actively performs the idea, whereas a tiny ticket holds its relation to the idea of air undercover. It's a tram ticket from Sydney during World War II that was used as a free transport pass by a very particular group. They were the Air Raid Wardens.

There's a lobby-card from Douglas Sirk's *Written on the Wind*, and a figurine from *Gone with the Wind*. There's an album of *Curved Air*, and there's a novel by Ruth Wind.

The collection becomes a thinking machine, and a picture puzzle. It's also a time capsule and a copy-world like that underwater aquarium on Captain Nemo's submarine. Like that aquarium, it's a physical manifestation of an idea. I've also assembled a *Museum of Space*, and a *Museum of Falling*.

Like Sunday painters and conceptual artists, I'm interested in the limits of representation. Now this might at first seem a little bit highbrow, or pretentious, but what I'm actually after is a conceptual lightness of touch—and I want to put the dad joke into conceptual art.

I'm interested in the extremes of listing and sorting out the world in words and in pictures. It is as if the world were a series of overlapping lists—as if it were a puzzle and if only we could assemble all the pieces we might even solve it. And, like all artists and novelists, I habitually substitute the problem of life with the problem of art. It's like that Raymond Chandler novel where the detective tells us that he hasn't solved the puzzle, but at least all the pieces are beginning to look like they belong to the same puzzle.

In the 2012 MUMA show I also displayed lots of examples from an ongoing collection I call 'Portrait of the wind'. It's compiled of hundreds of photos of people in the wind. I like the idea of photographs of something you can't see. You might notice a tie over someone's shoulder or a billowing dress. Again, a set of things are seen to hold and test an idea, like those novels that stretch the possibilities of description as if on a dare. A favourite example being Laurence Sterne's *The Life and Opinions of Tristram Shandy* (1759), in which Sterne employs a range of techniques that summon images from the book itself, as if it were a projecting machine. As a witty, yet melancholy, visual sign of grief he offers up a black page. Later, next to a marbled page Sterne writes: 'you will no more be able to penetrate the moral of the next marbled page (motley emblem of my work) than the world with all its sagacity has been able to unravel the many opinions, transactions and truths which still lie mystically hid under the dark veil of the black one'.[12]

One of the greatest examples of the limits of description is via its abdication. Further on, Sterne leaves us a blank space to paint our own picture of a desirable woman. He writes: 'To conceive this right,—call for pen and ink—here's paper ready to your hand.—Sit down, Sir, paint her to your own mind—as like your mistress as you can—as unlike your wife as your conscience will let you—'tis all one to me—place your own fancy in it.'[13]

Likewise, much later, Daniel Spoerri in his illustrated book of 1962 describing everything on his table has as its last entry a space for the reader to replicate the cigarette burn on his tabletop.[14] This brings to mind another playful shell of a description, that is a 'story' called *Suburbia* by an OuLiPo member, Paul Fournel (1996).[15] Fournel's story is made up solely of a foreword and footnotes, annotations, errata, an afterward and, even, a supplement for use in schools. All of these books activate the space between things and their representation.

While none of these examples belong in the science fiction genre, another exemplary book, Jonathan Swift's *Gulliver's Travels* (1726), clearly anticipates sci-fi.[16] It's filled with spatial play, time codes, scale shifts, and descriptive limits. At one stage, Swift physically exchanges pictures for words in an amusing bid to spell out the representation problem. Other novelists who inform my work also explore this territory, whereby the limits of representation are put to the test. While they are not sci-fi writers in any real sense, they press the real into hyper-real and fantastic patterns.

A work of fiction that is full of science and tests the limits of knowledge and description, but isn't science fiction at all, is Flaubert's *Bouvard and Pécuchet* (1881, 1896). Flaubert gives us two copy clerks who retire from gainful employment to try to explain the world for themselves.[17] They systematically attempt to work out by collection and practical strategies exactly how things work, from gardening to advanced science. They stumble methodically from one system to another, and end up none the wiser. These two nineteenth-century nerds are a parody of the enlightenment, and the positivist, if not utopian, view held out by the supposedly endless possibilities of knowledge.[18] There is, however, a poetry to their continuous failure.

One hundred years later, the OuLiPo group try writing by using literary constraints. Georges Perec's *Life A User's Manual* (1978), arranged according to several systems and constraints including the knight's tour of a chessboard (whereby the knight moves on all squares without repetition), is filled with numerous nods to Verne.[19] (It opens with Verne's 'Look with all your eyes, look'.) While far less readable, perhaps the most famous example of this type of exercise is Perec's novel *A Void* (1974), which was written without the letter e.[20] Another Perec favourite is *An Attempt at Exhausting a Place in Paris* (1976).[21] In this book, Perec goes to a single café, sits in the same place and exactly redescribes the scene he views. It owes a debt to Raymond Queneau's *Exercises in Style* (1947), where an incident on a bus is described ninety-nine different ways in ninety-nine chapters.[22] The chapter titles of that book are a performative example of the description problem, the first letter of each title being an amusingly illustrative pictogram. They avoid the illustration problem, whereby pictorial illustration re-enacts a piece of text. To illustrate a novel is, after all, to put a hat on a hat.

These fantastic feats of description all position the

world as if it were a puzzle. J.G. Ballard's *Crash* (1973) is another novel at the margins of sci-fi that has left something of an impression on me.[23] Like Verne, Ballard had a fundamental interest in the way a thing might be made to hold an idea.

The cover illustration of the first edition sets us rolling. The car becomes the female body, after a fashion. In Ballard's novel, we're given a perverted collector in a sinister blend of road research and sexual fetish. He's like a Captain Nemo for an overlit future. The novel opens with the narrator recovering in hospital after a car crash in which he's killed the husband of a young woman doctor. In pain-filled dreams, he finds himself dominated by strange sexual fantasies.

When he leaves hospital, he revisits the scene of the crash, and meets the now-widowed woman doctor. A little surprisingly, they have an affair, and begin an exploration of the motorcar in all its forms, conducting a variety of sexual experiments on London's motorways. They meet a dangerous character called Vaughan, who has a rather specific fantasy. He is a hoodlum scientist who's determined to die in a car crash with a famous film actress. Terrified of Vaughan, yet under his spell, the narrator joins his entourage of racing drivers, drug addicts, and airport prostitutes. They take part in stock-car races, watch test vehicles being crashed at the Road Research Lab, all the time being carried closer to the sinister climax of the novel, a disquieting vision of the future in which sex and technology form an exciting, if difficult, marriage.

The thing that stuck with me most, however, was not the sexy tech fantasy but the way Ballard describes his, and his narrator's, impression of things. He literally, and performatively, describes things using words to encapsulate physical impressions as if they were indexical codes. For example: he dwells on the impressions of car parts, on the flesh of crash victims and on the bodies of naked participants in sex acts in car interiors. Like the folded hulks of crashed cars, the human bodies are dented with the impressions left behind by things which press into them.

Ballard has his words do much the same. He works at the extreme end of how a set of words may be made to hold an idea. In his 1927 version of the poem *Paterson*, William Carlos Williams famously penned the line: 'No ideas but in things'.[24] Ballard captures something like this when he presses his words together to hold the impression left behind by things. He compiles his story with this network of traces, while describing the very act of observing and collecting such traces. Here's an example of the sort of thing I'm talking about: 'the automobile components shadowed like contact prints in my skin and musculature'.[25]

So, the car parts leave traces. Ballard plays on the limit of representation; the indexical trace. He's aware that words and pictures, like shorthand, are second-degree forms of representation, words being an arbitrary code that bear very little direct relation to the things they represent. They are a surrogate code. Onomatopoeic words attempt to leap this divide, as they mimic the sound they stand in for, like a hiccup. Photography is, of course, a first-order mode of representation. Sontag observed: 'Photographed images do not seem to be statements about the world so much as pieces of it'.[26] The photo is more like a rubbing—a frottage of light. Like indentations on skin, photographs are peculiarly indexical traces. Appropriately, Ballard turns to photography in his directly evidentiary system of description.

Extremes of representation are at the heart of all this fiction in extremis. Even sex is a dystopian stretch. Ballard writes: 'each ransacking the other's body like Crusoe stripping his ship'.[27] Crusoe being yet another exemplar of the type of microcosmic limit-case I'm talking about. Crusoe assembles a smaller boat from his wrecked ship, and then constructs a miniature world on his island, complete with a farm, and a library, and so on.

I've adopted this model in my work as well. Every photograph we take is in addition to the vast album of images that float about, unhinged, in the world. Each photo *graphs* the world in the form of a document. Photography has the innate structural order of the archive. Re-reading *Crash*, I noticed that Ballard says: 'Vaughan collected the grimaces of casualty nurses in his photographic albums'.[28]

For years I've collected other people's snaps and sorted them into categories. There's a box of photos of readers. There are hundreds of people in passing cars. I have twenty-six gas stations, and I have twenty-six crash scenes.

I have collections of bridges and of human bridges. I have a collection of upside-down people, and a collection of photos of photographers' thumbs. I have categories of cars, and of pets, and of people with pets and cars. There are photographs of people holding a single thing—a fish caught, a gift received, or something else—something worthy of being photographed.

I have accumulated hundreds of photos that include their photographer's shadow. There's also a whole set of photographs of amateur models with the impressions of their socks, or their waistbands embedded in their skin. That's getting close to an illustration of Ballard. It's another limit-case of indexicality. It certainly shares Ballard's territory. There are images that previous owners have marked to show where they are in the picture, or in which cabin they stayed, or just which bunch of flowers on a grave is theirs.

Photography is an art made in the wake of things. Again: Ballard's territory. I have a collection of photos of people from behind. I have photos of people carrying guns. I also have photos of people relieving themselves. I have photos that have been attacked. I have a collection of photo-booth images where the person wasn't quite ready. I also have a collection of interruptions. Each snap taken at just the wrong moment—as someone unexpectedly enters the frame. I have another collection of snaps taken at the perfect, pregnant, moment: just as someone walks through the door to their '*Surprise!*' party.

I have a huge set of photos of people who look dead but aren't. Probably. Again, this is Ballard's home turf. Not that Ballard drove me to this behaviour, of course.

Like Ballard's wound outlines, and Verne's submarine aquarium, my collections of found photos are a systematic copy-world. Each photograph taken offers the possibility of completing a set, as if to photograph is to work at a solution, of a type. The collections might add up to a world picture. It's as if only we could get all the pieces together, we could solve the puzzle. This is a condition of taking and collecting snaps.

In another set of optical illusions people appear to be giants amongst men. These are just a few of my categories. There are, of course, also photographs of people holding cameras—and of people holding photographs, and photographs of photographs. Like Nemo's submarine aquarium, this archive is doubly indexical.

You also notice that when you put things in categories you find categories within those categories—someone reading—listening to music—and in the wind—or a photographer's shadow and their thumb. If I ever find a photo that holds all of my categories maybe I could, perhaps, stop collecting.

I found a photo the other day of a boy in a boat. The boat was in a tiny round swimming pool. The pool was in his backyard. The boy was rowing the boat, but he only had one oar. It seemed to say everything– but not quite. Got to keep looking.

Notes

1. Jules Verne, *Twenty Thousand Leagues Under the Sea* (1870), trans. Mercier Lewis (Boston: James R. Osgood, 1873).
2. Jules Verne, *Twenty Thousand Leagues Under the Sea* (New York: The Heritage Press, 1956), 61.
3. Verne, *Twenty Thousand Leagues*, 1956, 80.
4. Verne, *Twenty Thousand Leagues*, 1956, 93.
5. Verne, *Twenty Thousand Leagues*, 1956, 78.
6. Verne, *Twenty Thousand Leagues*, 1956, 104.
7. Verne, *Twenty Thousand Leagues*, 1956, 113.
8. Wilson's illustration depicts details of glass cases. No aquarium is shown.
9. Jules Verne, *The Mysterious Island* (New York: Heritage Press, 1959), 535.
10. Jorge Louis Borges, *Dreamtigers* (Austin, Texas: University of Texas Press, a Condor Book, 1964).
11. Lewis Carroll, *The Hunting of the Snark: an Agony in Eight Fits* (London: Macmillan, 1876). The illustration of the empty chart is by James Holiday.
12. Laurence Sterne, *The Life and Opinions of Tristram Shandy*, Vol. III (London: Dodsley, 1759), 168.
13. Laurence Sterne, *The Life and Opinions of Tristram Shandy*, Vol. VI (London: Dodsley, 1759), 146–7.
14. Daniel Spoerri, *An Anecdoted Topography of Chance*, trans. Emmett Williams and illustrated by Topor (New York: Something Else Press Inc., 1966). First published as *Topograhie Anécdotée du Hasard* (Paris: Editions Galerie Lawrence, 1962).
15. Paul Fournel, *Suburbia*, in: *Oulipo Laboratory: Texts from the Bibliothèque Oulipienne* (London: Atlas, 1995).
16. Jonathan Swift, *Gulliver's Travels* (London: Benjamin Motte, 1726).
17. Gustave Flaubert, *Bouvard and Pécuchet* (London: H.S. Nichols, 1896).

18 I borrow the description of Bouvard and Pécuchet as nerds from Peter Brooks who titled a chapter on that book in relation to Henry James: 'Flaubert's Nerds'. Peter Brooks, *Henry James Goes to Paris* (Princeton: Princeton University Press, 2007).
19 Georges Perec, *Life A User's Manual* (London: Collins Harvill, 1987). First published by Hachette, in 1978, under the title *La Vie mode d'emploi*.
20 Georges Perec, *A Void*, trans. Gilbert Adair (London: Harvill, 1994). First published by Editions Denoel, in 1969, under the title *La Disparition*.
21 Georges Perec, *An Attempt at Exhausting a Place in Paris*, trans. Marc Lowenthal (London: Wakefield Press, 2010). First published as *Tentative d'épuisement d'un lieu parisien* (Paris: Christian Bourgois, 1975).
22 Raymond Queneau, *Exercises in Style*, trans. Barbara Wright (London: Gaberbocchus Press, 1958). First published under the title *Exercises de style* (Paris: Librairie Gallimard, 1947).
23 J.G. Ballard, *Crash* (New York: Farrar, Straus and Giroux, 1973).
24 Although its exact meaning was unclear, it went on to become something of a modernist catchcry. William Carlos Williams, *Paterson*, 1927.
25 Ballard, *Crash*, 38.
26 Susan Sontag, *On Photography* (London: Penguin Books, 1977, 1984), 4.
27 Ballard, *Crash*, 44.
28 Ballard, *Crash*, 24.

Anamorphic portage and the invisible match cut

Matthew Shannon

2001: A Space Odyssey

Why write about a book and film that has had so much written about it? Is there a point at which something can no longer be written *into*? Has it been overwritten? What can happen when writing on something that is beyond being written in? These are the questions we first face when looking to write anything further on the subject of Arthur C. Clarke's novel *2001: A Space Odyssey* and its filmic manifestation in Kubrick's *2001: A Space Odyssey* (1968). Can we discover a new economy of a place we know so well? Is a new dynamic possible?

When we consider *2001*, we should not separate the novel from the film or the film from the novel. We should not forget the novel was developed concurrently with the film version and was in fact only released in print after celluloid. From this perspective, the novel and film can be seen as part of the same collaborative multimedia work, allowing us to be free to jump indiscriminately between both texts even if they do follow a slightly different structure. Any contradictions between the two amount to a dialethic whole that can be explored and probed as one entity—neither one being the host of the other.

Arthur C. Clarke's novel is divided into six chapters: 'Primeval Night', 'TMA-1', 'Between Planets', 'Abyss', 'The moons of Saturn' and 'Through the Stargate'. Kubrick's film is divided into four movements: 'The Dawn of Man', 'TMA-1', 'The Jupiter Mission' and 'Jupiter and Beyond the Infinite'. Our received knowledge of these successive stages (in both the film and the novel) is of the odyssey of humankind, from pre-human to post-human, in successive stages of *becoming* and of *overcoming*.

The development of the human is defined by the

overcoming of subjection by an exterior reality. This culminates in the birth of the Starchild, a human somehow beyond the bounds of this exterior, even beyond time and space. The process of overcoming begins in the film with the infamous proto-human's (referred to as Moon-Watcher in the novel) use of a thighbone as an emancipatory device, a way of overcoming the ecological reality in which its species is embedded. By taking up the use of tools, Moon-Watcher's clan separates itself from all other Terran creatures. Unlike the other apes and animals around them, the clan is able to rapidly develop body modifications so as to adapt to new situations: 'Only the babies and the feeblest of the old folk were left in the caves; if there was any surplus food at the end of the day's searching, they might be fed. If not, the hyenas would soon be in luck once more.'[1]

2001's thesis of the human as the emergent factor of overcoming brings with it a formally romantic apprehension of an exterior reality. Reality is wild yet tameable. Hence, the infamous match cut between bone and spaceship proposes that the ultimate destiny of man is to overcome the reality of the terrestrial biosphere via more developed emancipatory devices, such as spacecraft.

The sections of the film and novel dedicated to the use of spacecraft show humanity in transition towards another level of abstraction, culminating in the film as the 'Beyond the Infinite' scenes of surreal and psychedelic imagery. This ambiguous ending to *2001* may have as much to do with strategically uncertain narrative consequences as it does with a more complicated meta-thesis that extends beyond the bounds of the medium of either film or novel: that we as a culture can only accurately image/imagine as far as the homeless and no-longer-on-planet-earth reality of the spaceship. Going beyond this traditional futurist expectation lies outside of our conceptual, linguistic and visual projections: a paradigm shift comparable to the jump from proto-human to human. For this reason it makes perfect sense for Kubrick and Clarke to manifest the 'Beyond the Infinite' sequence with signifiers of abstraction that we are able to understand, even if we understand them only as ideological visual signifiers of *that-which-cannot-be-fully-comprehended*. We could ask, what other choice did they have?

We should also remember that throughout the film and novel the events that create the narrative thrust of becoming and overcoming are always driven in part through the encounter with an occulted and abstract other. The proto-human, human and post-human are able to enter successive stages of alteration via encounters with this otherness. This proposes that the agency of the human defined by the overcoming of reality is completely exterior to the human itself. The Monolith signifies this existence in the film—an emissary that represents the non-embodied existence indirectly, in the way a lawyer represents a client. What exactly this abstracted non-embodied existence *is* can only be speculated about. A cosmic Gaia or consciousness seems possible, as does pure potentiality and becoming. The possibilities are endless, but restricted to speculation.

Discussions of *2001* tend to focus anthropocentrically on the successive stages of human evolution (pre-human, human, post-human). However, it is possible to invert the investigation and concentrate on the *anamorphic regimes* that exist around the three central characters of Moon-Watcher, Dr Floyd and Dave Bowman. So, rather than focusing on the changes occurring at the level of the human, we can also track the altering status of what is *around* the human. Describing what exists around each character as 'anamorphic regimes' is a purposeful way of avoiding using the term 'world'. As we shall discover, this is a particular kind of regime in itself. It is also a way of avoiding terms that are essentially substitutes for 'world', such as domain, globe or sphere—terms that convey similarly loaded connotations of enclosure and immunology.

An *anamorphological investigation* can then assist in establishing differences between what is around the three main protagonists of the novel and the film. This approach borrows in part from the preface to Eugene Thacker's 2010 book *In the Dust of This Planet: Horror of Philosophy, Vol. 1*, where an outline for a model of difference between 'World', 'Earth' and 'Planet' is proposed. The new economy proposed by Thacker questions the ability or inability of the mind to access the world, of its capacity to exist without the world, and what possibilities there are for it to think beyond the limits of the tools it has created. Although nearly all of Western philosophy reflects this problem to some extent, Thacker's proposal should be seen in light of an attempted suspension of this tradition and an attempt to introduce a new dynamic, a new economy of the same place. In this sense, Thacker's work is non-philosophical.[2]

Earth: 'Primeval Night' (novel) and 'Dawn of Man' (film)

Earth is the 'world-in-itself', a regime outside of the human that is not human-centric, a reality that exists outside our intelligibility. This world (Earth) is indifferent to human well-being, it is where climate change is taking place. It is a world that will attack us unprovoked in the form of disasters we call 'natural'. But it is also the world our material resources are drawn from. This is the world Moon-Watcher lives in. In the context of *2001*, it is by definition the world-in-itself by the presence of the human as pre-human. This world exists prior to the invention of humankind's ability to manipulate, represent or study reality.

The hunger this world beseeches upon Moon-Watcher's clan in combination with received but not perceived information from the Monolith is the impetus for the invention of a new anamorphic regime. By taking the thighbone and acting upon the world-in-itself (Earth) as a creative/destructive agent, Moon-Watcher artificially manipulates the trajectory of evolutionary, ecological Earth. As we know, *2001* proposes that this act produces the human, a human recognisable as a product of the Enlightenment. However, as Thacker argues, Moon-Watcher's act of tooled emancipation from hunger and thirst additionally creates a new type of regime: the 'World'. From this perspective the match cut from bone to spaceship is also a jump cut from one regime to another, or from Earth to World.

As Thacker states, 'The world-in-itself [Earth] is a paradoxical concept, the moment we think it and attempt to act on it, it ceases to be the world-in-itself and becomes the world-for-us'.[3] It's important to recognise that one type of world does not dispel another; it may displace it or create it anew, but it does not do away with it entirely. A new type of regime may have been created via the separation of the human from the Earth; the emergence of the human is co-dependent on the emergence of the World. This new 'World' around the human exists either alongside or inside the Earth.

World: 'TMA-1' and 'Between Planets' (novel), 'TMA-1' and 'Jupiter Mission' (film)

World (with a capital W) is the 'world-for-us', it is produced as an effect of the acting upon the 'world-in-itself'. It is constructed from our interpretations of the Earth; it is the phenomenological space built out of meaning and culture. And, by extension, it is the space our thinking can feel trapped in when we use purely phenomenological or linguistic methods of inquiry; a mental space contained by the limit point of our own perceptions and constructions. This is the world of representations: an immunological sphere through which the world-in-itself (Earth) can attack or threaten with natural and ecological disasters. The intersection of the World and Earth is the perpetual nature versus culture boundary negotiation.

The 'world-for-us' is perfectly embodied by the metaphor of the spaceship or space station where the exterior reality of the human reaches a limit point of the constructed, manufactured and scientific. Outside of this limit is an abyss, a void, or what we can now call Earth. In this World we must also consider how our constructions have the capacity to bite back. So, whereas Moon-Watcher has to battle hunger brought about by failed hunting, Dave Bowman must battle with HAL, an agent of his species' own creation. Portentously, the novel tells us, 'Discovery was no longer a happy ship'.[4]

The battle with HAL leaves Dave Bowman destitute, a condition only fully articulated in the novel. With Discovery no longer able to sustain his return, the ship would continue on its path to Saturn regardless of Dave's survival: 'It even seemed possible that he would survive until the Discovery reached Saturn—which, of course, she would do whether he was alive or not'.[5] It is at this point that the World (world-for-us) becomes unhinged. The world-for-us as manifested in the Discovery spaceship has gone beyond Bowman's control; it is no longer a World *for* Dave. What Discovery drifts towards is not the world-in-itself (Earth), although it does have some similar qualities. Discovery at this point (in both the film and the novel) becomes a vessel delivering Dave Bowman to the final anamorphic regime.

While Bowman and the Discovery float into the orbits of Saturn's moons in the novel and Jupiter's in the film (technical difficulties in rendering Saturn's rings meant Kubrick needed to relocate this section), the Monolith appears once again, this time floating in alignment with the moons of Jupiter. The camera pans up from this alignment, resting on a screen of complete black for approximately three seconds. From this black screen the psychedelic sequence commences. The kaleidoscopic images emerge out of a vanishing point that the swirls and lines of colour both propose and articulate. Rather than transitioning to the psychedelic sequence via a jump cut, the way in which the colours emerge slowly from the centre of the black screen suggests that an edit was made in the preceding three seconds of black. We can then identify here another match cut, symbolically akin to the regime change triggered by the infamous pairing of bone/spaceship at the start of the film. A cut from the blackness of deep space to the abstract blackness of a monochrome: a match so exact that it goes easily undetected.

We could call this the *impossible match cut*, as it is almost impossible to perceive. What takes place between these two black screens is a significant use of montage that creates a jump from either everything to everything, or from nothing to nothing, or possibly a jump from nothing to everything. We have reached the limit point of our comprehension. This epistemological limit represents an end point of the representational, phenomenological and conceptual fabrication that is the world-for-us (World). Via this match cut, the films leaves both the solar system and the 'world-for-us' of the spaceship to enter the ambiguous territory of the 'world-without-us'. This is the regime of the *Planet*.

Planet: 'Abyss', 'The Moons of Saturn', 'Through the Stargate' (novel) and 'Jupiter and Beyond the Infinite' (film)

The planet is the 'world-without-us'. As both 'spectral' and 'speculative', it is certainly the most ambiguous of all the regimes. In Thacker's words:

> The world-in-itself may co-exist with the world-for-us—indeed the human being is defined by its impres-

> sive capacity for not recognising this distinction. By contrast, the world-without-us cannot co-exist with the human world-for-us; the world-without-us is the subtraction of the human from the world.[6]

We should not take the proposal of the world-without-us (Planet) as 'the subtraction of the human from the world' as substitutable to the world-in-itself (Earth). This impersonal Planet is a result of the abstraction and dematerialisation of beings that have become pure thought and are no longer part of a material World or Earth. This scenario is made far clearer in the novel than the film. As Clarke tells us,

> A few mystically inclined biologists went still further. They speculated, taking their cues from the beliefs of many religions, that mind would eventually free itself from matter. The robot body, like the flesh-and-blood one, would be no more than a stepping-stone to something which, long ago, men had called 'spirit'.[7]

The use of the term 'spirit' here to describe the non-embodied entity that Bowman encounters provokes us to think of a possibility not considered by Thacker, that of 'us-without-world'. To consider 'us-without-world' would be to accept a mind existing independently of any world. This seems to fit our understanding of the abstracted entity that is controlling or producing the world in which Bowman finds himself.

This notion of us-without-world does not initially appear to sit consistently with the anti-anthropocentric economy of Earth, World and Planet. However, if we consider the us-without-world to be a mind we can call *Alien* then we can start to reconcile these ideas. What if Thacker's Planet can only be accessed by an *Alien* mind? This doesn't necessarily mean a mind extraterrestrial in origin, although this is a possibility. If Thacker's Planet is the 'subtraction of the human from the world' then maybe the 'spirit' described by Clarke can be characterised as the subtraction of the human from the mind.

At this point it may seem the application of Thacker's regimes to *2001* are reaching a limit point. However, what remains critical is to consider how the images Kubrick produced function in relation to a world-without-us and, by extension, to the possibility of thinking us-without-world. How can the final stages of both the film and the novel *eo ipso* represent an essentially unrepresentable image?

This is where we need to think about what it means to make psychedelic and, in the colloquial use of the term, surrealist images. These types of images are essentially speculative signifiers of *something unrepresentable*. They tend to express an excess of visuality that defines what they cannot—a thing or experience so excessive it cannot be directly communicated. This logic is extended particularly by the way in which the audience of the film experiences the psychedelic images largely from the point of view of Dave Bowman. Rather than seeing Bowman pass through from one reality to another, the audience *affectively* have the same experience of transition.

The psychedelic imagery starts with a kind of slit-scan wormhole that we speed through alongside Bowman. The kaleidoscopic patterns emerge organically from an invisible central point, never repeating. More ambiguous are the images of landscapes, with illuminated seas that evoke dream images, and the exploding astral bodies that could just as easily stand in for microbiological processes or gigantic super novae. All of this imagery can be seen as an attempt to connect the film to the optical and cerebral network of the viewer, so it's not surprising that stories of acid-tripping audience members proliferated on the first release of the film.

The images decompose the audience–film divide. The film spills out of the screen, creating the meta-thesis of *2001*, that the cognitive capacity to envisage a future paradigm shift lies beyond us. The mysterious shots towards the end the film of Bowman, jump-cutting through his old age in a kind of eighteenth-century villa with a clinical, illuminated floor, are given much greater articulation in the novel. In Clarke's telling it is clear that the environment Bowman finds himself in is entirely ersatz. Processed foodstuffs are presented to him in recognisable packages and forms (for example a cornflakes box) that all contain the same gooey or puddingy substance: a regime beyond the beyond. Astronaut Dave Bowman is in an extra beyond, one that is only able to present itself or be presented as an imitation, not having the ability to become visible on its own terms. This may be where *2001* takes us. Like the co-dependence of the human and the World, the regime of the Planet may only be able to show itself via indirect means to the human. To engage with the Planet directly is to acquire a post-human, Alien mind.

Notes

1 Arthur C. Clarke, *2001: A Space Odyssey* (1968), (New York: ROC, 2002), 3.

2 'Non-philosophical' in terms of François Laruelle's conception of an axiomatic practice that suspends all philosophy as essentially reflective. See François Laruelle, *Philosophies of Difference: A Critical Introduction to Non-Philosophy*, trans. Rocco Gangle (London and New York: Continuum, 2010).

3 Eugene Thacker, *In the dust of this Planet: The Horror of Philosophy, Vol. 1* (Winchester: Zero Books, 2011), 5.

4 Clarke, *2001: A Space Odyssey*, 71.

5 Clarke, *2001: A Space Odyssey*, 92.

6 Thacker, *In the Dust of This Planet*, 5.

7 Clarke, *2001: A Space Odyssey*, 95.

In space no one can hear you laugh

Nick Selenitsch

I headed to the local video store to hire *Spaceballs* as a prompt to write about comic science fiction. 'We have *SpaceJam*', the kid—who had never heard of *Spaceballs*—suggested, as if he was offering Boag's beer instead of Cascade. 'It's not really the same', I said, and hired *Sleeper* instead.

Sleeper is an odd film. It is early Woody Allen, so it has large sections of slapstick, à la silent films. Unless you are a devoted Mr Bean fan—and I'm referring to the films not the TV series—these Benny Hill-esque scenes seem pretty unnecessary, especially as the dialogue is so good. The script is brilliant, as it always is with Woody Allen, particularly his early 'funny' films. The plot of *Sleeper* involves a man, Miles Monroe (Woody), who is brought back to life two hundred years after he went into hospital for a routine ulcer operation.

> MILES: I can't believe this. My Doctor said I'd be up on my feet in five days. He was off by 199 years.[1]

Miles finds a world completely changed from 1973, where he was a part-owner of The Happy Carrot Health Food Restaurant on Bleecker St, New York ('Wherever that was', says the Doctor reading his file).

> DOCTOR 1: Has he asked for anything special?
> DOCTOR 2: Yes, this morning for breakfast he requested something called wheatgerm, organic honey and tiger's milk.
> DOCTOR 1: (Laughs.) Oh yes. Those are the charmed substances that some years ago were thought to contain life-preserving properties.

DOCTOR 2 (LOOKING CONCERNED): You mean there was no deep fat, no steak, no cream pies or hot fudge?
DOCTOR 1: Those were thought to be unhealthy; precisely the opposite of what we now know to be true.
DOCTOR 2: Incredible.

A character in Oscar Wilde's play *Lady Windermere's Fan* explains: 'Life is far too important a thing ever to talk seriously about it'.[2] The line has been popularised as an Oscar Wilde (mis)quote: 'Life is too important to take seriously'. The same applies to science fiction.

Science fiction is farcical. Seriously, why would anyone take it seriously? It is an endless roll call of ridiculousness: aliens, wars between worlds, worlds in which robots rule the earth, worlds where women rule the earth, a world where Big Brother rules (and is a TV success?), worlds without books. Waterworlds. Aliens. More aliens. Maybe no one *does* take it seriously (except for Tom Cruise?). This could explain why there are so few decent comic sci-fi films around. At a quick memory glance there is: *Mars Attacks*; *Sleeper*; *The Hitchhiker's Guide to the Galaxy* (though this is a million times better as a book); *Spaceballs* and *Galaxy Quest*. Strangely, *Hot Tub Time Machine* is listed by Wikipedia as comic science fiction. Maybe this scarcity is due to the fact that 'serious' science fiction is too easy to parody. To use an example from another genre: how do you parody somebody like Silvio Berlusconi? There is no need. Conversely, why would anyone spend time and money making a comic version of *Waterworld*?

Science fiction seems to be a way of addressing our perceived fears and anxieties (aliens) as well as our real fears and anxieties (global warming) via a projected past or future. Comic science fiction is a genre for making fun of these phobias. *Sleeper*, for example, is an opportunity to make fun of the social issues of 1970s, from health food stores to fears of communism to protest movements and the sexual revolution.

> LUNA (DIANE KEATON): I think we should have had sex, but there weren't enough people. We'll use the orgasmatron.

There are theories of humour that suggest that laughter happens because a perceived normality becomes incongruous, i.e., the King is wearing a nappy. In the TV series *Red Dwarf*, the last human alive is not a person of physical and mental superiority—as a eugenicist's fantasy would have it—it is Dave Lister, a slovenly, self-described bum, the lowest-ranking crew member on an abandoned spaceship. In *Sleeper*, the man who has been brought back to life after 200 years to heroically rescue citizenry from a brainwashing and 'mind reprogramming' totalitarian government is a meek-mannered clarinet player (with the 'Ragtime Rascals'), and part-owner of a health food restaurant in Greenwich Village.

Humour is also a way of dealing with unbearable situations. This is potentially why the Swedes are not famous for their comedy; what do they have to be worried about apart from long winters? I once went to an exhibition on Swiss humour at the Swiss National Museum in Zurich. The exhibition attempted to convince the audience that Swiss humour existed. I thought to myself: if you have to explain why a joke is funny, it generally isn't. In Australia, our comedy reflects the relatively small scale of our fears: fears of lawyers, of parking attendants, of finding the right plumber, and, in an international arena, of being provincial bumpkins (the two Barrys: McKenzie and Humphreys). Our strongest fears appear to involve being attacked by the native elements, including sharks, snakes, spiders, fire, the occasional collector of hitchhikers or fantasies involving invasion from the north. These fears and fantasies become horror films, such as the giant wild boar in *Razorback*.

But, Woody Allen's main concern in *Sleeper* isn't to provide therapy for an anxious society. It is to get a few cheap laughs at anyone's expense. The sobriety of sci-fi films and TV from the 1940s, '50s and '60s provides an easy target. However, the main thing you realise when watching *Sleeper* is that the gags are not about science fiction, they are about the dreams and discontent of modernity. This is a reminder that science fiction is an inherently modernist project: it is a story of utopia and its evil twin, dystopia. It is not a coincidence that the period of 'high' modernism (1940s/'50s/'60s) is paralleled by the heyday of science fiction.

Science fiction pushes modern life into spacey and futuristic extremes. This allows us to reflect upon our present situation, and to ponder where we might be heading. There is a scene in *Sleeper* where Miles is offered a seat on a 'futuristic' (i.e., modernist) chair, a singular S-bend thread of steel that resembles a chair in shape but is 10cm wide. Miles tries to sit down but instantly falls off. On the second effort, he manages to balance his body on the swaying thin piece of metal with his legs tucked up against his body, resembling a parrot on a thin branch. This brilliant scene is reminiscent of Jacques Tati's masterpieces of modern-world parody, *Playtime* (1967) and *Mon Oncle* (1958).

'The Future Lies Ahead'—Mort Sahl, 1958

Once he gets over the initial shock of not being alive for 200 years, Miles is cynically ambivalent about the future into which he has been thrust. Luna, who swings from passionate support of the totalitarian status quo (cue Yuppie) to revolutionary activist, is perplexed by his *laissez faire* attitude toward important societal concerns:

> LUNA: And you also don't believe that the political systems work? And you don't believe in God, huh, right? So then, what do you believe in?
> MILES: Sex and death; two things that come once in my lifetime. But at least after death you're not nauseous.

In *Sleeper*, Allen uses science fiction to suggest that even if there might be a totalitarian government that wipes our brains in the future, or potentially a paradise where everybody reaches enlightened nirvana via new technologies (or a return to 'nature'), either way, there will still be morons. There will still be people who just want to fit in, who follow a cause for the sake of following a cause, who are convinced they know better than others, or who are deluded enough to think they know the answer. In short, if humans exist, the stupidity of humanity exists.

Miles uncovers a Volkswagen Beetle that has been hidden in a cave for 200 years. He read aloud a bumper sticker stuck to the front of the vehicle:

> MILES: 'Register Commies, Not Guns.'
> LUNA: What does that mean? What?
> MILES: Oh, he was probably a member of the National Rifle Association. They were a group that helped criminals get guns so they could shoot citizens. It was a public service.

Sleeper was written in 1973. Thirty years have passed and we are still the same clueless idiots. If we weren't able to laugh, we would cry. It is best not to take life too seriously.

Notes

1 *Sleeper*, dir. Woody Allen, prod., Rollins-Joffe Productions, USA, 1973.

2 Oscar Wilde, 'Lady Windemere's Fan' (1892), in William Tydeman (ed.), *Wilde: Comedies* (Macmillan: Basingstoke and London, 1982), 113.

The coolest old tape worms never talk direct

Soda Jerk

Please note: No original text has been deployed in this cut-up treatise on the radical politics of the cut in The Nova Trilogy *of William S. Burroughs.*

Listen all you boards, syndicates and governments of the earth. And you powers behind what filth deals consummated in what lavatory to take what is not yours. To sell the ground from unborn feet forever.[1] Man has placed his token on every stone. Every word, every image, is leased and mortgaged.[2] It is obese. It has reached its limits, its maximum.[3] Now you and this cesspool you call a television station, and your people who wallow around in it, your viewers who watch you do it, they're rotting us away from the inside.[4]

The border between social reality and science fiction, social fiction and science reality, is an optical illusion.[5] Images are more real than anyone could have supposed.[6] If real is what you can feel, smell, taste and see, then 'real' is simply electrical signals interpreted by your brain.[7] Therefore whatever appears on the television screen emerges as raw experience for those who watch it. Therefore television is reality, and reality is less than television.[8] You are a programmed tape recorder set to record.[9]

The Nova Mob[10] keeps this tired old show on the road.[11] The board is a group representing big money who intend to takeover and monopolize[12] the Reality Studio.[13] Yes we know the front men and women in this organization, but they are no more than that…a façade… tape recorders…the operators are *not there*.[14] At any given time recorders fix the nature of absolute need and dictate[15] our sense of the past, present and future.[16]

All that was needed was an unending series of victories over your own memory. 'Reality Control', they called it.[17]

The basic nova technique is very simple:[18] If all records told the same tale—then the lie passed into history and became truth.[19] Suppose I make a recording of the conversation, alter and falsify the recording, and play the altered recording back to the two actors. If my alterations have been successfully and skillfully applied[20] the two actors will remember the altered recording.[21] 'Who controls the past', ran the Party slogan, 'controls the future: who controls the present controls the past'.[22]

This is obviously one aspect of a big picture…what looks like a carefully worked out blueprint[23] to falsify, misrepresent, misquote, rule out of consideration as a priori ridiculous, or simply ignore or blot out of existence: data, books, discoveries that they consider prejudicial to establishment interest.[24] Now you may well ask whether we can straighten out this mess to the satisfaction of any life forms involved, and my answer is this:[25]

> Their Immortality Cosmic Consciousness and Love is second-run grade-B shit.[26] Reality Film is the dreariest entertainment ever presented to a captive audience.[27] And you can see that the marks are wising up, standing around in sullen groups, and that mutter gets louder and louder[28]—What's this reality con?[29] Who the fuck are you and what are you doing in my image track?[30] Who monopolized Love Sex and Dream? Who monopolized Life Time and Fortune? Who took from you what is yours?[31]

It is true, what many of you have heard.[32] This machine strategy and the machine can be redirected.[33] The same technology that has constructed the audiovisual machine has put the means of configuring its products into the hands of the audience. But when two-thirds of global copyrights are in the hands of six corporations, the capacity to rework one's memories into the material symbolic form of individual testament and testimony is severely constrained. We rarely own the memories we are sold.[34]

Yeah. Well, that sounds like a pretty good deal. But I think I may have a better one.[35] The counter move is very simple.[36] If you want the world you could have in terms of discoveries and resources now in existence, be prepared to fight for that world.[37] We think of the past as being there unchangeable. Actually the past is ours to shape and change as we will.[38] The cut is the mechanism whereby[39] we transgress into the utopian terrain of time travel: back into history, forward into the future, or down into the depths of the 'now'.[40]

You are to infiltrate, sabotage and cut communications.[41] Breaking into and breaking up the film[42] creates, in this way, diverse futures, diverse times which themselves also proliferate and fork.[43] The more you run the tapes through and cut them up the less power they will have.[44] Remember you do not have to organize similar installations but merely to put enemy installations out of action or take them over—a camera and two tape recorders can cut the lines laid down by a fully equipped film studio.[45]

The experiments described here were explained and demonstrated to me by[46] William S. Burroughs.[47] But there wasn't any video then, not that people could get hold of. That was in '69.[48] The history of history-writing has come a long way since then.[49] What has happened is that the underground, and also the Nova Police, have made a breakthrough past the guards and gotten into the darkroom where the films are processed.[50] It's to do with technology, the Internet and the past that's put everything out there like an archival universe.[51]

Anything, in any medium imaginable, from any culture, which is in any way recorded and can be played back is now accessible and infinitely malleable and usable to any artist.[52] We are splintering consensual realities to test their substance: utilizing the tools of collision, collage, composition, decomposition, progression systems, random chance, juxtaposition, cut-ups, hyperdelic vision and any other method available that melts linear conceptions and reveals holographic webs and fresh spaces.[53]

Science fiction becomes the discourse best equipped to contend with this new state of things.[54] Wormholes, modes of teleportation, paranormal substances and mental powers of psychokinesis suggest that the rational behaviour of form and matter is open to infinite possibilities within the digital realm.[55] Nobody can control the whole operation. It's too complex.[56] Not even[57] Uncle Fishhook[58] understands what's going on in the system now.[59]

Without necessarily striking an alarmist or disapproving tone[60] I would like to sound a word of warning.[61] In the post-sampling post-Internet era[62] the presence of the past in the present is massively increased. But this spatialisation of time causes historical depth to drop out.[63] This leads to a tricky question[64]—how can we prevent this telescoping of cultures and styles from ending up in kitsch eclecticism, a cool Hellenism excluding all critical judgment?[65]

The key to this dilemma is in establishing processes and practices that allow us to[66] open up a space where ideas about history can be generated.[67] The cut-ups will give you new material but they won't tell you what to do with it.[68] Alongside it we will develop multiple metaphors, alternative principals of evidence, new loggias, catastrophe theories, and new tribal ways to separate our useful fictions and archetypes from useless ones.[69] It's the academic equivalent of Kurtz: the general in *Apocalypse*

Now who used unorthodox methods to achieve superior results compared with the tradition-bound US military.[70]

The crucial move today is to[71] upset the set patterns that plot the established moral and political orders of the entertainment.[72] It remains true that as soon as accident becomes a permanent possibility, history ceases to be programmable and predictable.[73] But this is not enough.[74] Tristan Tzara cutting Shakespeare sonnets up and pulling their words from hats is an exercise in randomizing. William Burroughs and Brion Gysin mixing poems in with sliced-up pages from *The New York Times* is quite another matter.[75] It generates a critique by using the material left behind by the enemy. Like jujitsu, using the weight of the enemy against himself...[76]

Listen: I call you all. Show your cards all players.[77] I offer you nothing. I am not a politician.[78] A revolution can be neither made nor stopped. The only thing that can be done is for one of several of its children to give it a direction by dint of victories.[79] Believe me when I say we have a difficult time ahead of us. But if we are to be prepared for it, we must first shed our fear of it.[80] Prisoner, come out. The great skies are open.[81] Wise up all the marks everywhere. Show them the rigged wheel of Life-Time-Fortune. Storm the Reality Studio. And re-take the universe.[82]

Notes

1 William S. Burroughs, *Nova Express* (New York: Grove Press, 1992), 3.

2 Sherrie Levine, 'Statement 1982', in David Evans (ed.), *Appropriation* (Cambridge: MIT Press, 2009), 81.

3 *Treatise of Slime and Eternity*, dir. Isidore Isou, 1951, in *Avant-Garde 2: Experimental Cinema 1928–1954*, Kino Video (2007).

4 *Videodrome*, dir. David Cronenberg, prod. Universal Studios, 1983.

5 Kodwo Eshun, *More Brilliant than the Sun* (London: Quartet Books Limited, 1999), 84.
6 Susan Sontag, *On Photography* (London: Penguin Books Ltd, 1979), 180.
7 *The Matrix*, dir. Andy Wachowski and Lana Wachowski, 1999, Warner Home Video, 2007.
8 Cronenberg, *Videodrome*, 1983.
9 William S. Burroughs, *The Ticket That Exploded* (London: Fourth Estate, 2010), 165.
10 Burroughs, *The Ticket That Exploded*, 44.
11 Burroughs, *The Ticket That Exploded*, 104.
12 Burroughs, *The Ticket That Exploded*, 108.
13 Burroughs, *Nova Express*, 59.
14 Burroughs, *The Ticket That Exploded*, 17.
15 Burroughs, *The Ticket That Exploded*, 43.
16 Arjen Mulder and Joke Brouwer, 'Introduction', in *Machine Times*, Arjen Mulder and Joke Brouwer (ed.) (Rotterdam: V2_Publishing, 2000), 5.
17 George Orwell, *Nineteen Eighty-Four* (New York: Random House USA Inc., 1998), 32.
18 William S. Burroughs and Daniel Odier, *The Job: Interviews with William S. Burroughs* (London: Penguin Books Ltd, 2008), 35.
19 Orwell, *Nineteen Eighty-Four*, 32.
20 Burroughs and Odier, *The Job*, 35.
21 Burroughs and Odier, *The Job*, 35.
22 Orwell, *Nineteen Eighty-Four*, 32.
23 Burroughs, *The Ticket That Exploded*, 16.
24 Burroughs and Odier, *The Job*, 177.
25 Burroughs, *The Ticket That Exploded*, 44.
26 Burroughs, *Nova Express*, 6.
27 Burroughs, *The Ticket That Exploded*, 116.
28 Burroughs, *Nova Express*, 14.
29 Burroughs, *The Ticket That Exploded*, 118.
30 Burroughs, *The Ticket That Exploded*, 31.
31 Burroughs, *Nova Express*, 5.

32 *Matrix Reloaded*, dir. Andy Wachowski and Lana Wachowski, Warner Home Video, 2003.
33 Burroughs, *Nova Express*, 74.
34 Victor Burgin, *The Remembered Film* (London: Reaktion Books Ltd, 2004), 110.
35 *The Matrix*.
36 Burroughs, *Nova Express*, 74.
37 Burroughs and Odier, *The Job*, 224.
38 Burroughs and Odier, *The Job*, 35.
39 Mary Ann Doane, *The Emergence of Cinematic Time: Modernity, Contingency, the Archive* (Cambridge, MA and London: Harvard University Press, 2002), 224.
40 Mulder and Brouwer, 'Introduction', *Machine Times*, 5.
41 Burroughs, *The Ticket That Exploded*, 86.
42 Burgin, *The Remembered Film*, 8.
43 Jorge Luis Borges, 'The Garden of Forking Paths', in *Labyrinths: Selected Stories and Other Writings* (New York: New Directions Publishing Corporation, 2007), 26.
44 Burroughs, *The Ticket That Exploded*, 168.
45 Burroughs, *The Ticket That Exploded*, 86.
46 Burroughs, *The Ticket That Exploded*, 167.
47 Jack Sargeant, *The Naked Lens: An Illustrated History of Beat Cinema* (London: Creation Books, 1997), 169.
48 Genesis Breyer P-Orridge, 'Throbbing Gristle Interview', in *Re/Search #4/5: A Special Book Issue* (San Francisco: V/Search Publications, 1982), 80.
49 Ellen Blumenstein, 'Andre Romao: The Vertical Stage—History, Theatre, Democracy', in *Andre Romao: The Vertical Stage* (Berlin: Künstlerhaus Bethanien GmbH, 2010), 76.
50 William Burroughs and Sylvère Lotringer, *Burroughs Live: The Collected Interviews of William S. Burroughs, 1960–1997* (Los Angeles and New York: Semiotext(e), 2001), 70.
51 Simon Reynolds in Dan Fox, 'Music', *frieze*, 140

(June–August 2011), 45.

52 Genesis Breyer P-Orridge, 'Thee Splinter Test', in Richard Metzger (ed.), *Book of Lies: The Disinformation Guide to Magick and the Occult* (New York: Disinformation Company, 2003), 33.

53 Breyer P-Orridge, 'Thee Splinter Test', *Book of Lies*, 32.

54 Scott Bukatman, 'Who Programs You? The Science Fiction of the Spectacle', in Annette Kuhn (ed.), *Alien Zone: Cultural Theory and Contemporary Science Fiction Cinema* (London and New York: Verso, 1990), 200.

55 Jose Da Silva, 'Sam Smith', in *Premier of Queensland's National New Media Art Award* (Brisbane: Gallery of Modern Art, 2008), 32.

56 Burroughs and Lotringer, *Burroughs Live: The Collected Interviews of William S. Burroughs, 1960–1997*, 81.

57 Burroughs and Lotringer, *Burroughs Live: The Collected Interviews of William S. Burroughs, 1960–1997*, 81.

58 Sylvère Lotringer and Jack Smith, 'Uncle Fishhook and the Sacred Baby Poo-poo of Art', in *Hatred of Capitalism. A Semiotext(e) Reader*, Sylvère Lotringer and Chris Kraus (eds) (Cambridge, MA: Semiotext(e)/MIT Press, 2001), 243.

59 Burroughs and Lotringer, *Burroughs Live: The Collected Interviews of William S. Burroughs, 1960–1997*, 81.

60 Simon Reynolds, *Retromania: Pop Culture's Addiction to Its Own Past* (London: Faber and Faber Ltd, 2012), 424.

61 Burroughs, *Nova Express*, 7.

62 Reynolds, *Retromania*, 420.

63 Reynolds, *Retromania*, 425.

64 Reynolds, *Retromania*, 424.

65 Nicolas Bourriaud, *Postproduction: Culture as*

Screenplay: How art reprograms the World, trans. Jeanine Herman (New York: Lukas & Sternberg, 2005), 44.

66 Bourriaud, *Postproduction*, 46.

67 Craig Baldwin in Kevin Attell, 'Leftovers/CA Redemption Value: Craig Baldwin's Found-Footage Films', *Cabinet Magazine*, No. 3 (Summer 2001).

68 Burroughs and Odier, *The Job*, 32.

69 Breyer P-Orridge, 'Thee Splinter Test', 34.

70 Simon Reynolds, 'Renegade Academia', *Sound Unbound: Sampling Digital Music and Culture* (Cambridge, MA and London: MIT Press, 2008), 171.

71 Reynolds, *Retromania*, 416.

72 Burgin, *The Remembered Film*, 8.

73 Sylviane Agacinski, *Time Passing: Modernity and Nostalgia*, trans. Jody Gladding (New York: Columbia University Press, 2003), 31.

74 Susan L. Hurley, *Justice, Luck and Knowledge* (Cambridge, MA and London: First Harvard University Press, 2003), 100.

75 Tom McCarthy, *Transmission and the Individual Remix* (Vintage Digital, 2012), eBook edition, 26.

76 Craig Baldwin in Kevin Attell, 'Leftovers/CA Redemption Value: Craig Baldwin's Found-Footage Films'.

77 Burroughs, *Nova Express*, 4.

78 Burroughs, *Nova Express*, 6.

79 'Napoleon Bonaparte Quotes', Brainy Quote: http://www.brainyquote.com/quotes/authors/n/napoleon_bonaparte.html. Accessed 22 July 2013.

80 *Matrix Reloaded*.

81 Burroughs, *Nova Express*, 4.

82 Burroughs, *Nova Express*, 59.

Black mirror, dirty infinitude

Edward Colless

> ... he shall see things not fit to be written...[1]
> —E. Ashmole, *Theatrum Chemicum Britannicum*, 1652

An ancient heresiarch in the shadowy lost world of Uqbar, recounts Adolfo Bioy Casares in casual conversation with Jorge Luis Borges, considered mirrors and copulation to be equally abominable because 'they increase the number of men'. This esoteric item, allegedly from an old entry in an *Encyclopedia Britannica*, spurs Borges's curiosity for arcana and spawns his celebrated essayistic story 'Tlön, Uqbar, Orbis Tertius'.[2] The heretic's censure sounds worthy of Leviticus; although there's no recoil here from impurity, let alone what we might diagnose to be a priestly pious disgust with the physiology of sexual intercourse. This prophet from Uqbar lucidly envisages how species expand their populations the way mirrors breed images, and it's the sanitary but phantasmagorical profiteering *ad infinitum* rather than any physical filth that makes reproduction in both modes identically, not just figuratively, abhorrent: it entails a deceptive accountancy, a laundered kind of swindle or usury behind the baroque amatory hocus-pocus.

And, of course, Uqbar is all smoke and mirrors. The geography, customs and culture of its world (and the heresiarch's quasi-Gnostic scorn for the evil nature of the created world) don't exist other than as details of a subversive metaphysical conceit inaugurated in the early seventeenth century: a plot to invent an entire new world, concocted by a secret British society of blasphemers whose vanity extended to matching the abilities of—and thus dethroning—that imposter demiurge, God the creator. An arcane plot but one which is virally dispersed through conspiratorial dynastic generations of scholars who have surreptitiously interleaved their forgeries in successive encyclopedias and in historical and philosophic literature, much in the way an urban myth accumulates its currency and supplants whatever real event triggered it.[3] Moreover, the forged history of the unreal Uqbar is itself the mirror image of its story's own baroque artistry. The formation, heritage and legacy of this exquisite secret society are all an emblematic invention by Borges himself—a metafictional plot hatched in a mirror that 'troubled the depths of a corridor in a country house', he reports, by reflecting an otherwise overlooked encyclopedia volume on a bookshelf (in which Bioy Casares searches in vain for the entry on Uqbar that he has read in another copy of the same book).

The trouble this mirror brings is the revelation that the world is the invention or inducement rather than the inventory of an encyclopedic knowledge, and this is knowledge which is little more than labyrinthine citation, appropriation, reflection and imitation populated with counterfeit beings (such as the Borges who narrates the story and his friend and collaborator, the real Bioy Casares) in a radiant mirror maze. But what consolation is there for those who comprehend their own complicity with the treachery of this simulacrum, in which metaphysical mystery is supplanted by the ironic enigmas and riddles of metafiction? In a vertiginously clever postscript to the story, Borges disowns any interest in his own fantasy even as it contaminates the real world, even as fanciful artifacts from Uqbar are reported turning up as real objects. He is distracted from this abominable contagion by devoting his retirement to a Spanish translation of Thomas Browne's stately, melancholic funerary meditations in his *Hydriotaphia* (*Urn Burial*). Little wonder that, in the multiple framed iridescent climaxes and seductive tenebrism of Uqbar's baroque *mise en abyme*, it would be heresy to suggest breaking the mirror of what should be called—using Schopenhauer's exquisite castigation—'the vanity of existence'. Heretical because this iconoclasm would entail not reforming the evil world but rather, having annulled reflection and copulation, it would mean losing the cause of the world. The end of a species transfixed in a mirror phase: the end of a humanity that regards its misrecognised self-awareness—its consciousness—as the necessary and sufficient condition for the existence of the world. In Gnostic terms, the broken 'uncreated' light released from the shattered mirror would spark a bonfire of all vanities of the eye.

Such a *gnosis*, however, is truly a lost cause. The Uqbar apocalyptic would entail not a redeeming, resplendent sublimation of the human but its dispatch toward a dark, corrupting infinitude: greater evil, even, than creation. It would require a speculative cosmological horror to unleash such a nihilistic plague, a catastrophic attractor like the dark flow now postulated to be dragging hundreds of galaxy-clusters at speeds of more than three-and-a-half million kilometres per hour in a single direction towards something indescribable in scale, gravitational power and make-up: what is pulling them might well be an inconceivably colossal, primordial structure of matter and energy born at the moment of the Big Bang but which exists exiled 'alongside' the known universe. Picturing such a dark entity (pitch dark in the terms of current astrophysics) seems more the province of a Satanic science fiction space opera than the delirious disquisitions and paradoxes of negative theology. And yet, hard to picture as it may be, there is an instrument in science fiction's repertoire of alien artifacts that commits the iconoclasm required of this type of monstrosity.

Is it that hard to picture the black Monolith from *Stanley Kubrick's 2001: A Space Odyssey*? Despite its custodial aura and sentinel-like silence, it seems also guileless, even artless and ineffectual as an object. The spoofs and tributes it occasions, simple-minded as they mostly are, capture something of the Monolith's ambiguous mystique. Montaged into tourist photos of standing stone circles and the footings of ruined archaic temples, the Monolith only discloses a self-evidently droll insinuation that was already there in the first place. One geek website, more sharply inspired, sells (with an allusion to the Japanese brand of 'Kubrick' figurines) the prank of an exciting '2001 Monolith Action Figure': an unadorned generic black plastic brick, the packaging of which dramatically advertises 'Zero Points of Articulation!'[4] Indeed, that fake sales pitch is right on the money. The hardest thing for most critics or fans of the movie to acknowledge about the Monolith is its monolithic inertia, its dumb and indifferent lack of articulation, since it seems both a black or blank hole in the film and also the old-school censor's patch concealing or, perhaps more vividly, eclipsing that nagging blind spot: something dirty, complicit with the censoring it enacts, and that induces in its devotees a fantastic compensatory allegorical significance—as well as unsustainable symbolic profundity. Inflated in reputation by its fallacious interpretation as a discrete instrumental intervention in human destiny from 'beyond the infinite' (the realm of the extraterrestrial 'gods' signposted by the movie's last chapter title), the Monolith is more like the mouth of an *oubliette*: a leering gag on the dark life and pseudo-immortality of what is tossed into the unconscious in an ancestral epoch, 'four million years ago'. 'A shaggy God story', complained one of the first generation of the movie's reviewers, disparaging *2001* for an epically bombastic religious scaffold made up of props including the Monolith, unaware of how precisely this quip actually captures the Monolith's command of deflating black comedy.[5]

Ironically, the Monolith's cultic fate as a fetish enacts the movie's thematic axiom expostulated by Kubrick and his script collaborator, science fiction novelist Arthur C. Clarke: that non-terrestrial life forms (whether intelligent or not) capable of interstellar travel would be so alien—unfamiliar, unprecedented, remote, and indecipherable—that we would not recognise them as life forms at all but would treat them as supernatural or even metaphysical entities.[6] As if under this very spell, some cineaste and fan bloggers have decoded the Monolith's flat surface as an allegory of the darkened movie screen, onto which the movie *2001* itself is projected.[7] The key to the movie's daunting transcendental enigma would be thus not an ultimately unpronounceable object of unquenchable desire that we will still futilely reach towards on our deathbed, like the surviving astronaut, but a coolly eloquent artistic credo accessible to cineaste initiates. Seen this way, the Monolith flickers as a *mise en abyme* within the movie to become a manifesto of modernist aesthetic reflexivity. It gives the labyrinth a loquacious cunning. That's clever, but posited as an intentional strategy it isn't quite convincing of a film which was exhibited originally in the curved, wrap-around anamorphic Cinerama format, rather than the flat screen it was subsequently shown on in roadshow release and later through repertory cinemas or letter-boxed on a monitor.[8]

Meanwhile, the movie's pre-production history gives an indication of the uncomfortable weirdness of this object, which makes its allegorical interpretation even less tenable. Initially developed by the art department as a black tetrahedron—a four-sided Platonic geometric solid that Clarke claimed deliberately invoked the atomic structure of carbon, while alluding to Buckminster Fuller's geodesic cells and Kepler's cosmological diagrams—versions of this prototype were tested against the set designs for the ape pit and the moon. 'Somehow', reports Clarke, 'they never looked right, and there was also the danger that they would arouse wholly irrelevant associations with the pyramids'.[9] Hardly surprising! But evidently, this particular symbolisation gave the alien artifact all-too-human legibility. Clarke's preference then turned toward an object that would be 'crystal clear', presumably lustrous as well as unfussy.[10] A transparent cube was constructed, ditched, and then Kubrick ordered a massive single three-ton slab of Lucite, a transparent new type of plastic, to be cast. But, despite the unique difficulty and considerable cost of this, it too was junked; '...banished to the corner of the studio'.[11] Curiously, the final prop used in the film is hardly mentioned in any reports on production or special effects. Also symptomatic of its peculiar status, for a prop that is so illustriously and emblematically identified with the movie, at each of its manifestations—prehistoric, historic and post-historic—the Monolith is first disclosed in extreme long shot, almost incidentally in the middle distance of the scene rather than heroically foregrounded. What made it finally suitable seems to have been its very lack of describable qualities rather than any technical, artistic, scenic or symbolic resolution. In production, it is an item overlooked; in reception, it becomes a featureless figure. It gleams, but reflects nothing. It absorbs anything. Although, that last verb is not all adequate to its obscure lack of activity. Not natural (like a crystalline mineral), nor industrial (like an engineered magnet), nor aesthetic (like a minimalist sculpture), it miraculously just appears on the set, just as it does in each of the narrative scenes: 'unmanufactured', 'unmade'. It's not by accident that the prefix on these last words carries the disconcerting ontological slippage we encounter with the term 'undead': a corpse that doesn't die. Can we be permitted to call the Monolith such a black corpse, a zombie object?

In the movie's penultimate scene located in the windowless, shadowless zone of what has been dubbed an 'eighteenth-century hotel room', the black Monolith stands impassively at the foot of the astronaut's deathbed. Impassive, but not disinterested. There is something undeniably portentous and angelic in this inexplicable advent, even if the slab looms more like a vulture than a sentinel. In this scene, not dissimilar its effect among the apes or in the moon's archaeological dig, the Monolith is as intimidating as a visitation from the angel of death or the angel of annunciation. Yet, while it seems to ceremonially superintend the evolutionary transfigurations of ape into human and then into 'overman'—a trinity Kubrick undoubtedly sourced from Nietzsche's *Also Sprach Zarathustra*—there is nothing patently providential in the Monolith's on-screen sullen manifestations. In the last shot of this hotel room sequence, the camera tracks rapidly toward the Monolith until its black surface engulfs the screen to become a backdrop of infinitely deep, unlit space in which for a moment camera movement and proportion are rendered utterly meaningless. The adamant, adamantine black depth of this Monolith is quite unlike the mystical or sacrosanct and pregnant black rectangles that occur in the spiritualising (notably, theosophical) abstraction of modernist art. For all its starkness, Malevich's black square is a solemn emblem of cosmic creation and artistic creativity. We would be mistakenly, stupidly, idealist to project this profound productivity into the stubborn gloom of the Monolith. There is black comedy with this monolith's murk but it is, no less, a horrible blackness. It is best approached as the dangerously paradoxical black mirror used by necromancers, in which we see neither reflections of our world nor ourselves but rather the conjuring of invisible creatures and unspeakable events.

Don't bother, then, looking into Malevich's or Ad Reinhardt's black squares for illumination of the Monolith since their blackness will be, in Reinhardt's reproof, 'not as black as all that'. We should turn toward objects associated irredeemably with 'black arts'; towards, for instance, the small circular black mirror used by the sixteenth-century magus and mathematician John Dee for 'skrying', for summoning angels, which he piously conducted with the mediumistic assistance of his impious, secretive, cagey collaborator and sociopathic Svengali-like muse, Edward Kelley. In his visions, Kelley's angels laboriously pointed to voluminous sequences of unintelligible glyphs constituting an Adamic, unutterable and virtually untranslatable language that Dee—fascinated by Kelley's epic transcriptions—called 'Enochian'. Improbable as these 'spiritual conferences' sound, Dee's sepulchral and unnaturally untarnished device is no legendary object, but a real thing sitting somewhat ironically in a cabinet in the Enlightenment salon of London's British Museum; there as a result of the mirror having been acquired in the late-eighteenth century by Horace Walpole for his antiquarian collection of curiosities. Walpole mistook Dee's mirror to have been made of coal. It is actually obsidian: a glassy volcanic rock that, when polished (traditionally, with bird shit), appears to be shiny yet barely reflects any discernable forms; appears to soak up light but is slick and thick as a blot of congealed sump oil. Imported to Europe by the late 1520s in the wake of Cortes's imperial conquest of Mexico among countless 'new world' treasures, the mirror has an Aztec pedigree associated with the god of sorcerers and sovereigns, Tezcatlipoca (translated as 'smoke-filled mirror', the smoke from beneath the earth), and Dee's use of it was not estranged from its original magical milieu in which devices like this—some in rectangular slab forms—were employed to conjure things from the underworld and from the unknown regions of men's hearts, from their unconscious.

Dark mirrors are conductors for this kind of divination or prophecy, and not too far from this opportunity comes the allure of commanding the 'evil eye'; and, beyond that, the invitation to necromancy. Even the innocuously fey 'Claude glass' has a demonic ambiance. Named after the seventeenth-century artist Claude Lorrain, this was a pocket-sized portable shallow convex mirror with a dark tint or tain used by painters and Grand Tourist connoisseurs—primarily throughout the eighteenth and early nineteenth centuries—as a device to abstract their view onto a landscape, ingeniously rendering the prospect in the narrow tonality and compositional conventions of picturesque aesthetic sensibility associated with Claude. Far less cumbersome than the perspective instruments used by Brunelleschi, Durer or Vermeer for linear perspective, use of the Claude glass however required a particular perversion of vision in its handling. Holding the mirror aloft, one turned one's back on the actual view in order to stare into the palm of one's hand, which is held to the side of the shoulder over which the scenery is being reflected. Thus, to use the Claude glass properly, the artist or tourist would inevitably strike the distinctively affected pose of a dandy in a suspended tableau of salutation, to no one. The connotations of this pose could not be further from the circumstance of a character whose viewing platform seems so similar: a slave chained up in the shadows of Plato's cave. Moreover, as Arnauld Maillet has sardonically suggested in his subtle investigation of the Claude glass, this posture embodies a peculiar form of vanity. Transfixed in a mode of auto-hypnosis, this is an aesthetic sensibility configured in the gesture of single-handed self-pleasuring.[12] Yet this is also a macabre auto-eroticism since it acts out the seductive *memento mori* motif in medieval Christian *vanitas* iconography of a deceptive maiden luxuriously looking into the mirror she holds up in front of her, to escape the frame of her pictorial space by locking into the viewer's eyes—a *vanitas* embodying a most persuasive reprimand and incitement to iconoclasm because it so prolifically reflects the narcissistic misidentification founding the ego.

But perhaps the most pertinent assessment of the black Monolith's monstrous black art lies entangled in the linguistic contortions of St Paul's famous 'dark glass' in his first epistle to the Corinthians (13: 12): 'For now we see through a glass, darkly; but then face to face: now I know in part; but then shall I know even as also I am known'. In this *King James Version*, its most consolatory expression, Paul's 'glass' sounds more like a description of the eye's lens than an accusatory (let alone macabre) *vanitas*. Modern, prosaic translations reduce the elusive figuration of the glass to the irresolution of an image, to 'a poor reflection as in a mirror' or the chastened similitude of 'a dim image'.[13] The verse in the *KJV* concerns hindrance to a consummation of soulful knowledge and obstruction to Grace, the diagnostic vocabulary and erotic overtones of which evidently have Platonic ancestry. What causes the darkness is the innate density, or sensuous partiality, or selfish sensibility of the corporeal body. And because mirrors are habitually associated with the duplicity and sinister luxuries of a devil, corrupting self-knowledge and self-scrutiny with the sensuous partiality of egotism, most Christian biblical criticism of this Pauline 'glass' has endowed it with the moral treachery of the mirror. Adam Clarke's conscientiously Methodist commentary on *Corinthians* published in his monumental 1817, six-thousand page biblical philology unashamedly appeals to his own sense of 'rhetorical suitability' for understanding the source Greek word, *esoptrou*, as a 'mirror': 'The word is not used for a glass to look through;' he insists, 'nor would such an image have suited the apostle's design'.[14] Any association with transparency, he adds, would also be inappropriate to the polished metallic or mineral surfaces used for mirrors in antiquity.

But in a tangential concluding remark Clarke identifies Paul's 'glass' also with an Aramaic term which, although he doesn't mention this, would presumably be pre-classical rabbinic and Talmudic in usage and which denotes a medium ambiguously reflective as well as translucent: *aspaclaria*. A revelation of the will of God, in clear and express terms, is called [by the Jewish writers] *aspaclaria maira*, a clear or lucid glass or *specular*. An obscure prophecy they termed *aspaclaria dela naharia*, 'A specular which is not clear'.[15] Ezekiel's vision of God in the whirlwind would be an instance of the latter: an obscure image, but not untrustworthy or marred for that. Only Moses, in the canonical literature and according to the Jerusalem Talmud, uniquely experiences the former.[16] He sees 'face to face'. But if one exceptional instance of this *specular* is purely transparent and all others are dense or cloudy this doesn't exactly make the medium reliable. Moreover, this rabbinical usage of *specular* would respect the Deuteronomist author's verdict that the voice of God had primacy as the font of lucid divine revelation. Visualisations of God are necessarily obscure, inasmuch as they are perplexing and esoteric (even if naturalistic or anthropomorphic), so as to shield the prophet transcribing them from the transgression of idolatry associated with paganism. Through a Jewish hermeneutic of theophany not at all inimical to nor excluded by Paul, the Pauline 'glass' in Clarke's philological sidestep is thus identified with prophetic vision that remains a riddle (*ena aenigma*) rather than a blur or storm or conflagration. And this is not only Clarke's opinion. 'The *aenigma* of the Apostle of the Gentiles', explains Jurgis Baltrušaitis in his iconological study of the mirror, notably in science fiction,

> is not a confusion but an encrypted figuration that signifies one thing by another. It is a catoptric prodigy enabling one to see the invisible and the immaterial

> images revealed in it, which are transfigured and vanish at the least inflection of the metallic surfaces.[17]

With this formula the dark, clouded vision of prophecy can be treated and cured by optical adjustment, in effect by an optometrist's prescription. Divination is a procedure of decipherment like decoding a cryptic crossword clue, and any obscurity in its mediumistic process is clarified by getting the right angle or enlightening perspective, rather like looking at a daguerreotype or perhaps at Freud's 'mystic writing pad'.[18] There is no dark magic, no impenetrable secret, to this, only a solution to a problem, which is disguised in the technique of a magic trick delighting the innocent and gullible or luring those susceptible to hypnotic captivation. Not a magic mirror, continues Baltrušaitis caustically, but the magic of mirrors.[19] In cinematic terms, particularly for science fiction cinema, this might be the province of optical 'special effects' which, surely, involves a mode of dandyism and vanity comparable to the hypnoid aesthetic dispensation of the Claude glass. Keep in mind, however, that the special nature of the cinematic 'special effect' is that it is spectacularly illusionistic. It ceremonially draws attention to itself, like the posturing required of a magic act, as a heightened instance of cinematic illusion that makes it all the more obviously deceptive. And yet, our judgment on its success requires assessing a correlative capacity for deceiving us into believing it to be real—that's to say, believing it to be indistinguishable from the rest of the deception that constitutes the movie. (After all, any movie, in its entirety, is *ipso facto* a 'special effect'; although acknowledging this turns the entire movie into a black mirror.) The aesthetic specialty of the 'special effect' assumes a surplus of deceit or unreality, along with a counterbalance surfeit of reality and conviction. We see through its technique, but darkly. Naturalistic illusion and a willful suspension of disbelief are not what inspire this peculiar vision. The 'special effect' is not a riddle. And it cannot be decontaminated as a catoptric technique, no matter how prodigal. It is instead, and in the archaic sense of the word, prodigious. Monstrous. Anomalous. Infectious. Satanic. Its pathology should be diagnosed as 'unnaturalism'.

This is how the black Monolith appears, both on the set and on the screen. A special effect worthy of staging prophecy. But what is crucial to its prodigious obscurity is that it is untrustworthy, not simply enigmatic or allegorical. Its advent is the entrance of a black angel: and not the angel of Annunciation but, to coin a mad term, a Satanic angel of 'Unnunciation'.[20] Perhaps this was the angel conjured from an infernal unconscious by Dr Dee's obsidian mirror, from the telluric blackness of a mirror that can never be lit no matter how much light falls upon it; and an angel which, through its unintelligible glyphic communiqués, would undo the primacy of the inception of God and the world in the luminous word of Creation:... *fiat lux et facta est lux*.[21] Accordingly, the 'unmade' complexion of the black Monolith may bear comparison with the Gnostic speculation of an 'uncreated' light, which lies as far beyond the universe of Creation as does the monstrous attractor, exiled from our contemporary universe, which is the source of a cosmically catastrophic 'dark flow'. And yet we should equally acknowledge that the blackness of this monolith has, strictly speaking, nothing to do with light of any kind or its incidental deprivation.

To pursue this weird qualification, we need to turn not to the Gnosticism that abominates the mirrors of Uqbar, but to the descent of an even more arcane metaphysics—and, eventually, an even more abominable conjecture—developed by the Neo-Platonist philosopher Plotinus. In his *Enneads*, Plotinus differentiates two modes of light in order to elucidate his ontological doctrine of emanations: there is light that is a body, identical with it and essential to it as unchanging, unmoved substance; and there is light that shines from that body and illuminates other bodies as changing images. Only the latter is accessible to the senses; that's to say, is visible. Even staring directly at the sun we still would not see its substance but only its image. Plotinus's medieval Latinate commentators (notably Robert Grosseteste and Albertus Magnus in the thirteenth century) provide us with a surprisingly more familiar—even contemporary—lexicon for this partition, derived from the Arabic Plotinian natural philosophy of Ibn Sina and al-Kindi, and recruited in service to Christian theology.[22] *Lux* is the primordial substance, source and form of Creation which, because it cannot be seen, is singularly obscure, hermetic and opaque. This is the light of God, the plenum, the Good: identical in essence to each of them. It is different to illumination, luminance, to the sunlight or moonlight that radiates the bodies of planets and people. This *lumen* is multiple and partial and distributed across all scales of the universe, as mass and energy clot into fireball pools and nebulae or condense into auroral bands, or flare in meteoric streaks, or shimmer on scurrying feathers beneath a jungle canopy. We perceive its radiance as splendor. We experience its deprivation as shadow, as dusky gloom, as nighttime, as the cold darkness in deep space or in the depths of an ocean trench or a subterranean dungeon.

Darkness is most commonly thought of as the obscuring of *lumen*, even when taken to its coldest and most remote pole. But as Alexander Galloway points out, there is a corresponding darkness for *lux*. And if *lux* is identified with Being as the source of the world and Creation, then its shadow realm, its obscuring blackness, is the extinction of Being. 'Such is the infinite darkness of the abyss', says Galloway, 'the void and the vacuum, the darkness of catastrophe and cataclysm. It is a cosmological blackness, the black of Satan, the black of absolute evil, the black of nonbeing.'[23] Nonbeing, however, sounds too consoling for this infinite darkness, since this infinitude is dirty, obscene, and far more abominable than the hygienic mirrored reproduction of men and the world. The apocalyptic eclipse of *lux* is the world 'unmade', the world like a zombie corpse, the world lost with the unaccountable advent of the black Monolith. 'Extinction', remarks Eugene Thacker in an exquisite dictum, 'is the non-being of life that is not death'.[24] And yet, again, the 'non' of 'non-being' negates with almost too much facility and composure. Awkward as it sounds, 'un-being' might show us what the horrible, dirty blackness of the Monolith occasions, even if this is a thing unfit to be written.

Notes

1 'In fine, if any man be so blest as to discover and availe our *Diana*, he shall finde and confesse that he was beholding to Naturall Magick for directions at the *Beginning*, *Midle* and *End*; and when it is wrought up to his highest degree of Perfection, *he shall see things not fit to be written*; for (may I aver it with awfull Reverence) *Angelicall wisdom* is to be obteyned by it.' Elias Ashmole, *Theatrum Chemicum Brittanicum Containing Severall Poeticall Pieces of our Famous English Philosopher*, who have written the Hermetique Mysteries in their owne Ancient Language ('Annotations'), (London: J. Gismonde for Nath. Brooke, 1652), 447.

2 Jorge Luis Borges, 'Tlön, Uqbar, Orbis Tertius', trans. James E. Irby, in Donald A. Yates and James E. Irby (eds), *Labyrinths* (Harmondsworth: Penguin Books, 1970), 27. A page later, Borges's narrator states that

Bioy Casares calls him from Buenos Aires with a copy of the encyclopedia entry in front of him to read out the correct citation: 'For one of those gnostics, the visible universe was an illusion or (more precisely) a sophism. Mirrors and fatherhood are abominable because they multiply and disseminate that universe.'

3 Urban legends are generated as modern folklore (requiring narrative example, belief in the possibility of an event, and a degree of moral or practical lesson), disseminated not only through the networks of oral culture but also through mass media channels. See Jan Harold Brunvard, *The Vanishing Hitchhiker: Urban Legends and their Meanings* (London: Pan Books, 1983), 15–25.

4 See Sam Biddle, '*2001: A Space Odyssey* action figure will leave your other toys in cosmic awe', 2010, *Gizmodo*: http://gizmodo.com/5668811/2001-a-space-odyssey-monolith-action-figure-will-leave-your-other-toys-in-cosmic-awe. Accessed 14 April 2013.

5 John Simon's phrase is quoted in one of the few reviews among the movie's first generation of responses that not only intuited but also enjoyed Kubrick's snarling Swiftian satire: F.A. Macklin, 'The Comic Sense of *2001*', reprinted from *Film Comment* (Winter, 1969) in Stephanie Schwam (ed.), *The Making of 2001: A Space Odyssey* (New York: The Modern Library, 2000), 183. Disappointed early reviewers had noticed the characterless, sexless, unmotivated, unmemorable—and in three cases, inactive—human cast, but usually objected that this de-dramatised tone was due to failure by an inept, negligible and didactic script ostensibly withered under the smothering hubris of directorial grand designs. Early enthusiasts for the movie's psychedelic special effects and their purported Aquarian-age religiosity were equally incapable of comprehending

that, as Macklin had noticed, this barren emotional background of human life and death was expert comic artifice, highlighting the irony of computer HAL's inscrutable, softly spoken, poignantly jealous sexual villainy and the pathos of his demise. The Monolith's comic artifice, however, still remains generally unsounded.

6 Kubrick's most eloquent and extended presentation of this proposition was in his 1968 *Playboy* interview, reprinted as Eric Norden, 'Playboy Interview: Stanley Kubrick', in Gene D. Philips (ed.), *Stanley Kubrick: Interviews* (Mississippi: University Press of Mississippi, 2001), 47–74. With little eloquence and even less intelligence, this was also presented as the prefatory criterion for the pseudo-archaeology of Erich von Däniken's notorious first two books *Chariots of the Gods*? and *Gods from Outer Space*, both coincidentally released in 1968, co-authored with screenwriter Wilhelm Roggersdorf. Von Däniken proposed that famous epiphanic episodes in the archaeological record (iconographic) and ancient religious literature were depictions of 'close encounters' with extraterrestrial life, but decodable in his ludicrously prosaic, literal terms. The Biblical chariot or throne of God, for instance, was an alien spacecraft misrecognised in the lens of ancient mythology and theosophy. There is a ludicrous, but beguilingly innocent, anachronism in von Däniken's proposition: that in 1968 such ancient imagery of alien tech geared for near light-speed interstellar travel could be uncovered behind its mythological guise and identified through its resemblance to contemporary NASA tech of the Mercury, Gemini and Apollo space programs (which at the stage of von Däniken's writing had put astronauts only into orbital space).

7 For instance, Rob Ager, 'Chapter 2: The meaning

of the monolith' in *Kubrick: and beyond the cinema frame. An in-depth analysis of 2001: A Space Odyssey* (2008): http://www.collativelearning.com/2001%20chapter%202.html. Accessed 27 April 2013.

8 The Cinerama process launched in 1952 required three synchronised cameras shooting on 65mm, projected onto three screens with a ratio of 1:2.59. *2001* was shot in Super-Panavision (1:2.21 ratio) anamorphic 70mm as a single projection to allow for flat screen roadshow release after its initial run in Cinerama theatres internationally. Thomas E. Brown, '*2001*'s Original Projection Format', *Visual Memory*, http://www.visual-memory.co.uk/amk/doc/brown1.html. Accessed 5 July 2013.

9 Arthur C. Clarke, 'Monoliths and Manuscripts', in Schwam (ed.), *The Making of 2001: A Space Odyssey*, 62.

10 Clarke, 'Monoliths and Manuscripts', 66.

11 Clarke, 'Monoliths and Manuscripts', 62. And, one might mischievously suggest, if the Monolith was intended as a slyly reflexive rebus of transcendent directorial intelligence why was this second pre-production manifestation discarded: the cube-brick?

12 Arnauld Maillet, *The Claude Glass: The Use and Meaning of the Black Mirror in Western Art*, trans. Jeff Fort (New York: Zone Books, 2009), 61–65. Maillet proposes a neoclassical genealogy of the 'perversion' in this gesture: antique commentators such as Seneca prosecute the mirror, which ought to be used to gain knowledge, for turning toward luxury and voluptuousness, as if the mirror had been invented solely for 'touching up one's looks' (Seneca, cited 71). The absorptive intensity of the hand's clasp of the mirror in luxurious aesthetic distraction might, we could speculate, also correlate with the contemporaneous (eighteenth- and early nineteenth-century) iconog-

raphy of feminine subjectivity affectively typified in sophisticated, literate auto-erotic reverie induced from the leisure of private, secular reading. Carried away by a Romantic sensibility, these female readers are frequently depicted relaxing into a reflective pause from reading, the book resting in their lap or held beside a hip, with a finger sensuously inserted between the book's unfurled pages to mark a place.

13 *The Bible: New International Version* and *Good News Bible* respectively.

14 Adam Clarke, *New Testament of Our Lord and Saviour Jesus Christ; containing text taken from the most correct copies of the present authorized translation including the marginal readings and parallel texts with a commentary and critical notes. Volume II* (London: J. Butterworth & Son, 1817), n.p., see notes to 1 Corinthians, Chapter 13, Verse 12.

15 Clarke, *New Testament*, n.p.

16 Clarke's scholarship on this passage, despite his notorious anti-Semitic inflection and contempt for Jewish mysticism elsewhere, is actually not that divergent from some current Jewish historical theology: for a comprehensive study of the linguistic usages of the 'specular' in visionary experiences composed in medieval Kabbalistic literature and their rabbinic and apocalyptic sources, see Elliot R. Wolfson, *Through a Speculum That Shines: Vision and Imagination in Medieval Jewish Mysticism* (Princeton: Princeton University Press, 1994).

17 Jurgis Baltrušaitis, *Le mirroir: Essai sur une légende scientifique: révélations, science-fiction et fallacies* [1978], cited and translated in Maillet, *The Claude Glass*, 70.

18 Sigmund Freud, 'A Note Upon the "Mystic Writing Pad"' (1925), in James Strachey (ed.), *The Standard Edition of the Complete Psychological Works of*

Sigmund Freud Vol. 19 (London: Hogarth Press, 1974), 227–32.

19 Maillet, *The Claude Glass*, 70.

20 On 'unnunciation' see Edward Colless, 'Transdisciplinary Aesthetics: An Occultation and Occultism', 2011, *Transdisciplinary Arts Research: University of New South Wales*: http://blogs.unsw.edu.au/tiic/leaf/leafrewire/darren-tofts-being-indisciplined/leafisea/edward-colless-transdisciplinary-aesthetics-an-occultation-and-occultism/. Accessed 21 July 2013.

21 *Latin Vulgate Bible*: Genesis 1, 3. '…let there be light, and there was light.'

22 'Plotinus's conception of unity and multiplicity as the root to the medieval distinction between *lux* and *lumen*.' Yael Riazman-Kedar, *Studies in the History of Philosophy and Science*, Vol. 37 (2006), 379–97.

23 Alexander Galloway, 'What is a Hermeneutic Light?' in Ed Keller, Nicola Masciandaro, and Eugene Thacker (eds), *Leper Creativity: Cyclonopedia Symposium* (New York: Punctum Books, 2012), 171.

24 Eugene Thacker, *In the Dust of this Planet: Horror of Philosophy, Vol. 1* (Winchester: Zero Books, 2011), 126.

This project has been assisted by the Australian Government through the Australia Council for the Arts, its arts funding and advisory body, for their London Writers' Residency in conjunction with ACME Studios, London.

Telepathic communication in *Planet of the Apes*

Lauren Bliss

Do not be fooled by the comic façade of the *Planet of the Apes*, at least the first five films from 1968 until 1973—they have much to say about communication and language.[1] The films tell the story of a civilisation of intelligent apes living several thousand years in the future, after a nuclear war in our own time almost destroys the entirety of the human race. The only humans left are mute brutes, and the apes, conversely, have been anthropomorphised, a process exacerbated and parodied by the fact that they are obviously human actors dressed up in ape costumes.

This blending of human with ape lends the films their comic value. Humans as humans have sexual relationships with humans dressed as apes; humans dressed as apes have sexual relationships with each other; humans as humans acting like apes have sexual relationships with humans as humans; and a human dressed as an ape gives birth to a real chimpanzee. The incessant threat of apocalypse seems to be a simple reference to the Cold War and the threat of nuclear catastrophe. Similarly, the viewer may experience delight at the sight of Charlton Heston kneeling before the broken Statue of Liberty, the irony dripping off his NRA card, as he screams: 'You idiots, you blew it up!' However, to call these films a reflection, a metaphorical mirror image of history, or an ironic take on the nature of the human, is to miss the point. The series must be read in terms of its continuity or rather repetitiveness: each film more or less repeats the same story. This repetitiveness forms an unlikely telepathic narrative, a message received from some distant Other, which occurs on multiple levels: of film to film, of the human to human-as-ape, and of human in the past to the human in the future.

Telepathy is the transference of affective and cognitive phenomena from discrete beings at a distance. It primarily refers to prophesy, that is, to what will happen rather than what has already passed. Freud cautiously made mention of the possibility of telepathic communication in a number of essays and lectures.[2] He was quick to insist that telepathy in the occultic sense, as a communicative operation to merely confirm belief, is neurotic fantasy.[3] However to consider it as he did, as extrasensory thought-transference, via the unconscious marked by unfulfilled desire and necessary repression, as a manifestation of something that then really takes place, is to think through the connectivity and disconnectivity that plagues everyday encounters with the world.[4] Telepathy in this sense is 'the desire to affect or feel *while* maintaining distance'.[5] For Freud, the possibility of telepathic communication lies in the distanced relationship between two communicators. In psychoanalytic terms this is the analyst and analysand: 'the analyst must turn his own unconscious like a receptive organ towards the transmitting unconscious of the patient'.[6] However, as I will suggest, in the case of *Planet of the Apes*, telepathic communication occurs within the structural relationship of film to film.

Telepathy brings out what was previously repressed. According to Freud, it

> teaches us that what has been communicated by this means of induction from one person to another is not merely a chance piece of indifferent knowledge. It shows that an extraordinarily powerful wish harboured by one person and standing in a special relation to his consciousness has succeeded, with the help of a second person, in finding conscious expression in a slightly disguised form—just as the invisible end of the spectrum reveals itself to the senses on a light-sensitive plate as a coloured extension.[7]

In psychoanalytic thinking, repression is maintained by the drives. Through the structure of the unconscious, telepathy and repression are inextricably linked in an intra-subjective loop. Telepathy cannot occur if there is a direct line between receiver and sender. A measure of distance, however material or immaterial, needs to be maintained. What is revealed is a form of desire, at once both necessarily repressed and non-repressed. To consider telepathy in this sense is not to consider it as the opposite of repression, but as its enigmatic return.

The telepathy we see operating throughout the *Planet of the Apes* is conditional on the repetitive structure of each film. In each case, the telepathic message is one of impending destruction that is delivered by the Other (whether by human, ape-as-human, or human-as-ape). The destruction is denied, the apocalypse takes place and the narrative then resets itself in some other time period so that the game can begin again. The first film opens with a cunning restaging of the conventional Oedipal drama, recalling the psychoanalytic account of the entry into language. Some years into the future, things are running smoothly on board a spaceship travelling at the speed of light, until a beautiful female astronaut dies in unusual circumstances and the three remaining men on board, Taylor, Landon and Dodge (Charlton Heston, Robert Gunner and Jeff Burton) crash-land their spaceship on an unknown planet (later revealed as Earth). Discovering themselves in the year 3978 AD, the trio embark on a quest to return back to their own time. Exploration leads to an encounter with a species of intelligent apes who treat humans in much the same way we tend to treat primates now: as subjects defined by their taxonomical or scientific status.

The problem that the astronauts encounter is that the humans of the future cannot speak; they are mute like the apes we know today. The astronauts' attempts to communicate challenge both the apes' perceived superiority and their definition of humans as inferior, leading to brutal violence. The apes capture, imprison and perform operations on the humans—medical, legal, scientific and psychological—with tragic results; one is lobotomized and the other killed in a battle. Only Taylor (Heston) manages to survive by befriending two researcher-apes, Cornelius and Zira (Roddy McDowall and Kim Hunter), who hide him from public view. But once his ability to communicate is made public in the apes' court of law, and he openly challenges the definitional status of the human (the judge cries out during the tribunal: 'Humans don't speak, this is heresy!'), he is threatened with lobotomy and forced to flee.

Communication between disparate beings, alongside the impossibility of representing teleological ends, is thus the subject of these films. Two motifs are important in this sense: the scarecrows that sit at the border of the apes' civilisation, attempting to ward off the Other; and the broken Statue of Liberty embedded in the sand in the so-called 'forbidden zone'. This is the place where New York City once stood, a site now reduced to nothing more than a beach, a series of caves and a ruined subway. The apes seem to fear this place not because of the radioactive fallout, but because it represents the Other of the past that haunts the borders of their civilisation. The forbidden zone is akin to the unconscious as the locus of destruction, a spectre that disturbs each subsequent film. It is also what incites the possibility of telepathic communication.

Taylor escapes to the forbidden zone and hides until the apes eventually catch up with him in the second film, *Beneath the Planet of the Apes* (1970). In this story Taylor and his mute, human-as-ape girlfriend Nova (Linda Harrison) encounter a group of telepathic humans—descendants of fallout survivors—who are guarding a leftover nuclear bomb. When the apes find the humans, a battle ensues. Nova disrupts the battle by screaming her first word, 'Taylor!' This is one moment of telepathic rupture in the narrative; it anticipates what is about to occur without preventing anything. Repression returns, the apocalypse recurs, the bomb is detonated by a mortally wounded Taylor, and the earth is destroyed.

Additional sequels reverse and scramble the narrative procedure, but the spectre of destruction remains the same. The problem of a species almost, but not quite, lost—a species of human and human-as-ape continuously under threat—is repeated throughout the series as the protagonists, in their various forms, reproduce and travel into different time periods, always skirting the real apocalypse through reproduction and time travel. What was destroyed cannot be returned to and the humans-as-apes and humans-as-humans act out the same structure over and over until, in the fifth and final film *Battle for the Planet of the Apes*, the destructive ends of the previous four films are diluted into a caricature (figured as a tear rolling down the face of a statue of the dead ape leader, Caesar).

Freud believed that telepathy could not occur without a 'conscious bridge'. He used the structural analogies of the light prism and the telephone, as well as the relationship between analyst and analysand, to illustrate his thesis on the subject. In film, it is the writing of early cinema theorist Jean Epstein who best outlines how the cinema is 'psychic', or an agent of telepathy. Epstein argued that the camera, as a machine which records and projects with exact likeness, created an immaterial distance between what was on screen and the mind of the viewer; resulting in the viewer perceiving their notion of self through the Other. 'I had never been seen this way before and I regarded myself with horror. I understood those dogs that bark and the apes that fly into a rage in front of the mirror. I thought myself to be one way, and perceiving myself to be something else shattered all the vain notions I had acquired. Each of these mirrors presented me with a perverse view of myself, an inaccurate image of the hopes I had. These spectating mirrors forced me to see myself with their indifference, their truth.'[8] Telepathy in the cinema is not only the revelation of some future event, but a deeper interrogation of what was repressed, what was unknown but nonetheless always there. As film theorist Nicole Brenez reminds us: 'In the same way that Freud turned telepathy into a prototype to investigate the various states of the image (from the passing of an image as memory to image as volition, affective prospecting), thought transmission [for Epstein] constitutes an archaic model of choice used to express the symbolic powers of the cinema'.[9] In this sense, the telepathic powers of the cinema exist not as a reordering or restructuring of signifiers, but as what could paradoxically be termed as a *reminder of the unknown*, or by what Brenez calls the exhuming of 'the unconscious of the referent and the effect of its transposition into a motif; cinema is a "photo-electric psychoanalysis".'[10]

Insofar as telepathy can be considered as an anachronism, the deliberate perceptual ruptures and scrambling of the repetitive narrative fractures the possibility of direct one-to-one communication. These are the telepathic moments where what was repressed is revealed. If mainstream cinema seeks to avoid the disconnectivity of telepathic communication through the creation of seamless image worlds, then telepathy attempts to disrupt this process by exposing the structural 'break' at the heart of the cinematic apparatus. Put another way, as the film repeats itself—albeit with a number of structural reversals—it gives rise to an attempt to communicate telepathically, somewhat ironically, at the expense of an occultic belief in film to confirm and seal-over some aspect of reality for us.

Following Epstein's comment on the fractured image of himself on the cinema screen, when taken as a series, *Planet of the Apes* materialises the disconnectivity between film and subject, between film and film, between human and ape and between human and human. Its telepathy lies within the connection that this causes, the continuity—cinematised as the film repeats itself over and over. But through their particular figuration of human reasoning through the repressed spectre of the ape, the individual films also make a mockery of how the relations between communication and language are perceived in conventional legal, scientific and anthropological conceptions of one-to-one communication. As telepathy is encountered in the form of a message from the Other (the speaking ape, the speaking human), it must be denied and the Other destroyed.

Should the return to destruction be cast as crudely nihilistic? It appears to me that the figure of the apocalypse exists as a necessary negation, allowing what was constructed as critique to be destroyed so as to further interrogate the affective valences involved. Telepathy—particularly as Freud and Epstein see it—can challenge our thinking and dissolve the falsehood of faith and confirmation, a falsehood regularly deployed in the approach taken by Hollywood to communication and language. To investigate telepathy is thus to 'avoid robbing the mind and spirit of their still unrecognized characteristics...to exclude the wishes of mankind from material reality'.[11] As Dr. Zaius reminds us of the human, '[H]is wisdom must walk hand in hand with his idiocy. His emotions must rule his brain. He must be a warlike creature who gives battle to everything around him, even himself.'

Notes

1 The Tim Burton remake (2001) and sequel *Rise of the Planet of the Apes* (dir. Rupert Wyatt, 2011) are not

telepathic. These films seem to deliberately block the possibility of telepathy, likely as a result of the power of the original five films. This is something I discuss with reference to Hollywood later in this essay.

2 See Sigmund Freud, 'Psychoanalysis and Telepathy' (1921/41) in James Strachey and Anna Freud (eds) *The Standard Edition of the Complete Psychological Works of Sigmund Freud Vol. 18: 'Beyond the Pleasure Principle', 'Group Psychology' and Other Works* (Vintage, London 2001), 177–93; and Sigmund Freud, 'Dreams and Telepathy' (1922), *SE 18*, 197–220. See also Roger Luckhurst, *The Invention of Telepathy* (New York: Oxford University Press, 2002), 269–72.

3 Sigmund Freud, 'Psychoanalysis and Telepathy' [1921/41] *SE 18*, 177–93.

4 The importance of telepathy in terms of love and connectivity is explored by Melbourne-based artists Sean Peoples and Veronica Kent in their ongoing work *The Telepathy Project*. This essay is partially inspired by the encounter I had with the artists, which involved an artistic interrogation of the subject of primates and communication (a screening of television show *Monkey Magic* while the Speech & What Archive performed their work *What the monkey says no one pays attention to* at TCB art inc., Melbourne, November 2012).

5 Veronica Kent, *The Telepathy Project*, unpublished PhD diss., (Melbourne: Victorian College of the Arts and the University of Melbourne, 2012), 14.

6 Sigmund Freud, 'Recommendations to Physicians Practising Psycho-Analysis (1912e), in James Strachey (ed.), *The Standard Edition of the Complete Psychological Works of Sigmund Freud: Vol. 12* (London: Hogarth, 1978), 115.

7 Sigmund Freud, 'Psychoanalysis and Telepathy' (1921/41), *SE 18*, 184.

8 Jean Epstein, 'On Certain Characteristics of *Photogénie*', trans. Tom Milne in Sarah Keller and Jason N. Paul (eds) *Jean Epstein: Critical Essays and New Translations* (Amsterdam: Amsterdam University Press, 2012).
9 Nicole Brenez, 'Ultra-modern: Jean Epstein, or "Cinema Serving the forces of Transgression and Revolt"' trans. Mireille Dobrynzski in Keller and Paul (eds) *Jean Epstein: Critical Essays and New Translations*, 2012.
10 Brenez, 'Ultra-modern', 235.
11 Freud, 'Psychoanalysis and Telepathy' (1921/41), *SE 18*, 179.

Dhalgren

Dylan Martorell

When I was a kid, the dissolution of '60s counterculture was everywhere. Failed open relationships, missing fathers, addictions, attempted suicides. When I moved back to Scotland we lived in a council house, the old park caretaker's house. Our front yard was bowling greens, pine forests, mini-golf, soccer fields, playgrounds and, across the fields, 'the Penny' or the state penitentiary, the UK's main facility for the incarceration of the criminally insane. My friend's uncle had been killed by an escapee with an axe a few years before we settled. One day, someone from The Penny came to our house. They were worried that one of the prisoners was using reflections of light as Morse code to communicate to an outside party.

Our backyard was separated from the local dump by a tall wire fence. The dump was my real playground. High cliffs of bulldozed dirt and years of refuse compacted into stratified layers. I loved everything about it, except for the gang of Cro Mags from the junction who had a locked shed full of pornographic magazines. I think my Mum got the shed demolished. I remember the gang coming to our house one Sunday afternoon threatening violence.

Sometimes we would chase rabbits. In winter, the tip became a frozen scape of jagged drops.

Samuel R. Delany's *Dhalgren* (1975) is a long book, but not a difficult book. Apparently Phillip K. Dick threw it against the wall in disgust after reading it. Self-indulgent, absence of a narrative arc, meandering, unfocused, no tightly-wound-amphetamine-logic: no puzzles to be solved, no. An unnamed American city has suffered an unnamed disaster in an unnamed time. The protagonist is a young man, apparently schizophrenic and suffering amnesia. It feels and reads like the early

’70s but also sounds like the near future. Like *The Road* for bisexual acid casualties. The American military have consulted science fiction writers for years to help develop weaponry and robotics systems. Books like *Dhalgren* are guidebooks, not works of fiction. Scenes in this book are probably being enacted right now in austerity-affected Mediterranean towns, the streets of Jakarta, Syria, Johannesburg…

In his exegesis, Dick talks about the concept of orthogonal time: ‘Everything which was, just as grooves on an LP contain that part of the music which has already been played; they don’t disappear after the stylus tracks them’.[1] This is an underlying concept of time that doesn’t exist in the past or the future. It is a constant now which lies beyond the wall of everyday illusion. Dick believed in an underlying reality which could only be grasped by a process of esoteric enlightenment. *Dhalgren* seems to exist on a plane similar to Dick’s: a concept of a more ‘real’ reality that is slowly bleeding into our world.

Reading *Dhalgren* for the first time, I recognised in Delany’s text the same types of adults I’d associated with as a kid. Adults high on LSD asking me to decipher their drawings of symmetrical women/witches, having screaming fistfights in the front yard, crashing cars in their sleep, burning soup in the kettle, walking around nude in the snow crying, losing their false teeth in the toilet, slashing their wrists in the bathroom.

The topography also resonated. Growing up in Perth I’d track down derelict sites, abandoned buildings, wastelands. Amazing spaces, like the old premises of *The West Australian Newspaper* with all the typesetting trays, clocks and furniture still set up like a six-storey Mary Celeste. In a couple of these spaces I set up temporary studios or conducted improvised musical performances with friends on abandoned cars and oil drums. In Melbourne, I set up in a dilapidated church in Collingwood; a small two-storey shed near the Clifton Hill railway line; a saw factory in Fitzroy.

These were all spaces outside of the confines and concepts of public/private space, places without electricity, open to the weather, free of charge, with a history of objects, smells, light and sounds that were perfect for creating works in the moment with whatever was around. Sometimes you'd find someone sleeping in your space, or that someone had destroyed or graffitied your work, or left a gift of beer bottles and shit, or that it was being knocked down, or that security or dogs had been installed on the premises: always an exciting prospect that led to some of the more thrilling aspects of free rent.

Sometimes I'd stay for a couple of months, sometimes a couple of days. Some were spots to return to over and over, like the top of the grain silos of the old Carlton Brewery, a spot where you could drink beer, listen to music and watch pigeons. Most of them are now luxury apartments.

I didn't finish *Dhalgren*. I'm not even sure I enjoyed it, but maybe that's not necessary, and who wants know how some things are going to end anyway.

Note

1 Philip K. Dick, in Pamela Jackson and Jonathan Lethem (eds), *The Exegesis of Philip K. Dick* (Boston; New York: Houghton Mifflin Harcourt, 2011), 929.

Adrian Martin is Distinguished Visiting Professor of Film Studies at Goethe University, Frankfurt, and author of *Last Day Every Day* (punctum books: English, Spanish and Portuguese editions).

Amelia Barikin is researching the intersection of art and science fiction at the University of Queensland. Her book *Parallel Presents: The Art of Pierre Huyghe* was published by MIT Press in 2012.

Andrew Frost is a writer, art critic and broadcaster, whose doctoral thesis *Science Fictional: SF Beyond the Limits of Genre* studied the historical relationships between contemporary art and science fiction. Frost has written and presented a number of TV programs, the most recent of which, *The A–Z of Contemporary Art*, screened on ABC1 in June 2013. Currency Press published Frost's monograph *The Boys* in its *Australian Screen Classics* series in 2010.

Anthony White is a Senior Lecturer in the School of Culture and Communication at the University of Melbourne. His book *Lucio Fontana: Between Utopia and Kitsch* was published by MIT Press in 2011.

Arlo Mountford is a Melbourne-based visual artist whose practice reinterprets art historical events, works and ideas. He has exhibited throughout Australia and internationally and is represented by Sutton Gallery, Melbourne.

Brendan Lee's photographic, filmic and written works delve into the ever-changing nature of Australian cultural identity, and the elusive subject matter of the quintessentially Australian spirit. Drawing from Australian literature and popular culture, particularly mainstream film, Lee presents humorous narratives of stereotypical Aussies living on the urban fringes. Lee has written two novels with a third on the way.

Charles Green is Professor of Contemporary Art and Head of Art History in the School of Culture and Communication at the University of Melbourne. He is also an artist, working in collaboration with Lyndell Brown.

Chris McAuliffe is an Honorary Fellow at the Australian Centre, School of Culture and Communication, the University of Melbourne. He was Director of the Ian Potter Museum of Art at the University of Melbourne from 2000–13.

Chronox is an ongoing, earnest attempt to build a time machine. Creating works across music, installation and text since 2008, Chronox have exhibited in such forums as MONA FOMA, PICA and the Now Now.

Damiano Bertoli is an artist.

Darren Jorgensen lectures in art history in the Faculty of Architecture, Landscape and Visual Art at the University of Western Australia. He publishes on both Australian art and science fiction.

Dylan Martorell is an artist and musician whose work is influenced by the natural world, human rituals, ethnography and mythology. He has exhibited and performed in numerous solo and group exhibitions in Australia, Singapore, Indonesia, Thailand, and India, including at the Jakarta Biennale and the Kochi-Muziris Biennale, 2012. Martorell is a member of the Slow Art Collective, and part of the experimental music groups Hi God People, Snawklor and The Donkey's Tail.

Edward Colless has worked in film and theatre and writes art criticism. He is Head of Critical and Theoretical Studies at the Victorian College of the Arts, University of Melbourne.

Helen Hughes is a PhD candidate in Art History at the University of Melbourne. She is co-editor of *Discipline* and an editor of *emaj*.

Helen Johnson is an artist and writer based in Melbourne.

Justin Clemens's recent books include *Psychoanalysis is an Antiphilosophy* (EUP 2013) and the new edition of *The Mundiad* (Hunter 2013). He teaches at the University of Melbourne.

Lauren Bliss is a PhD Candidate at the University of Melbourne, working on the figural theory of Nicole Brenez. She has written for magazines such as *Discipline*, *Arena*, and *Screening the Past*, is a regular contributor to online magazine *Desistfilm*, and has a monograph with re.press.

Matthew Shannon is an artist living in Amsterdam.

Nathan Gray is an artist and experimental musician who uses objects and installations to explore the overlap between the two disciplines and their shared histories. He has exhibited widely internationally and is represented by Utopian Slumps, Melbourne.

Nick Selenitsch is a Melbourne-based artist who has exhibited extensively in Australia for the past ten years.

OSW is a collaborative group comprising Terri Bird, Bianca Hester and Scott Mitchell. Projects emerge from exploratory workshops focused around a collective interest in forces of formation involving the social, political, geologic and economic that are registered variously across material events.

Patrick Pound is a Melbourne-based artist who collects books and other things which might be found to hold an idea or two.

Philip Brophy writes on killing people, among other things.

Rex Butler teaches in the School of English, Media Studies and Art History at the University of Queensland. He is presently completing a Reader's Guide to Deleuze and Guattari's *What is Philosophy?*

Ryan Johnston is Head of Art at the Australian War Memorial, Canberra. He has worked as an art history lecturer at the University of Melbourne, as a curator at La Trobe University, and as Acting Director of Shepparton Art Museum. He is currently finalising his PhD dissertation on Eduardo Paolozzi at the University of Melbourne.

Soda_Jerk is an Australian two-person art collective that works with found material to trouble formulations of cultural history. Taking the form of video installations, cut-up texts and lecture performances, their archival image practice is situated at the interzone of research, documentary and speculative fiction.

Index

Making Worlds: Art and Science Fiction
Edited by Amelia Barikin & Helen Hughes

Designed by Brad Haylock (MADA)
Cover by Joe Shakespeare & Brad Haylock

First edition 2013
ISBN 978-1-922099-07-5
Edition of 1000

Printed by BPA Print Group
Published by Surpllus

European distribution:
Motto Distribution—www.mottodistribution.com
Australian distribution:
Books at Manic—www.manic.com.au

Surpllus Pty Ltd
PO Box 418
Flinders Lane 8009
Victoria, Australia

www.surpllus.com

Surpllus #14